COLD WAR WARRIOR

Canadian MI-6 Agent Lawrence Fox

ROBERT POPPLE

To Jay & Liz,
With kindest regards,
R Popple

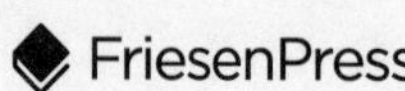

Suite 300 - 990 Fort St
Victoria, BC, V8V 3K2
Canada

www.friesenpress.com

Copyright © 2016 by Robert Popple
First Edition — 2016

All rights reserved.

No part of this publication may be reproduced in any form, or by any means, electronic or mechanical, including photocopying, recording, or any information browsing, storage, or retrieval system, without permission in writing from FriesenPress.

ISBN
978-1-4602-8383-7 (Hardcover)
978-1-4602-8384-4 (Paperback)
978-1-4602-8385-1 (eBook)

1. BIOGRAPHY & AUTOBIOGRAPHY, MILITARY

Distributed to the trade by The Ingram Book Company

Table of Contents

Acknowledgements

A credible narrative on Lawrence Fox's missions as an MI-6 agent in the 1956–1967 window would not have been possible without the timely effort of Lawrence Fox's second wife, Georgette (Vezina) Fox. They met in 1968 and married in 1974. She encouraged Lawrence to write down his MI-6 exploits while they were still fresh in his mind. She then promptly typed them out, thereby forming the starting basis for this book—including the many verbatim conversations.

Over time, many people undoubtedly examined that work. The route it took to me began when Lawrence passed it to one of his Midland Sixth Street School Grade 1 classmates, Ruth (Foote) Moore. She passed it to a friend Rose Ball, who passed it to Paul McDonald, who passed it to me. By that time, it was the spring of 2015.

Lawrence clarified and added detail in one-on-one interviews and innumerable telephone conversations to round out his story. That input included bridging material between his MI-6 missions, thereby providing insight into the complications arising from his double life—caused largely by the secrecy involved.

Fred Hacker provided his insight, guidance and comments on the first draft manuscript. Fred also put me in touch with Major-General Lewis MacKenzie, who kindly provided the Foreword.

The input on the first two drafts provided by my friend and neighbour Barbara Proctor-Hartley was invaluable. Her perspicacious comments and strategic approach improved the clarity, conciseness, and consistency of the imagery and detail throughout. Thank you, Barbara.

George Bereznai, a fifteen-year-old resident of Hungary at the time of the 1956 Revolution, provided perspective on that historic event.

Artist-architect Manley LaFoy assisted greatly with the Front Cover design through his rendering of Lynx, advancing in full MI-6 regalia, coming out of Hungary in 1956.

Preface

I first became aware of Lawrence Fox in the spring of 2015 through Paul McDonald, a friend from high school (and later Facebook) who I had not seen since 1959. He said that he had a bridge-playing friend who was a few years older than us who had grown up in Midland, Ontario, that this person had been an MI-6 agent and had written up his experiences.

A few weeks later, I received an electronic copy of Lawrence's manuscript from Paul, written in the first person. It read like a screenplay that Clint Eastwood would be attracted to, because it matched Eastwood's penchant for making movies out of true stories—*Letters from Iwo Jima, American Sniper,* and *Million Dollar Baby*, for example. Here was a true Canadian story in that very vein.

The manuscript had an undeniable ring of truth to it, and the action aspect made it a page-turner. The detail was of the sort that could only come from first-hand participation. I was intrigued.

Paul arranged for me to meet Lawrence in Midland on May 16, 2015. In a fifteen-minute meeting, a friendship was struck. We agreed that I would attempt to transform Lawrence's manuscript into a non-fiction thriller and sealed the deal with a handshake.

I returned to Midland on July 20 and 21, 2015 for taped, detailed discussions and clarifications with Lawrence in a Midland Public Library meeting room—kindly arranged by Fred Hacker.

The outcome of that process is this narrative, which is unique inasmuch as the events described here actually happened. This is non-fiction espionage—unlike Ian Fleming's James Bond, and even the John Le Carré series, which are primarily fictional.

The basis of its authenticity is Lawrence's word. His tendency to exaggerate is *zero*; anyone who has met him is aware of that. Even today, the details are embedded vividly in his mind. He has full and consistent recall, no matter which aspect is called into question in a first-handedness that is uncanny—much like that required in the taped, double debriefings following each MI-6 mission.

All code names and most proper names used—except Lawrence's real name, of course—are fictitious. All characters are (or were) real people. All conversations did take place, were witnessed by Lawrence and were written down when they were still fresh in his mind. They are considered accurate to within a few words of what was actually said.

This is a true story.

Robert Popple
October, 2015

Foreword

Anyone who enjoys reading military history—whether fiction or non-fiction—has many choices, particularly those dedicated to wartime exploits. My observation has been that wartime non-fiction written by rank and file soldiers is typically more articulate and interesting than that of high-ranking soldiers. Perhaps this is because their personal experience is much closer to real, first-hand action. Some have told their story soon after their exposure to armed conflict, while others have waited decades in order to soften the memories.

Little known and far less acknowledged are the recountings of our specially trained agents on missions behind the Iron Curtain (1946–1989). Details of their exploits are, by and large, missing from the vast library of non-fiction military literature, most likely because there are comparatively few of them written. On the other hand, fictional, highly romanticized dramatizations of the exploits of the Secret Service—particularly those of the United States (CIA) and the United Kingdom (MI-6) in both movies and print, featuring heroes like James Bond, George Smiley, and Harry Palmer—have been widely successful.

The fact is that Canadian forces played a significant role during the Cold War years—and is similarly under-acknowledged. Our Army, Navy, and Air Force were among the largest in the world, only exceeded in scale by the United States, Russia, and the United Kingdom. Even after the massive demobilization following World War II, Canada maintained a large Navy at sea, including two aircraft carriers. Our Army included a sizeable military capability as part of the British Army on the Rhine, positioned to face down the Soviet Union at the East German border. We also fielded a large Air Force component that was trained and equipped to deliver nuclear weapons deep into the Soviet Union.

During the Cold War, with tensions frequently high between the East and West, particularly in Europe, there was a crying need for information and intelligence gathering on the east side of the Iron Curtain. Surveillance from the air was limited—even with the U-2's high altitude photography, impressive as it was for its day. Any insertion of forces on the ground was fraught with danger, and the detection methods used by the Soviets to intercept any such incursion, no matter how modest, matched the sophistication of that fielded by the West. However, the consequences of being caught spying were brutal (to put it mildly), unless those captured were of sufficiently high profile to be bartered in exchange. The recent real-life, espionage thriller *Bridge of Spies* features a notable example.

Lawrence Fox has been reluctant to write about his clandestine activities during the height of the Cold War for over fifty years; the fear of violating the Official Secrets Act was uppermost in his mind. However, the obscure "document" he signed when he was recruited in 1956 had nothing to do with the Official Secrets Act—and the passage of time has made it irrelevant.

Describing himself as an espionage courier—a term not generally known to the public—he was sent behind the Iron Curtain on at least five occasions to retrieve secret information, or to bring important individuals out to the West. Those assignments were dangerous and required a high diversity of skill for successful completion. Lawrence recalls each mission vividly, including many verbatim conversations that were recorded on a timely basis; they make his story a highly readable and entertaining first-hand account of his Cold War experiences.

Although Lawrence Fox's missions were not great in number, their intensity contained more excitement, action, fear, pain, and satisfaction than most military personnel pack into an entire career. Lucky for us, he is still around to share it.

Major-General Lewis MacKenzie, C.M., O.Ont., M.S.C. and Bar, C.D.
October, 2015

Prologue

November 6, 1956, mid-afternoon.
An abandoned airstrip near Vienna.

An MI-6 agent operating under the code name "Lynx" walks toward a waiting military aircraft. He is to be its sole passenger. Born and raised in Midland, Ontario, he had enlisted in the RCAF four years earlier, at seventeen. Distinguished by his outstanding marksmanship from the beginning of his military career, he had been selected immediately as a candidate for dangerous espionage work. He is dressed in a camouflage jumpsuit, tight-fitting boots, a heavy shirt, a black tuque, and his face is blackened with paste. A thirty-pound pack sits heavily on his back.

Armed to the teeth, he is carrying four weapons—two tailor-made carbines, and two small weapons—an automatic .45 pistol and a double-edged combat knife. The latter two are hanging on his waist. One carbine is slung on his back, the other is cradled on his right forearm, finger on the trigger. In his other hand, he is carrying a black briefcase for delivery to his MI-6 superior in compliance with the instruction: To be brought out of Hungary, at any cost.

One carbine belonged to his mission partner, "Nomad", who was shot in the back by a Russian military officer only a few hours earlier.

He stows his gear methodically, and straps himself into a seat. The crew have been instructed not to enter the passenger compartment under any circumstances, lest they see his face—standard MI-6 procedure.

At cruising altitude, Lynx removes the black paste from his face and changes into civilian clothes, which have been carefully laid out for him by others. His change of visual identity complete, he shoves his .45 automatic and combat knife into his backpack and stows the pack.

It has been over twenty-four hours since he last slept, and he is exhausted. The steady hum of the aircraft engines soon cause him to doze off. The next thing he knows, he is jarred into full alertness as the aircraft touches down, the result of an imperfect landing. His nerves still raw from a harrowing escape earlier that day, he instinctively reaches for his .45 automatic, and then suddenly remembers that it has been packed away. His nervous reaction evaporates when he realizes that he is still the only person in the passenger cabin of the aircraft. Out the window, he can see only dreary afternoon weather on what looks like yet another abandoned airstrip.

He studies the situation through the aircraft window and sights a black, British-built car idling near the end of the runway—a car similar to the one that dropped him off the night before. A thin wisp of exhaust indicates that its engine is running.

The aircraft taxis alongside the waiting car. He opens the aircraft door, extends the dismounting ladder, and carrying all his gear, he climbs down onto the ground. Still apprehensive, his eyes dart nervously from side to side as he closes the door behind him.

As soon as Lynx is well clear of the aircraft, the pilot—who is operating under his own set of orders—manoeuvres the aircraft into the wind, gives both engines full throttle, releases the brakes, and in a cloud of dust the aircraft lurches forward for take-off. Moments later, it has disappeared into the overcast, lead-blue sky.

Lynx carries his full gear—the all-important briefcase in one hand—as he walks to the waiting car, its driver sitting motionless, staring straight ahead, undoubtedly also under orders not to look at his pick-up. A Secret Service agent sits in the back seat wearing sunglasses and also looking stoically straight ahead.

Lynx opens the rear car door opposite the passenger, carefully places the carbines on the car floor, puts his backpack on the seat between himself and the agent, and still holding the briefcase tightly in one hand, gets in. In a British accent, the agent asks Lynx, "Is it all there, Laddie?"

Still livid that he would be misled on the danger inherent in this, his first assignment, Lynx snaps back a "Yes, sir!" in as sharp but subdued a regimental bark as he can muster. Without acknowledging his response in any way, the agent ignores Lynx for the rest of the car ride.

The car proceeds for about thirty minutes, slows as it approaches a series of classically elegant Georgian estates, and turns into one of the driveways. It stops in front of a beautiful grey stone mansion with a façade covered with ivy. A gardener is busily trimming a rose garden in full bloom and another is cutting the lawn. Lynx quietly marvels to himself that this peaceful, classical home in suburban London is a debriefing centre for Her Majesty's Secret Service.

The Secret Service agent speaks for the first time since his abrupt initial greeting, instructing Lynx, "Bring only the briefcase, Laddie. The rest of the equipment will be looked after."

The agent proceeds to the front door, opens it, and instructs Lynx: "At the end of the hall, last door on the left."

Lynx walks down the hall and opens the designated door. He steps into a huge vestibule and is drop-jawed by the sheer majesty, the opulence of the room, the polished marble floors, the spiral staircase, the delicate ornate woodwork, and the plush furnishings—luxury unlike any he has ever seen before. As the oak door closes behind him, he is suddenly overcome with the empty loneliness that only an MI-6 agent can know.

His mind casts back momentarily to his first few days as an RCAF recruit four years earlier, a wet-behind-the-ears, small-town kid from Midland, Ontario, and the incredible, ensuing drama.

Lynx, who has just been to hell and back in the dozen hours following the parachute jump that began his first MI-6 mission, is reporting for the required debriefing.

Chapter One:
A Midland Boyhood, Enlistment, and Training

Lawrence Arthur Fox was born in Midland, Ontario, on September 5th, 1935, the second son of Grace and Reginald Fox. He had one sister (June) and two brothers (William and Walter). He attended grade school at Sixth Street School, where he was reportedly "a little devil."

At age eight, Lawrence got a job pumping gas at Steer's White Rose station. In those days, the gas pumps were fitted with a ten-gallon glass tank with calibration marks to indicate how much gasoline had been pumped into it. The gas then ran by gravity into the car's gas tank. It was wartime, and rationing was in effect.

On the first day of Lawrence's tenure as a gas jockey, "Sam Weiner," as the local kids called him, pulled up in his 1930 Model "A" Ford and put up two fingers. Lawrence took that as a signal that Sam wanted two dollars worth of gas, and with the owner's help, proceeded to pump eight gallons up into the glass tank (which came to $2.00) and feed it into Sam's gas tank. Sam, who only wanted *two* gallons of gas at twenty-five cents a gallon, was livid when he found out what young Lawrence had done and he stomped up and down in a screaming rage.

The station owner, Alvin Steer, just laughed it off and let Sam have the gas for free.

At age fourteen, Lawrence's father gave him a Winchester Cooey single shot, .22-calibre rifle. On the first day out with his gun in George Ingram's sugar bush along outer Hugel Avenue, he aimed at anything that moved. That included a squirrel that he shot out of a tree, the rodent squirming and flinching in pain as it lay mortally wounded. Lawrence watched it die a slow, pathetic death; he decided then and there that he would never again hunt for anything that he wouldn't eat. Going forward, his targets would be either partridge or rabbit.

When he shot his first partridge in the breast, his father pointed out two drawbacks—not only did it ruin most of the meat, but it also possibly tainted it with lead. Far better, he counselled his son, was to shoot partridge in the head and thus save the meat.

Taking his father at his word, Lawrence missed a lot of game at first, because the partridge head is a very small target that jerks erratically as the bird walks about. But the boy persevered. He learned to breathe correctly when aiming, mastered the technique of a proper trigger squeeze, and eventually honed his marksmanship skills to the extent that he rarely missed a clean headshot.

Lawrence's mother was a staunch Baptist and, of course, on good terms with the local minister. She home-schooled her children on the fundamentals of the Protestant religion—including the importance of the Ten Commandments. One in particular was to surface at critical junctures as Lawrence's military life took shape.

In the summer of 1949, Lawrence wanted a bike badly, but family money was tight. His mother suggested that he ask the minister for a job cleaning and cutting the grass for five dollars a month. He did, and the minister agreed. Lawrence's mother ordered a CCM bike from the Sears catalogue, staked him for the needed fifty-five dollars, and he repaid her over the ensuing eleven months.

He and his boyhood pal Al Bath rode their bikes everywhere together. One time they went all the way from Port McNicoll to the fall fair in the Midland arena grounds—each with a girl on the crossbar!

At fifteen, Lawrence got his first real summer job on a farm, plowing, disking, and harrowing fields for two dollars a day at "Stoney Lonesome," as the owner called his acreage, a tract of land loosely strewn with rocks and boulders. Lawrence was at the wheel of a Cockshutt machine from dawn to dusk. He was so tired one day that he fell asleep at the wheel and drove the machine right into a wire fence. The big machine became so entangled with the fence that a lot of wire cutter work was needed to cut it free.

In the 1950s, a large sightseeing and supply boat called the *Midland City* ran a daily excursion out of Midland to provision the cottagers and lodges among Georgian Bay's 30,000 islands. In the summer of '51, Lawrence sailed on her as wheelsman at one hundred dollars a month, room and board included. Later that year, Lawrence got a job at the Roxy Theatre, taking tickets, opening and closing the theatre, and doing other duties as manager Al Perkins required.

The following year, Lawrence was working in Toronto at the Coca-Cola plant and decided to enlist in the RCAF. He met the age requirement on September 5th when he turned seventeen. He then needed to secure four signatures—those of both parents', the Midland Chief of Police, and the Midland Baptist church minister.

He reported for duty with the RCAF on Monday, October 20, 1952. His first posting was to Bootcamp in Saint-Jean, Quebec, for eight weeks.

Some Bootcamp aspects such as marching drills held little attraction to Lawrence, but he considered them simply part of his commitment to the military. On a typical day, with the platoon in its three-rank formation and standing at ease, the Corporal would walk up and down the platoon, dressing down anyone who exhibited poor decorum in "old school" fashion by making humiliating remarks.

One day, the Corporal stopped in front of Lawrence, looked quizzically at him, and asked, "Did you shave this morning?"

"No, sir," Lawrence answered, peach fuzz being the only growth on his face that he shaved off about once a week.

The Corporal moved his face inches from Lawrence's, their noses almost touching, and barked, "From now on, you will shave each and every morning! Now Private, have you got that?"

"Yes, sir!" answered Lawrence.

Five weeks into this routine, excitement was running high among the new recruits when they were told that Ground Defence exercises would soon begin. That meant that they would get to fire the coveted .303s. They had all been eyeing the firing range for some time in eager anticipation of this milestone.

On the appointed day, the Corporal halted the platoon of fifty recruits in front of the firing range and ordered them to "stand easy." The first group of five walked through a rigorous procedure to check each rifle before firing, and Lawrence, who would take his turn in the second group, listened carefully to ensure he knew what to do when the time came.

As he waited his turn, he remembered his precious Cooey .22 single shot, the only rifle he had fired to date. He couldn't help but notice how much bigger the .303 shells were.

Once the first five recruits had finished firing their ten rounds, a Sergeant, who had been studying the targets with binoculars and standing to one side, pointed out two of the riflemen. The Corporal immediately ordered them to stand over near the Sergeant. At that moment, Lawrence had no inkling how that particular Sergeant would eventually become the dominant force in his life.

As the selected duo went and stood beside the Sergeant, the Corporal ordered the next five—which included Lawrence—to take up their positions. After walking through the required procedure, Lawrence was ready to fire at his target.

He held his breath as he gently squeezed the trigger on the Corporal's "Fire" command, just like he had done hundreds of times with his Cooey. The "kick" of the .303 took him aback when the weapon slammed into his shoulder, coincident with the bullet release. *Wow! Way more powerful than my old Cooey,* he thought.

His first shot hit the white of the target, two inches above and one inch to the left of the bullseye. Carefully aiming two inches lower and one inch to the right, his second shot had to be a "bull." The only shot that he could see in the white of the target was his first one. Firing the remaining shots at that same aiming point, all nine were "bulls."

On the Corporal's command, Lawrence got back onto his feet. He froze apprehensively when he realized that the Sergeant was now pointing at him.

The Corporal ordered Lawrence and another rifleman to stand over near the Sergeant. Most unnerving was the fact that the Sergeant was now staring at Lawrence exclusively—almost hypnotically, making him feel very uneasy. By the time everyone in the group had taken a turn, five of the original fifty had been directed to stand over near the Sergeant.

When the Corporal had dismissed the platoon and departed, the Sergeant finally spoke—in a distinctly British accent.

The Sergeant immediately began organizing his five selectees into trying out several more "pieces"—military jargon for guns. Notably, his demeanour suddenly changed from friendly to abusive as he yelled at the young recruits, depending on their performance.

Lawrence simply ignored the Sergeant's yelling, because none of it was intended for him. Instead, he concentrated on calibrating his weapons, quietly thinking to himself *No two guns fire the same* as he went from weapon to weapon. Carefully compensating for whatever feedback he got from his first shot, he easily put nine of the ten rounds into the "bull," using whichever rifle he selected.

The Sergeant had noted Lawrence's marksmanship from the beginning, and soon had dismissed the others so that he could study it exclusively. Alone, the two spent the rest of the day shooting .303s, hitting bullseye after bullseye. It wasn't long before Lawrence's shoulder was aching from the "kicks" that accompanied each shot.

After that afternoon together, Lawrence resumed his training and would not see the Sergeant until he was stationed at Camp Borden, Ontario, a few months later.

On New Year's Day, 1953, Lawrence lay on his bunk at CFB Camp Borden, listening to Hank Williams' many hits, including *I'm So*

Lonesome I Could Cry. That tune registered with him because he was missing his girlfriend, Alda Laurn. The news of Williams' death just after midnight was headlined on the radio. Lawrence's squadron had just reported for duty.

When the weekly routine started the following day, it was clear that his training would include classroom and hands-on maintenance work on Lancaster V-12 (1,345 horsepower) engines. The learning environment was relaxed and well ordered. Lawrence felt some satisfaction that his decision to join the military had been the right one; after all, this mechanical training had been a prime reason for enlisting.

One day, he was called out of the classroom and there was the Sergeant waiting for him, the one whom he had met a few months earlier at the CFB Saint-Jean rifle range. After the briefest of exchanges, the Sergeant told Lawrence that they would be back on the rifle range "tonight after dinner."

That night, and for many more in the ensuing weeks, the two of them were at the range, Lawrence firing dozens of rounds on "a beautiful .303 with a scope." However, before long, Lawrence began developing some apprehension about doing so much range work. The focus on marksmanship was pulling him away from his goal. He attempted, almost sheepishly, to express that concern a few times to the Sergeant—but he was ignored.

Soon, Lawrence was excused from drilling with the rest of the platoon so that he could spend the day at the range with the Sergeant. He was firing all sorts of weapons—Bren guns (which gave no "kick" whatsoever, but wanted to "jump ahead"), Sten guns, .303s, and even pistols of a variety of calibres.

Then the targets ceased being just concentric circles. For example, one night at the range, Sarge had three dummies, human forms from the waist up, arranged beside an on/off light system that would illuminate for three seconds at random. The exercise called for Lawrence to shoot all three dummies within that time limit using a 30/06 semi-automatic—no problem for Lawrence. More such intense range drills followed.

One day, the Sergeant was unhappy with Lawrence's Bren gun work. Evidently seeking to impress the young recruit and to demonstrate a particular technique with the weapon, the Sergeant grabbed a Bren gun, folded the tripod, inserted a full magazine, and fired all thirty-two rounds from the hip in one blast. His barrage of bullets totally obliterated the bullseye some fifty feet away.

Greatly impressed, Lawrence noticed that, instead of using his right index finger on the trigger, the Sergeant had used his middle finger for that purpose while his index finger was set above the trigger, parallel to the gun barrel and pointing at the target. He deduced intuitively that this had aided the hand–eye aiming aspect considerably.

When the Sergeant asked him if he would like to try that, Lawrence placed his fingers exactly as the Sergeant had done, and of the thirty-two bullets in his magazine-emptying blast, only two missed the "bull."

The Sergeant was pleased—not only with the results, but also with Lawrence's observation skills, namely how he had accomplished the feat using his third finger (and not his second) as his trigger finger.

Bayonet drills, again one-on-one with the Sergeant, followed. However, one day, Lawrence could hang back no longer and asked him outright, "What's all this 'special training' for?"

"Well, Laddie-Buck," replied said the Sergeant, taken as he had to calling Lawrence by that time, "I'm training you to be a sniper. And you are to tell no one what you are doing. Have you got that?"

Taken aback, seventeen-year-old Lawrence was shocked by this reply. He said, "But Sarge, a sniper is a killer, and that's not for me. I can't kill. I didn't enlist to become a killer. I want to get my aeronautical engine mechanic qualification so that I have a trade—and a future. And besides, there's no war on now."

The Sergeant's face reddened and his eyes bulged, almost as if they were about to pop out of their sockets. He was suddenly shouting at Lawrence from close range at the top of his voice: "Killing is in all of us. Get it? All of us! You will bloody well do as I say! Okay? If I put a dummy up and tell you it's a man with orders to kill, you will bloody well do it when I tell you to! When I say shit, you will say, 'what colour, sir?' Now, have you got that?"

"Yes, sir!" replied Lawrence, shaken by the Sergeant's explosive outburst.

The next day at a bayonet drill, still somewhat traumatized from that unexpected dressing down, Lawrence's concentration failed. Outraged, the Sergeant suddenly picked up a rifle, fixed a bayonet to it, and ordered Lawrence to "charge me and bloody well mean business." Lawrence did as he was ordered. With a sudden manoeuvre, the Sergeant feinted to one side and struck Lawrence on the jaw with the butt of his rifle. Lawrence was on the ground so fast that he scarcely knew what had hit him.

After exchanging expletives, Lawrence got to his feet, mad as hell, and taking the Sergeant at his word, charged with his bayonet aimed directly for the kill. The wily Sergeant kept his bayonet aimed low, and Lawrence feinted a move towards his legs that the Sergeant tried to counter. Capitalizing on the split-second opening that resulted, Lawrence swung the butt of his rifle up, caught the Sergeant full on one cheek, and down he went.

To Lawrence's great surprise, the Sergeant started laughing, saying, "Now you've got it, Laddie-Buck. You bloody well did it. I do believe me little bird is catching on."

Alone with the Sergeant one Friday night, the two had a shouting match over the issue of Lawrence being groomed as a sniper. In the course of the heated exchange, Lawrence's relationship with three fellow recruits with whom he had become good friends surfaced. It had been eating away at the Sergeant, who wanted Lawrence to cut off all social contact. He shouted at Lawrence, "You're going to start telling them what you're doing, and that can't happen!"

Back at the barracks, Lawrence was totally turned off with this treatment. He simply didn't want to become the social leper that the Sergeant was insisting on. Consequently, Lawrence packed a suitcase, got a pass, and left camp. He had had enough. If he got caught AWOL, it would mean guardhouse time, or military prison—maybe both—but he didn't care.

He hid out in the village of Port McNicoll with his girlfriend, Alda Laurn, near his hometown. On the thirteenth day, Lawrence was walking down the street, and out of nowhere, somebody tapped him on the shoulder. It was the Sergeant.

It suddenly registered with Lawrence: He would not be able to make a move or do anything that the Sergeant would not know about as long as the Sergeant had earmarked him to become a military sniper. He was being singled out for this military career path because of his marksmanship. This direction was in strong conflict with his personal preference, which was to pursue a career as an aeronautical mechanic. Even at that stage, his prime work passion was airplane engines; it was to become life-long.

The Sergeant persuaded Lawrence to return to base and he served fourteen days in the guardhouse. Lawrence was quite popular with his fellow inmates during this brief jail term—a social plus, as it turned out. He repeatedly opened their cells by reaching through the meal slot, unbolting his cell door, and freeing his fellow inmates; such was security at the base jail. Sarge's timely intervention did, however, have a silver lining; its timing enabled Lawrence to avoid serving time in the base's dreaded 12-SDB prison. Had he been AWOL a single additional day, 12-SDB time would have been mandatory. That would have meant hard time military prison, subsisting on bread, water, and boiled eggs—not to mention a brutal exercise programme. One of his friends had experienced that treatment with a resulting weight loss of sixty pounds in sixty days.

Once he was released, Lawrence complied with Sarge's wishes and ceased all social contact with his few friends. He became a loner. He had thereby forfeited a prime reason for joining the military in the first place—namely, the social benefits. Instead, he became a fixture at the rifle range with the Sergeant almost every evening.

Lawrence still wanted to get his aeronautical mechanic certification for the added job security benefits, but his marks were disappointingly low. With all the range work the Sergeant demanded, there was little time left for study. Nevertheless, he managed to scrape through. In April 1953, he was deployed to CFB Lachine, Quebec, where he commuted to and from Dorval on the bus each day for engine maintenance work assignments.

Those work assignments included maintaining North Star DC-4 engines (1,749 horsepower), an engineering marvel that had a dry weight of 1,740 lbs. and therefore a weight-to-horsepower ratio of less than 1 lb. per horsepower. *Wow! What a beautiful machine,* he thought repeatedly as he studied its features and worked at developing the skills and knowledge of his chosen trade. Finally, the young recruit was working at what he wanted to do.

Then, without warning, as would become typical, the Sergeant appeared out of nowhere. This time he wanted to broaden Lawrence's training into the area of explosives; specifically, the Sergeant wanted him to focus on plastic explosives with timers. Just for good measure, he also had Lawrence throw a live grenade to "get the feel of it." Once paired with a timer, nitro-glycerine-based plastic (C-4) explosives were quite delicate, and some near-disasters occurred. However, none were consequential. Blessed with the innate ability to learn quickly, Lawrence had soon mastered the technique of setting them up—specialist's knowledge that he would eventually put to extensive use.

As the informal aspects of their relationship had grown, Lawrence became accustomed to addressing the Sergeant as "Sarge," and they went to a few different military bases together. Lawrence was impressed that Sarge moved in and out of those bases with ease. The gatekeepers would see him coming, raise the barrier well before he had reached it, and simply wave him on through.

Lawrence began to wonder, *Who is this guy, anyway? How did he get such clout? Am I really being trained as a sniper, or is there more to it than that?*

By July 1953, Lawrence had been in the RCAF the best part of a year and was yearning for some down-home relaxation. He hitchhiked from Dorval to Midland, a 450-mile trip, arriving at 5:00 a.m. on a Saturday morning and slept until 10:00 a.m. He had just started to enjoy his mother's home cooking and was sitting on the front porch when the young brother of friends he had gone to high school with rode up on a bicycle.

"Got a telegram for you," he announced.

Lawrence tore the envelope open and it read:

> Return to camp immediately.
> Signed: Your Commanding Officer.

Excited, Lawrence was on a bus to Toronto within the hour and barely made the bus connection to Montreal. When he identified himself at the camp guardhouse, he was handed an envelope with a message inside that read:

> Meet me tomorrow at 0800 hrs. with your heavy
> winter clothing together and your kit bag.
> Signed: Sarge.

The following morning in the warm July weather, Lawrence felt slightly foolish carrying his winter clothing in a kit bag. He met Sarge who, as was now becoming usual, was tight-lipped about what he had in the works. Then, when Sarge instructed Lawrence to act as if "you don't know me," he was perplexed. Lawrence thought to himself, *What's with this guy? And what's all this 'You don't know me' stuff about?*

Nevertheless, Lawrence recognized the airplane they were about to board as one belonging to his squadron that was scheduled that day to fly to Resolute Bay. *We are going to Resolute Bay?* he thought. *Why? It's at seventy-five degrees of latitude, for crying out loud!*

Sure enough, the airplane took off as scheduled later that morning, made one stop at Fort Churchill, and proceeded a thousand miles north to Resolute Bay with Lawrence, Sarge, and a cargo of supplies on board.

In the Cold War era, CFB Resolute Bay was in the early stages of becoming a Canadian High Arctic military and weather outpost. Manning it would enable the country to claim rights over the area, when the subject of sovereignty would inevitably come up in discussions with the Russians. It remains one of Canada's northernmost settlements, and one of the coldest inhabited places on earth. The average daytime temperature in July is 4 degrees Celsius.

One of its principal safety hazards is the polar bear. They roam the area freely in a mostly desolate landscape of ice, snow, and low-lying shale rock. There are no trees in Resolute Bay. A sign on one building there said rather poetically, "It's miles and miles of nothing but miles and miles."

Located *north* of Baffin Island, almost in line with the North Pole, the outpost housed a minimal number of year-round military personnel in 1953, likely less than twenty-five. Plane wrecks that had crash-landed nearby—typically in thick fog that could descend in minutes—surrounded it. A military purgatory, its commanding officer was "doing time" for erroneously navigating a North Star into Russian air space.

One memorable event early in Lawrence's extended Resolute Bay visit featured the arrival of sixteen Lancasters (four twelve-cylinder engines, 1,350 horsepower apiece) from 408 Squadron of CFB Torbay, Newfoundland. Every windowpane in the tiny military outpost shook as the sixteen aircraft, their sixty-four engines at top revs (3,000 rpm), flew over the base in formation at treetop level. They landed and looked terrific, parked in a row, their propeller spinners—the shallow cones that centre the props—painted a trademark red. As a rip-roaring booze-up proceeded late into the night, someone painted all sixty-four spinners robin-egg blue.

The next morning, all visiting pilots, co-pilots, and base staff were promptly assembled outside in military formation for the inquiry. The base commanding officer and the chief pilot from 408 Squadron paced—together—up and down the columns of airmen, wanting to know who had pulled the prank. The chief pilot shouted at the top of his voice that he would "find out, even if you have to stand here all day" in the freezing cold. No one spoke up. Among the base staff, everyone knew that their commanding officer had pulled the prank. He may have committed a snafu that was unacceptable to the military brass, but at least he had a sense of humour.

After their initial arrival together at Resolute Bay, Sarge had no contact with Lawrence for a week or ten days. Lawrence was left entirely on his own—a good fraction of that time wondering why he was there. With flights arriving and departing daily, Sarge could easily have flown out onto other business—and probably did. Wherever Sarge was, Lawrence didn't see him

To pass the time, Lawrence spent days—alone—gazing across the vast landscape of Resolute Bay. In the course of that time, Lawrence befriended a female dog named Nicky. They bonded heavily, no doubt aided greatly when Lawrence started feeding her fine T-bone steaks directly from the base kitchen. In return, Lawrence came to appreciate Nicky's ability to give warning whenever a polar bear was in the vicinity. They became inseparable.

One bright August morning at 5:30 a.m. and without warning, Sarge approached the sleeping Lawrence. Nicky, sleeping on the floor alongside Lawrence's bed as had now become customary, bared her teeth at Sarge as he neared the bed—the beginnings of what was to become an unbeautiful friendship. For that reason and because Sarge wanted Lawrence to be on his own for the day's exercise, he refused to let Lawrence take the dog with him.

"Shake a leg, Laddie-Buck. We've got business to attend to," said Sarge as he roused Lawrence from his sleep, oblivious to not having seen Lawrence in over a week.

As he spread a map of the island out on a table, Sarge outlined the objective of the day, which was to be a major orienteering exercise.

"The task is the retrieval of a container ten miles away marked by a metal stake, without a compass," he explained. "Compasses don't work up here anyhow. Besides, this will test your ability to survive without the dog, because her natural instincts would enable her to come straight back here. I want you to do it by yourself. You've got eight hours."

Lawrence refused to back down on having Nicky accompany him, and continued to press his case with Sarge over coffee before setting out. Sarge finally agreed—"but only for this one exercise." Lawrence felt some pride that he had stood his ground and achieved a reversal of one of Sarge's typical domineering dictates.

The orienteering exercise was going to be tough in the circumstances of low temperature, desolate landscape, and Arctic hazards. Nevertheless, by 06:00 hours, Lawrence was off, aiming to cover the twenty miles in eight hours. He attempted to maintain as straight a course as possible and reached the container in four and a half hours—a half hour behind schedule. He thought it unlikely that he would make up that time on the return leg. Nevertheless, he started back at a trot with Nicky running alongside. Before long, her feet were bleeding from the sharp rocks, but she soldiered on without complaining.

The rolling terrain gave the impression that the camp couldn't be far away, an illusionary effect created by the hills and valleys that looked similar in every direction. That feature of the terrain could easily disorient an inexperienced traveller. An hour into the return leg, Nicky stopped unexpectedly and started growling, baring her teeth; she had exhibited the same behaviour when she had detected a polar bear a week earlier. Lawrence froze. Without a gun, avoiding a polar bear had to be top priority. He could neither see the animal, nor knew its location. He watched Nicky standing statue-like, ears up, nose sniffing, head moving to the left.

"Okay, girl. Let's go," he said out loud, detouring to the right in the belief that that course alteration would avoid the bear. His hunch had been right—at least to the extent that he didn't encounter a bear.

Setting a brutal pace in the circumstances, three hours of smooth sailing later (and with only five minutes to go), he reached the top of a knoll and sighted the camp in the distance. When Lawrence arrived, Sarge merely looked at his watch and—consistent with his unusual approach to motivation—remarked tauntingly, "Five minutes late."

"The hell with your five minutes late," said an exhausted Lawrence, gasping for breath. "I damn near ran straight into a polar bear. Nicky warned me just in time, and I detoured around it. She didn't just make straight for camp, but stuck with me." Lawrence had made the point that perhaps it was foolhardy—even irresponsible—to send an unarmed trainee on an orienteering exercise in this area of the world that, in addition to its remoteness, featured serious safety hazards.

When Lawrence asked Sarge if he could take a gun on his next orienteering assignment, Sarge replied, "Laddie, there'd be hell to pay if you ever shot a polar bear up here." He did, however, concede that it was worthwhile for Nicky to accompany him on future exercises. Further, as a safety precaution, Sarge eventually agreed to allow Lawrence to take a rifle with him on these excursions.

Still at Resolute Bay on his eighteenth birthday (September 5th, 1953), Lawrence was riding on the forks of a forklift, moving cargo, when a hydraulic line broke and sprayed hydraulic fluid in his eyes. A Leading Aircraftsman was functioning as the site doctor and he washed Lawrence's eyes out. When Lawrence mentioned that it was his eighteenth birthday, he gave Lawrence six ounces of pure alcohol and warned him to dilute it with plenty of juice before attempting to drink it.

When he needed more juice for dilution to the recommended concentration, Lawrence had to go to another building to get the top-up. When he wanted back into the building he had left, a polar bear was contentedly eating out of the garbage cans beside the Mess Hall door, thereby making re-entry unsafe. Lawrence had to wait several minutes for the magnificent creature to leave before he could get back in.

After topping up the jug with plenty of juice, he and five buddies promptly polished it off and proceeded to the bar for birthday-beer chasers. All six passed out after only a few sips of beer.

On September 12th, Lawrence retrieved his fifth and final container. Sarge had re-appeared to set up each exercise and witness the results. Between exercises, he had probably left and flown back in when needed. Wherever he was, Lawrence only saw him on exercise days. Notwithstanding, Lawrence was still confused. *Was this part of a sniper's job?* he pondered at length, reluctant to raise the subject again with the temperamental Sarge. The day after that final orienteering exercise, an aircraft headed south to CFB Lachine with Lawrence aboard. Sadly, Nicky stayed behind. Winter was setting in, the snow was four inches deep, and the temperature registered minus-20 degrees Celsius.

In January 1954, Lawrence's squadron moved to CFB Trenton, Ontario, about one hundred miles east of Toronto. Nestled in the Bay of Quinte area, it is still one of Canada's largest military bases and the

RCAF hub of air transport for the country. Every month or so, Sarge would appear without warning. He and Lawrence would train together for a day or two, sometimes to assimilate new material, sometimes to review past training. Sarge consistently avoided casting any light onto the full-intended purpose of Lawrence's special training. He would then disappear as mysteriously as he had appeared. Whenever Sarge wasn't there, Lawrence, for his part, continued working diligently towards his aeronautical maintenance specialist qualification.

Still only nineteen years old, Lawrence had the youthful attraction to the thrill of speed that most kids do. In the spring of 1954, he bought a 1936 Ford coupe and stripped it down into a stock car. As an aggressive driver in races, he had no hesitation about nudging the competition to improve his position at the finish line whenever the opportunity arose.

One night at the local racetrack, the car ahead of Lawrence spun out of control. With no chance of taking evasive action, Lawrence crashed into it, broadside. As the struck car rolled over, his Ford coupe nosed up, went clear over the rolling car and came crashing to the ground on the other side of it. As the crash sequence cascaded, Lawrence managed to keep his Ford upright with adept handling of the steering wheel and the brake pedal. However, the other driver was strapped in and when his car finally stopped rolling on its side, it suddenly burst into flames. Without a second thought, Lawrence scrambled out of his car and ran towards the blazing car. The driver was only dazed but needed help to get out; Lawrence managed to drag him to safety.

Sarge was sitting in the stands and had been an eyewitness to the entire event. He took a rather dim view of Lawrence engaging in such "dangerous forms of play," and made no secret of it. He shouted at Lawrence afterwards, "I've spent away too much effort training you to have you get killed on a racetrack! Look what happened tonight!"

What happened that night was tame compared to a few nights later, when Lawrence had another, far worse accident with potentially fatal consequences. He rolled his car over three times sideways on top of other cars, then three more times end-over-end out onto the infield of the oval track. Fortunately, he was well strapped in.

Both accidents had been dangerous, the second one obviously more so than the first. After it happened, Sarge outlined some rationale for Lawrence that centred on the military's "self-inflicted wounds" policy that encouraged the avoidance of such activities. He convinced Lawrence to sell the Ford coupe. However, neither Lawrence nor even Sarge could know how valuable Lawrence's driving skills acquired in those stock car races would be on future assignments.

That same spring of 1954, Lawrence met a brunette named Elsie one night in a restaurant in Belleville. Her father was a master dynamiter working for McFarlane Construction; he masterminded many of the rock cuts on Highway 401. She was very social, bowled with her girlfriends weekly, loved to party, and was still living at home on a farm north of Belleville. She and Lawrence hit it off—to the extent that he promptly forgot his Port McNicoll girlfriend Alda Laurn and started dating Elsie.

Elsie was intrigued with the racetrack and never missed any of Lawrence's stock car performances. In fact, she—along with Sarge for the first accident, although they never met—had been an eyewitness to both of Lawrence's rather spectacular stock car collisions.

In September 1954, always secretive about what training was imminent, Sarge made another appearance. This time it was to teach Lawrence the art of parachuting.

When Lawrence arrived at Goose Bay, Labrador, without knowing why he was being sent there, he was shocked to learn that Sarge wanted him to jump out of an airplane. "Way more dangerous than stock car driving," Lawrence contended in a futile effort to talk Sarge out of the assignment. Lawrence was given no choice and was essentially *ordered* to take the parachute training.

The next morning, Lawrence met his instructor, Richard Brant, who had a mock-up arrangement in a loft to simulate parachute jumping. Lawrence still could see no connection between this training and being a sniper. However, if he had given the matter some creative thought, could he not have imagined a sniper being dropped somewhere before undertaking the obvious final step of delivering a bullet to its intended target? Many targets would not be readily accessible from everyday vantage points. Such were the side effects of wondering endlessly—incommunicado—about the purpose of his diverse training. Lawrence, perhaps in awe of Sarge, followed his orders obediently and never discussed the matter with anyone.

After some preliminary instruction, Lawrence and his instructor were soon aloft and looking out the open door of an aircraft. Lawrence's stomach was doing back-flips with anxiety. He was reluctant to go; Richard finally pushed him out of the aircraft. His worst fears seemed to be realized immediately. There he was, suddenly tumbling towards the ground in mid-air, feeling absolutely out of control. Despite Richard's repeated assurances, he was terrified of the prospect that his chute might not open.

Then the static line connected to the aircraft bottomed out, the chute opened, and what a sensation! One second he was in free-fall, the next he had been jerked to what felt like a sudden but painless stop. Richard had jumped right behind him and as he and Lawrence floated earthward, Richard taught him how to steer the parachute.

Lawrence's first jump wasn't a good one—or so he thought. Despite experimenting on the way down with steering, he barely missed landing on top of a tree.

"Your landings will get better as time goes by," Richard reassured him. *Bullshit,* thought Lawrence. *This is not for me.*

After another jump that day and two a day for the next three days, Lawrence was glad when the assignment was finally over.

As a teenager, Lawrence was fascinated by the occult, and when a fortune-teller predicted that he would marry a raven-haired beauty with whom he would have five children, Lawrence somehow connected that prediction with Elsie. On September 4, 1954—the day before his nineteenth birthday, and without a word to Sarge or nearly anyone else—Lawrence and Elsie got married. Over the course of the next seven and a half years, they had would indeed have five children. To this day, Lawrence believes the fortune-teller had been right.

Their first child arrived on April 8, 1955, a son named Carl. Lawrence was thrilled with the birth, but said not a word to Sarge—likely because he sensed that such a family matter would contravene Sarge's counsel to abstain from ". . . making lasting commitments" and could involve a rebuke in some form; Lawrence was more looking — consciously or unconsciously — for Sarge's approval at this stage.

Soon after, in search of therapeutic respite (perhaps from the effects of adding an infant to the family), Lawrence was about to leave for Huronia with his wife and newborn son. His intended destination was to be some of his favourite boyhood fishing holes.

Just as they was about to depart for Huronia, Sarge appeared with Jack, a dark-skinned east Indian man with whom he wanted Lawrence to take some training. Jack was dressed in British Army summer dress and short trousers. He was wearing what looked to Lawrence like an American cowboy hat with one side of the brim pinned up against the upper hat.

Jack was Nepalese and a special breed of fighter—a Gurkha, famous for their forward-curving knife and a well-known reputation for fearless military prowess. In deference to Sarge's wishes—and signalling where they were in his priority list—Lawrence cancelled his family trip to Huronia. The eclectic threesome—Lawrence, Sarge, and Jack—went camping in the bush north of Trenton (between Marmora and Madoc) for a stealth training exercise, leaving Elsie at home in Belleville with their newborn son.

Jack's initial attempts to interest Lawrence in this aspect of military tactics were simply unsuccessful. Sarge could order Lawrence around, but he couldn't order him to be interested; that required content, stimulation, and motivation, of which "sneaking around" possessed none, as Lawrence saw things. Consequently, in order to convince Lawrence that Gurkha stealth skills were indeed worthwhile, Jack and Sarge challenged Lawrence with a wager. Their proposed bet was that, with Lawrence standing guard at night, Jack could get back into camp without Lawrence's knowledge. Always up for a challenge, Lawrence readily agreed and Jack left camp.

That night, a quarter moon shone but it nevertheless was quite dark, particularly in the woods under the canopy of branches in full leaf. With a small fire going, Lawrence stationed himself where he thought he could see everything happening around the campsite. He watched and listened for anything suspicious. An hour passed, and there was not a sound—a second hour, nothing. Then, to Lawrence's great surprise, Sarge popped out of the tent with Jack right behind him.

Sarge summoned Lawrence over to them. Lawrence stood up and fell flat on his face because his bootlaces were tied together. Jack had tied them together and circled back around to enter the tent from the rear while Lawrence stood guard.

Now convinced that Jack's methods were worthwhile, Lawrence changed his attitude towards stealth training completely, even though he could not see any connection with a sniper's abilities. The training suddenly took on a high intensity and Jack's counsel became gospel. When Jack moved in stealth mode through a woodland carpet of twigs and dried leaves with his boots off, he would advance millimeters at a time.

They practised at length in daylight until Jack was satisfied with Lawrence's progress. Then they moved into night-time work.

"Remember this," counselled Jack to his young, eager protégé, "no one has eyes in the back of their head. If they have no reason to, they won't turn their head. That's why silence is your best ally."

Two weeks later, after persevering under Jack's tutelage, Lawrence secured Jack's approval of his stealth methods.

The frequency of Sarge's visits increased after that exercise, and further training followed, including a Flight Engineer's course held in Trenton. When Lawrence asked why he was being given the course, Sarge just walked away from the question. But when Lawrence failed the exam, Sarge was furious. Within a day or so, Lawrence was notified that he had been granted a second chance; this was an unheard of precedent, but almost certainly a result of Sarge's intervention. More significantly, it signalled the importance that Sarge was placing on

Lawrence's training for whatever plans he had for him—something that evidently surpassed the bare necessity of sniper marksmanship.

On passing the course, Lawrence's flights suddenly took on an expanded international flavour. Over the next few months, he flew cargo flights to Seven Islands (Quebec), Vancouver, Newfoundland, Chicago, Miami, and the months rolled on. Lawrence was enjoying his first taste of the high-flying lifestyle among military airmen.

In the spring of 1956, Sarge made arrangements with Lawrence to go to CFB Goose Bay. At that time, it was one of the largest military bases in north-eastern North America, even though it was located almost smack-dab in the middle of Labrador.

After a few drinks in this remote base's canteen, Lawrence was feeling their effects, and he retired to the barracks at about 11:00 p.m. At midnight, out of nowhere, Sarge was suddenly standing over him, proposing what Lawrence thought to be the most harebrained training exercise so far.

Sarge insisted that they go directly to Stores, where they proceeded to the Parachute Loft and selected the latest design—a jet-black, steerable, state-of-the-art parachute.

"You're going to use it tonight," Sarge announced to Lawrence's dismay. "And that's an order."

Never having jumped at night, Lawrence protested, but Sarge simply ignored him. Instead, he produced a map and started right in with the pre-exercise briefing.

"Here's where the Canadian Army Regiment is waiting for an intruder. That intruder is *you*, my little Laddie-Buck! The aircraft will drop you one-quarter mile from their line, marked with a flare. Right here! Now, here's where all the training I've given you will demonstrate its worth. Your assignment is to get back into their territory, undetected."

Perplexed, Lawrence asked him, "Now, tell me, Sarge. It's not for sniping, is it?"

Hesitating noticeably, Sarge answered, "You get through 'em successfully tonight, Laddie-Buck, and I'll answer all your questions. Okay?"

Lawrence agreed reluctantly, but in reality, had no choice. With the black chute bunched under his arm, Lawrence then asked Sarge, "Where's the chest pack?"

"Well, there ain't gonna be any chest pack on this jump," replied Sarge.

"What? No safety chute? What the hell do I do if this contraption doesn't open? Flap my arms?"

"Do what you want with your arms, Laddie. Flap them. Do whatever you please with them, but you *are* going to make this jump," replied Sarge.

Railroaded into action, a frightened Lawrence was soon aloft and peering down into the black of night. He could see a target flare flickering faintly below.

To say Lawrence was nervous would be an understatement. More accurately, he was terrified. Nevertheless, following orders, when the jump light came on, out he went. He had completed other jumps without an instructor, but without a static line to automatically pull the ripcord in case of some mishap, this one felt like suicide. This was a surprise, middle-of-the-night, trial-by-fire jump unlike any he had yet completed.

As he had been trained, Lawrence counted—1000, 2000, 3000, 4000, 5000—held his breath, and pulled the ripcord to open the chute. It opened and handled beautifully. What a relief! He readily steered the parachute towards the flare and landed about fifteen feet from it.

Now to get through the line of soldiers, he thought.

Sarge had given him black paste for his face, which he applied immediately. His Gurkha-Jack training now took over. Senses energized, he started off. Thinking that they would expect him to penetrate from the flank, he decided to go straight for the middle of the line. He reasoned that there would be minimal depth there, essentially a line only one person deep. *Get past that one person and penetration would be achieved*, he thought. To a great extent, he was also motivated by the thought that *Sarge will finally level with me about why I am being given all this training, why he singled me out, and more importantly, for what.*

His first action was to remove his boots so that he could feel every twig and leaf underfoot, Gurkha-Jack style. The bush was thick and he moved slowly, inching his way forward. Soon, to his right, he could hear two men speaking in whispers, but he couldn't make out what they were saying.

Then he heard a man say audibly, "Who are we looking for?" The voice was to his left and close. He froze, statue-like. He inched forward at a snail's pace. Placing each foot in front of the other with great care, he passed the two men without a sound. *How deep was their line?* He wondered. *Was it a single file line? I hope so.*

He heard a twig crack just ahead. Straining with both eyes and ears, he waited for any detectable movement; then he saw a soldier just ahead, leaning against a tree. Inching by him, he could have easily reached out and touched him. Gurkha-Jack's words of counsel flashed through his mind: "When you need to, crawl into your own shadow and disappear."

Creeping along, inching forward, careful step after careful step, stopping, listening, straining his eyes to make sure no one was ahead, Lawrence was within a few yards of completing penetration of the demarcation line. Once through, he headed straight for the hangar where he knew Sarge would be waiting.

Lawrence sighted Sarge and thought he would give him a scare, just to shake him up. He crept up behind Sarge and reached out quickly, clamped his right arm around his neck in a chokehold and simultaneously placed his left hand over Sarge's mouth. Quick as a flash, Sarge took his right arm in a firm grip and threw Lawrence over his shoulder. Sarge had mastered a few hand-to-hand countermoves of his own.

The two men broke out laughing. Sarge blew a few blasts on his whistle, picked up his radio and ended the exercise. All involved converged on the hangar, greatly impressed with Lawrence's penetration feat.

Still clad in black, face blackened, and black tuque on, none of the dozen or so "defenders" could imagine how he had pulled it off. But he had.

Almost four years had elapsed since his enlistment in the RCAF, and a lot had happened. Lawrence had become a qualified aeronautical engine mechanic, had married Elsie, now had a son (Carl), and had undertaken a wide range of specialized military training—marksmanship skills, explosives, orienteering in difficult terrain, flight training, stealth methods, parachuting, and some hand-to-hand and weapons-based combat work. With this latest successful test of his penetration skills, Sarge had committed to levelling with him about what was really going on—something that Lawrence was looking forward to, with great anticipation.

Chapter Two: **Operation Retrieve**

Later that morning at about 4:00 a.m. after washing up, Lawrence and Sarge met in the Mess Hall for their agreed meeting. Sarge approached the subject gingerly, beginning by praising Lawrence for his latest evasion manoeuvre. Then, he began summarizing why he had decided that Lawrence had the aptitude and ability to take on difficult assignments—such as what would be coming his way if he agreed to go ahead with the proposed venture.

But the youthful Lawrence was impetuous, anxious to get on with it (whatever "it" was). He wanted Sarge to get to the point. Whereupon Sarge complied and dove right in, saying, "I see you as an espionage courier."

"A what?" replied Lawrence.

"An espionage courier. It's an agent who takes important papers or information in a variety of forms, microfilm for example, from one place to another, often under dangerous conditions, and is trained on how to deal with most anything that might occur. You are on your own or with a partner, and once you are out there, it's up to you to make it back. That's why I have been giving you such a breadth of training. I hope you will decide to go ahead with this, but in the end, it'll be up to you."

Sarge expanded minimally on the secrecy aspect of this work, and told Lawrence that if he accepted the offer—made only to those chosen few with exceptional ability—he would become an agent for Her Majesty's Secret Service. Further discussion and clarification were allowed, of course, but for the venture to proceed, signing of an oath of lifetime secrecy would be required.

Hesitant but intrigued, Lawrence was advised to sleep on the idea, and they met again later that day at noon in the Mess Hall. Lawrence was unclear on the time frames involved and thought he might consider participating for a year or so. He was taken aback when Sarge told him that this would be a multi-year commitment. Lawrence was still apprehensive about the risk of having to kill, which remained implicit—and would be in contravention of the Thou-shalt-not-kill commandment that had been drilled into him as a child. Sarge, ever ambiguous, underplayed it as a "might happen" possibility.

To some extent under Sarge's spell, twenty-year-old Lawrence chose to interpret "might happen" as "won't happen," because he wanted to. Deep down, in a convoluted way, Lawrence also wanted Sarge's approval, and his youthful enthusiasm overtook any residual moral concerns that he continued to harbour. Consequently, he adopted a spare-me-the-details approach to this life-changing decision. With scarcely any further elaboration by Sarge, Lawrence announced that he was ready to sign.

They proceeded to another hangar that contained an office. Sarge unlocked it, then unlocked a desk drawer, pulled out a briefcase, opened it, and put a document in front of Lawrence. It was a declaration that he promptly signed. With that single stroke of a pen, Lawrence Fox became an MI-6 agent of Her Majesty's Secret Service. Within minutes, he had been assigned the code name "Lynx," which he would carry for the next twenty-two years.

The frequency of meetings in Trenton with Sarge suddenly rose and more training ensued—some one-on-one (judo, jujitsu, the use of coding for messages and how to read secret messages that appeared on blank paper), some as group exercises including survival in the bush. The Marmora-Madoc area north of CFB Trenton became the site of the field exercises. Lynx consistently achieved excellent results in every area, to Sarge's great satisfaction.

One exercise near Bancroft, Ontario, involved five fellow squadron members being dropped into an out-of-the-way location to simulate an airplane being forced down in difficult circumstances. They were given rations for nine days, but when they were picked up, they had plenty of rations left over. Lawrence had caught fish in the lake nearby to supplement the rations. At the debriefing, on being told that they had caught fish, the instructor grinned and informed the team that the fish in that lake were unsuitable for human consumption, because they were quite wormy. On hearing this, one of the officers who had been in the exercise promptly retched on the spot.

His reaction was purely psychosomatic. No one had eaten any fish for three days. They had been well cooked; all bacteria had been killed.

On June 24, 1956, Elsie and Lawrence had a second son, Lawrence Jr. He was a little brother for Carl, who was then only fourteen months old. They were building a family together, and life was good for Lawrence both on and off the job.

Lawrence had no contact with Sarge for several months and was simply going about his normal engine maintenance duties on the base. Then, in early November ('56), Lawrence was getting into his car and on the seat was an unaddressed envelope. As soon as he saw it, he knew immediately that it was from Sarge. Tearing the envelope open, there was a blank piece of paper inside—their code for a mission assignment. Rushing back to his room, he locked the door, turned on a table lamp, took off the shade, and slowly passed the piece of paper near the bulb, taking care to not singe it.

Hand printed in block letters, it read:[1]

> *AT 0700 HRS TOMORROW YOU ARE*
> *SCHEDULED ON A FLIGHT TO THE UK FLIGHT*
> *ENGINEER THAT WAS SCHEDULED SICK CHECK*

---

1 Written in lemon juice and invisible to the naked eye, the printing would only appear in front of a naked light bulb.

INTO CUMBERLAND HOTEL WITH THE FLIGHT CREW STAY PUT SEE YOU IN LONDON

SARGE

As he had been trained to do, he immediately lit a match, burned the note, and powdered it with a cigarette butt, leaving no chance that it could be read. Unable to sleep, he tossed and turned all night until his alarm clock went off. He arrived at the aircraft ahead of the crew, stowed his suitcase, and started his usual pre-flight checks in the already loaded aircraft. It took off as scheduled and stopped at CFB Goose Bay for refuelling. It then flew to Prestwick in the UK—where Lawrence and the crew overnighted—after a ten-hour trans-Atlantic flight that met with heavy headwinds.

Early the next morning, they flew to Langar, England (near the Sherwood Forest of Robin Hood fame), unloaded their cargo, and took off for Orly Airport, France, where they unloaded more cargo. They then flew back to London for a layover, and Lawrence checked into the Cumberland Hotel with the crew. After the crew had checked out (November 4th), Lawrence met Sarge in the hotel cafeteria as instructed. Sarge behaved strangely at first; he pretended that he didn't know Lawrence.

What's with this guy? thought Lawrence. After some awkward preliminaries, Sarge finally informed him in hushed tones that they would meet in the lobby the following night (November 5th) at 9:00 p.m. sharp to attend a pre-mission briefing. Sarge refused to elaborate any further on the matter.

Perplexed as to what was up, Lawrence went back to his room, opened a bottle of Seagram's VO, poured himself a few drinks, decided to do a little sightseeing, and took a cab to Piccadilly Square. Strolling about, he declined offers from a few roaming hookers and went back to the hotel where—alone in his hotel room—he proceeded to polish off the remainder of the Seagram's VO.

November 5, 1956

The next morning, harbouring a terrible hangover, Lawrence went to a nearby fish 'n' chips shop for a coffee that he promptly upchucked. He tried the fish and chips; they tasted fine and he managed to hold them down.

He was back out on the street, studying the marquee of a movie house that advertised a French film with English subtitles when he noticed an usherette watching him. They struck up a conversation, and she invited him for tea across the street later in the day at 4:00 p.m.

Her name was Jenny, a shapely nineteen-year-old, about five-foot-five with long blonde hair. Lawrence arrived early at the teashop and watched her cross the street as he waited for her there.

Jenny, of course, wanted to know all about Canada and Lynx complied—within bounds. When Lawrence indicated that he had had a tough time locating a good eatery, she offered to cook dinner in her flat. With Sarge's 9:00 p.m. deadline in mind, Lawrence indicated that he would have to leave by 8:00 p.m. "at the latest." Jenny indicated that she, too, would have to leave by 8:00 p.m. for her two-evenings-a-week modelling job. They had a compatible time fit.

Lawrence reassured Jenny that no womenfolk were involved, and indicated that he had a flight to catch—which turned out to be true, even if he didn't know it at the time. After an excellent dinner, his watch read 6:30 p.m. and they chatted about her situation. She wanted to be free of her parents and on her own. She told Lawrence how the high cost of living required her to have two jobs to make ends meet. Her parents lived nearby and she had a young brother, age twelve.

When Jenny turned the conversation towards him, Lawrence gave her a few nondescript comments on Canada's climate. His comments simply reinforced the reputation that Canada has in the UK of being a rather cold place to live.

When the time reached 7:55 p.m., Lawrence announced that he had to go. When he told her that he would be back in London "in a few days," she pulled a key for her flat from her purse and gave it to him, saying, "When you get back, come right over. It would be nice to come home and have someone here." Then, reaching up, she pulled his face down to hers and kissed him tenderly.

Once out the door, Lawrence hailed a cab and arrived ten minutes late for his meeting with Sarge in the hotel lobby. Sarge was furious, and wanted an explanation. Lawrence recounted what had happened, and Sarge, taking no chances, undertook to have Jenny screened. Sarge was paranoid about Russian agents, their far-reaching network of contacts, and essentially trusted no one—a behavioural pattern that Lawrence was to observe often in the coming years.

En route to the pre-mission briefing in a Secret Service car, Lawrence assumed his MI-6 code name Lynx for the first time. Sarge had Lynx empty his pockets into an envelope, which he put in his briefcase. A twenty-minute ride later, they arrived at a warehouse door. The driver gave two long and one short blast of the horn, the door opened, and the car entered the warehouse. The room was devoid of furniture except for three chairs sitting facing a large, internal window that looked blank and black. Lynx placed a hood with eyeholes—a balaclava of sorts—over his head at Sarge's insistence to conceal his identity before he got out of the car. Sarge indicated that Lynx take one of three chairs; Lynx sat down and removed the hood. A few minutes passed, the door opened, another man wearing a hood entered, and he was seated next to Lynx. Sarge sat in the third chair. Sarge removed the hood on the latest arrival and introduced Lynx to the man under it as Nomad, his mission partner. Lynx noted his features mentally, as was his wont: Nomad was about the same age as Lynx, had black hair, and was six feet tall—a big man in comparison to Lynx.

Sarge instructed that the two only use their code names when communicating, and forbid them from giving any further information on each other. He stressed the importance of this because "If you are caught, you will know nothing that you can tell your captors."

Lynx and Nomad agreed. Then, as if cued by an invisible baton, lights went on in the adjacent room behind the large glass window. Six army officers, one wearing a moustache and carrying a swagger stick under one arm, entered the room, followed by two high-ranking majors. They all sat at a table, papers in front of them, their every sound amplified by a microphone beamed into the room where the MI-6 triumvirate—Sarge, Lynx, and Nomad—sat.

On cue from Sarge, one of the officers started in: "Lynx and Nomad, this is 'Operation Retrieve.' The Russians are preparing to move on the Freedom Fighters in Budapest, and we have some important papers there—two envelopes—that we need brought out before the Russians move in and squash the revolution or occupy the city."

"You will be flown to a neutral country on a fast aircraft where you will board a light, single-engine plane. You will then be dropped into Hungary approximately fifty miles from Budapest. Contact will be made at the jump target. If the right man is there, he will say, 'The sun rises on Hungary tonight.' You, Lynx or Nomad, will answer, 'It shall indeed.'"

After a nudge from Sarge, both Lynx and Nomad confirmed receipt of this vital information with responses in the affirmative.

The officer went on: "If he doesn't give the password, you'll have to assume he is an enemy—probably a Russian. I hope you know that you will then have to shoot him."

No mention of the word "kill," thought Lynx. *Is it a taboo word?*

"Once he gives the proper identification, he will drive you into the city in a Russian staff car. In the car, there will be two Russian coats. Slip them on over your clothes. Once in the city, your contact will introduce you to their leader who has the documents. Leave the city and carry on out of Hungary immediately. We shall have a pick-up awaiting you at the Austrian border."

He then pulled down a gridded military wall map of Hungary and its borders and indicated the point of exit as coordinates "C12 down, G4 across." It was notably the closest exit point into Austria from Budapest.

"Our intelligence tells us that the Russians won't move into the city for at least two more days, so this should be a milk run—a piece of cake. Good luck, chaps. Any questions?"

Now into the swing of things, Lynx piped up with, "What time do we start?"

"You'll board the aircraft in about twenty-five minutes. It's parked only five minutes away. Your ETD is 2205 hours."

Sarge promptly announced that "Operation Retrieve is on," the meeting was adjourned, and the room behind the glass window went black. Turning to Nomad and Lynx, Sarge then opened the only other door in the room. It led into what looked like an indoor rifle range. Sarge pointed at two black cases on a table saying, "These are for you two. Go ahead. Open them up."

Lynx opened one case and inside was a beautiful Sterling Arms, state-of-the-art carbine, disassembled into eight parts:

- Barrel, 30/06, 18 inches long
- Breach block and pistol grip trigger mechanism
- Adjustable tubular stock and metal butt plate
- Scope, the most powerful Lynx had ever seen
- Magazine with a capacity of ten rounds of large diameter casings
- Second magazine, already loaded
- Screw-on silencer
- Shoulder carrying sling

Lynx lifted the barrel out of the case carefully, mated it with the breach block, then the stock, installed the silencer, adjusted the stock, and installed the scope. He took aim, fired one shot. *Zip!*—a bullseye. No adjustment necessary. *Zip! Zip!*—two more bullseyes.

Nomad did the same with the same result. Sarge promptly replaced the spent shells in both rifles and marked the case that each mission partner had picked—one mark for Lynx, two marks for Nomad.

False identification papers were then handed out—one set Russian, one set Hungarian—and a change of civvies that each man placed into his packsack. Both men also put in two loaded magazines, several plastic explosives with timers, black face paste, rations, a medical kit, a map of the area and a compass. They both put on wristwatches and slung .45 automatic pistols and eleven-inch, double-edged knives in scabbards on their belts.

They then got into their camouflaged jumpsuits and jump boots, shoved a black tuque into one pocket, picked up a parachute and proceeded to "walk"—such as they could, each carrying a carbine case and all related gear—towards the waiting car. Then, Sarge began his last minute instructions, as would become habit: "Bury the chutes after you land, also the carbine cases. Nomad, no offense, but Lynx is in charge, only because he has more training. Okay?"

"Sure," said Nomad, winking at Lynx, who was elated at first with his "promotion," and then annoyed when he suddenly realized he was now responsible for getting the papers out *and* for Nomad's safety. He glared at Sarge, to no avail.

"Finally," continued Sarge as he handed a briefcase to Lynx, "this briefcase never leaves your hands. It comes directly back to me only."

After a five-minute ride, they reached the waiting aircraft, boarded quickly, and Sarge passed an envelope to Lynx just before the door closed, with his final instruction: "Open it when you get airborne."

As the plane took off, Lynx read his wristwatch as 2205 hours—right on schedule.

The two mission partners, who had known each other less than an hour, exchanged nervous small talk as the flight began.

Once at their flight altitude, Lynx remembered Sarge's last minute envelope and opened it to find two folded notes, each with a capsule taped to it—one for himself, and one for Nomad.

Opening his note, it read:

> Lynx:
>
> Do not smoke while reading this note. The paper is highly flammable. You and Nomad are to be paired up on each mission from now on. He is well trained, dependable, and can be counted on. He is an expert in explosives. You have qualities that fit well together.
>
> The capsule contains cyanide, for use at your discretion. If either or both of you are caught, you could be shot on the spot. You would be tried as spies. After torture, during which they would suck everything you know from your brain, you would be jailed or sent to Siberia.

The capsule has a hard shell and will not melt in your mouth. Bite down on it. When the shell is broken, swallow the fluid. It takes twenty seconds to work. Keep it within easy reach at all times.

You are a good pair. That's why we are not sending a seasoned courier with you. Lynx, you call the shots, so use your head. Those documents must come out, at any cost.

Another thing: Agree on a new code name for me. My suggestion is either "Mom" or "Mother."

After reading this note, place it back into the envelope, put the envelope into the toilet, light a match, throw it onto the envelope, and stand well back. It flares up quickly.

Best of luck. See you at debriefing in about eighteen hours.

Mother

Shocked, Lynx wanted out right then and there, but that was obviously not an option. He and Nomad conferred, Nomad light-heartedly—that was his way of coping with the tension while Lynx was in a state of high anxiety. They spent the remainder of the flight in small talk—women, food, their training, Sarge—getting to know one another. Nomad did the honours of destroying the note in the toilet, and as warned, it disappeared in a dramatic *Swoosh!* without a trace.

November 6, 1956

The captain flew above a storm at increased throttle to maintain their rendezvous schedule. He advised that they would make their target rendezvous at 0240 hours.

Lynx dozed off, only to be shaken awake by Nomad pointing out that the "Fasten Seat Belts" sign was on. Lynx glanced at his watch; it read 0230 hours—ten minutes ahead of schedule. The flight began its descent. Nomad had already buckled his knife and .45 automatic onto his waist. Lynx buckled on his waist weaponry. He then helped Nomad with his chute straps to ensure no entanglement. They blackened their faces, sighted a double row of flares below, and braced for a grass airstrip landing. It was a rough one, but short.

They deplaned quickly, five minutes ahead of schedule, and were directed to a small-engine aircraft, a Cessna-like, high-wing monoplane with a side door removed and its engine already running. They climbed in and sat on their packs somewhat apprehensively, making sure that they sat where their weight would not affect any plastic explosives timers.

They held on to the metal reinforcing on the inside of the fuselage as the plane bounced over the grass and became airborne. It climbed rapidly to altitude, turned sharply, and headed across the country. Lynx noticed that the engine sound was muffled and that there was no flame from the exhaust, probably because a flame damper had been installed in the muffler.

Lynx sat in silence, thinking back to his early Midland days, and how his parents would never think that their son was in any danger. He was jarred out of his daydreaming by the rapid descent of the aircraft as the pilot announced that they would have to fly lower in order to get under the Russian radar. Twenty-five minutes from the target, he announced, "Get ready."

0315 hours[2]

As the tiny aircraft bounced around between air pockets just above treetop height, sometimes turning, Lynx and Nomad readied for the jump. The pilot put the plane into a steep up-climb in readiness by

---

2 These time markers are taken from Lynx's wristwatch readings and written recollections.

gaining a lot of altitude and had soon sighted a flare on the ground. He then cut back the engine, and within a minute, Nomad and Lynx were descending into the black of night. Counting down as he left the aircraft—1000, 2000, 3000, 4000, 5000—Lynx pulled the release, the chute unfolded, and he steered his chute towards the flare. He sighted a man standing beside it. Grasping his .45 automatic, he landed with a thud, rolled, and dropped the briefcase, keeping an eye on the dark shape of the man—throughout—as best he could. Releasing the chute harness and the safety on his .45 automatic as the man ran up to him with no gun visible, Lynx approached him cautiously, his .45 aimed at his head. The man said, "The sun rises on Hungary tonight."

"It shall indeed," replied Lynx. Nomad had readied his knife, which he sheathed. "What's your name?" asked Lynx.

"Dob," said the man.

That quick exchange was to be the first instance of Lynx's "Sixth Sense"—a form of ESP—kicking in. His gut twinged and started churning, alerting him to be wary. Something was off the rails, but he did not yet know what it was.

After quickly snuffing out the flare, removing the black face paste, assembling the carbines and burying the chutes and carbine cases as instructed, Lynx went a-prowling Gurkha-Jack style to verify that all was well. About a hundred yards away, Lynx sighted a car. He circled it quietly and found no one nearby. His uneasy feeling about the situation would not go away.

The car was the Russian staff car that had been mentioned at the pre-mission briefing, complete with a red star on each door, red hammer-and-sickle banners flying from each front fender—a big and powerful vehicle. Once inside the car, Lynx and Nomad slipped on Russian overcoats and hats, as instructed.

Dob took the wheel and started at high speed towards Budapest. Dob was undeterred by Lynx's comment that he was going too fast. Lynx's nerves were as taut as banjo strings and his uneasiness persisted. Small talk continued as they careened along the road towards Budapest. Nomad amused the happy-go-lucky Dob with his raunchiest jokes, until the boom of large guns could be heard intermittently in the distance. A sombre mood descended in the speeding car.

When Lynx heard Dob say, "Russians ahead of schedule," he anticipated the worst, wondering whether that was why his Sixth Sense had been nagging him. Dob drove on and the car skidded around a curve, only to reveal six men with submachine guns at the ready. Dob slammed on the brakes and the car swerved left, then right when he suddenly announced, "Don't shoot! They're not Russians. They're Freedom Fighters—part of our group."

Dob shouted something in Hungarian. They lowered their guns. Dob jumped out of the car, his tongue wagging in a continuous flutter of Hungarian. He returned and announced—nay, confirmed—the already ripe rumour that, "The Russians are in the city ahead of time."

Ten years had elapsed since the Iron Curtain was lowered on Hungary in 1946; widespread, seething discontent with Russian domination had been brewing below the surface ever since. The first public evidence of it surfaced on October 23, 1956, when Budapest university students had staged a protest.[3] The Kremlin antennae immediately went up and they began assembling tanks on the edge of the city, awaiting developments. Within a matter of days, one thousand tanks had arrived, signalling their iron-fisted intention to maintain control of the country.

At dawn on November 4, two days before Lynx and Nomad were dropped into Hungary, those Russian tanks advanced into Budapest under orders to crush the upstart revolution before things got out of hand. That mass invasion of the city had occurred at least a few days earlier than MI-6 intelligence expected.

Lynx reluctantly accepted that as the cause of his anxiety, thinking: *My stomach thoughts had been correct. Something is amiss. This will be some milk run, all right. Now, we'll have to wing it the rest of the way.*

The working class—who would emerge as the core of the Freedom Fighter faction in the coming battle—had long since abandoned hope

---

3 This was fourteen days before Lynx and Nomad had jumped on Operation Retrieve.

that they would ever prosper under a communist regime. Instead, they had been ruthlessly exploited by the dictatorial Russian regime, primarily through low pay and gruelling hours. And just to make sure there was unquestioning obedience throughout, the Russians deployed their secret police to keep everyone in line.

A boiling point had clearly been reached.

The six Freedom Fighters joined Dob and his team but it soon became obvious that the Russian staff car was a liability—it was too conspicuous, but was still a suitable getaway car for Lynx and Nomad once they had made their pickup. It would have to be stashed somewhere. Lynx and Nomad doffed their Russian coats and hats, changed clothes, and pulled out their Hungarian identification papers.

Now, what to do with the big, Russian staff car? Hide it, obviously—but where?

Dob decided that a good hiding place for the car was a barn just down the road. With seven armed men on the big Russian staff car—two in the front seat, three in the back, and two on the fenders—they made their way down the road to a house in ruin. Old growth trees surrounded it and a nearby barn, making it a perfect place to keep the car out of sight in readiness for the getaway.

To lighten his load, Lynx pared down to the .45 automatic on his belt, his knife in its sheath strapped to one leg and partway inside his boot, his carbine, two extra mags, and the briefcase. Nomad did the same, both also taking several plastic explosives in one pocket, timers in another to prevent accidental detonation. They left their packs with the staff car.

With one man left to guard the car, the remaining six trotted off towards the city. Dob knew of a car, hidden a half-mile down the road, that would save time. They headed for it and all six managed to shoehorn into the small European model. Both Lynx and Nomad took as much care as they could in the crammed quarters to avoid putting pressure on the plastic explosives.

0420 hours

They proceeded towards downtown Budapest with the car's headlights out to avoid drawing attention. They sighted a tank straight ahead. The driver turned into an alley, and then around a corner into another alley. They hoped they hadn't been seen.

0435 hours

Sneaking through alleys in the car as furtively as possible, they spotted another tank. This time, they had been seen. The big gun turret swung towards them as the tank's machine gunner started peppering bullets in their general direction. The car took off, swinging from one right-angle turn to the next in the grid of alleyways and streets, tires screaming at each corner. Another tank opened fire and narrowly missed the car, but the massive shell destroyed a wall behind it.

They abandoned the small car. Seconds later, it took a direct hit by a tank shell and exploded.

Leaving two men behind to distract the tank, the remaining four pressed on towards their designated rendezvous point. They moved from building to building, waiting for breaks in the action as they approached the centre of Budapest. Rifle and machine gun action continued in the background.

They reached an alley and met more Freedom Fighters with whom they joined forces in the hope that numbers would make a difference.

Within a few hundred yards of the pick-up spot, Freedom Fighters were firing rifles from apartment windows at the tanks below. Their bullets had no effect, ricocheting harmlessly off the massive armour of the lumbering behemoths. Several dead bodies were strewn where they had fallen in the street, a mixture of civilians and Freedom Fighters. To Lynx, the scene was grotesque.

The Freedom Fighters attempted to distract the tank's attention from one of their own who was bravely tossing a wine bottle filled with gasoline—a Molotov cocktail—onto a tank. It burst into flames and the fire somehow spread into the tank's interior. The tank crew opened the top hatch and scrambled out. The Freedom Fighters opened fire from point-blank range, killing them all.

Lynx had just witnessed his first cold-blooded killings. He reacted with revulsion, in contrast to a small group of civilian onlookers who openly cheered. However, their jubilance was short-lived as another tank approached from a different direction. Nomad offered to take it out by attaching a plastic explosive under the rear of the tank, planning to then "run like hell."

"Too risky," declared Lynx, who was in charge of the mission, only to hear an offer of "I'll do it" from behind him. He turned to see a teenager, one of the Freedom Fighters with whom they had joined forces at the last alley, his hand outstretched, saying, "Give me bomb. I'll do it."

Nomad pressed Lynx to "let the kid do the deed." Lynx cautioned him, saying, "You want to get him killed? Look. He's only sixteen years old."

"Fifteen, sir," the kid corrected.

Now Dob spoke up. "Let him try, Mister Lynx. We can't go anywhere until we take out that tank."

Caught in the middle of an intense situation, Lynx reluctantly agreed to let the youngster take his chances. The thought of sending a fifteen-year-old to his death gave him acute remorse. His gut twinged but—this time—he knew why.

Nomad, highly trained in the use of plastic explosives, asked the kid, "How long will it take you to go under the tank?"

"About five minutes."

"Okay. I'll set the timer for seven minutes. That means you have less than seven minutes to get this thing under the tank, and then get yourself as far away from it as you can."

The kid nodded. Nomad set the timer, placed the plastic bomb in the kid's hand, slapped him on the shoulder, and said, "Okay, Tiger. Go get 'em."

As the kid disappeared into the darkness, a minute passed, then two, Lynx timing him. Suddenly he appeared on the full run from behind a building farther down the street. Three minutes. He ran in a crouch to avoid being seen by the rear gunner on the tank. The four-minute mark. With a sudden burst of speed, he rolled under the tank as it lumbered forward, got between the tracks, stuck the explosive in place, popped out from under the tank, and was instantly again on the full run.

The group stood watching, their anxious hearts in their mouths, when the inevitable happened. The tank's rear gunner sighted the kid in full flight and immediately opened fire with his machine gun.

The boy tumbled and rolled over several times, came to a stop in the gutter, and lay still. *Just fifteen years old*, thought Lynx, *and now dead because I said to do it.*

Instinctively, to draw attention away from the kid, Lynx vented his frustration by opening fire with all ten rounds from his carbine, the bullets ricocheting off the tank's armour without effect. Hoping the kid was still alive, deep down Lynx's gut told him that he was gone. As Lynx ducked back into cover to change his empty magazine, Nomad took his place and opened fire.

Suddenly the plastic bomb detonated with an ear-piercing explosion, engulfing the tank in flames.

Lynx had looked away momentarily when Nomad suddenly shouted, "Lynx! Lynx! The kid's all right! He was playing dead!"

Sure enough, the kid had been using the curb as a partial shield, but was now up and running as fast as he could towards them, grinning from ear-to-ear.

Once the kid was safely back and as the group continued talking, mostly congratulating each other on the outcome of this riveting encounter, the group suddenly realized that there were four men running across the street towards them.

"Lynx, here comes Jules now. He's your contact man," said Dob, pointing him out.

A huge, muscular man, Jules' immediate priority was to debrief the fifteen-year-old kid. He then turned his attention to the MI-6 contingent and said with a grin, "Nomad, Lynx, you have made the boy a hero." Some welcoming pleasantries followed and he ended his greeting with, "How many more bombs do you have?"

"Seven," answered Nomad. Lynx instructed Nomad to give them four, leaving three in Nomad's possession and several spares still with Lynx. Jules' advice was to hide the two MI-6 agents in a safe place until he could pick up the documents, and he offered to take them to a hideout a short distance away. Lynx agreed, and Jules led them to a cellar in a nearby house that had been heavily shelled. Jules indicated that he had other commitments that he must attend to immediately, and that he would be back as soon as he could with the pickup package for Lynx. He exited the cellar, taking the others with him.

Lynx and Nomad sat alone in the cellar. Lynx lit a match to look around and observed solid overhead beams, old chairs, a dresser, and some other furniture, even a wine cellar. Positioning themselves for best advantage should anyone enter, Lynx discouraged Nomad from sampling the wine and handed him some rations.

Suddenly there was the unmistakable sound of a tank moving by on the paved street. Knowing full well that a tank blast in their direction would be fatal, they nevertheless both pointed their carbines—pea-shooters against a big tank gun—towards the door. Then, for reasons unknown, the tank moved on.

Lynx instructed Nomad to get some shut-eye and moved to the left side of the door. Five minutes later, Nomad was snoring noisily—too noisily, in fact—but Lynx let him slumber on.

0550 hours

Nomad awoke, and he and Lynx suddenly went into full alert when they heard footsteps approaching. Lynx quietly screwed the silencer onto his carbine as the footsteps got louder. Nomad—a highly accomplished knife thrower—stood well back in the shadows, ready to throw his knife at whoever came through the doorway.

Hearing only one set of footsteps as they came ever closer, Lynx concluded that it was a lone walker. The approaching visitor stopped again on the other side of the wall from Lynx, who carefully set his carbine down and prepared to attack with his hands. Nomad nodded in agreement, his knife still poised above his head. The visitor moved again and stopped, this time fully in the doorway.

As Lynx readied to deliver a fatal chop to the throat, the visitor stepped into the cellar—a youngster in his early teens. Lynx changed tactics instantly, and with a sudden burst of action, took him by the front of his clothes with one hand, grabbed his left wrist with the other, and flung him to the floor. Leaping onto his back with a cat-like swiftness, Lynx clamped one hand over his mouth. Nomad also closed in as backup and signalled the youngster to remain quiet by putting an index finger to his pursed lips. The youngster whispered something in Hungarian, which neither Lynx nor Nomad comprehended, and then indicated that he understood some English. They determined through the boy's broken English that he was Jules' young brother.

Lynx mimed that he should sit at the back of the cellar and, after checking to see if he was armed, sent him there. He sat wide-eyed as Lynx and Nomad talked in whispers.

While Lynx stood guard at the door, Nomad became the resident "baby-sitter" with the youngster and whined to Lynx about his new-found "role."

With daylight fast approaching, Lynx wondered, *How will we get back to the waiting getaway car and out of Budapest without the advantage of darkness? Waiting until nightfall—a long way off—does not seem like an option.*

Then the early morning sounds included those of something approaching through the rubble. Readying his carbine, Lynx heard, "Lynx, Nomad—it's me, Jules." Suddenly there he was, entering the cellar with two heavily armed men. Apologizing for the time taken, Jules promptly passed the vital documents—two sealed manila envelopes—to Lynx who quickly put them into his briefcase. As he was doing so, the boy spoke to Jules who indicated that he had told the boy to lay low, indoors, for safety. Snapping at his brother, Jules scolded him in Hungarian—and then stopped abruptly.

Jules raised his hand for silence, and all weapons were instantly pointed at the door. The sounds of two or more people approaching grew in volume. Someone outside spoke in Hungarian, Jules answered, and in they came—two Hungarians and a Russian prisoner, cowering in fear, his hands on top of his head as they prodded him into the cellar. Jules spoke to the prisoner in Russian. When he did not answer, one of the Freedom Fighters poked him with a rifle and he responded.

Jules wondered aloud why they had taken a prisoner—something they generally did not do—when even more footsteps were heard coming from outside. Nomad clamped a hand over the prisoner's mouth and held his knife across his throat with the other. The Russian's eyes were like saucers, bulging with fear.

The latest visitor, a Hungarian, his head and one upper arm bandaged, spoke to Jules while Nomad continued holding the Russian prisoner. Turning to Lynx, Jules told him that getting out of the city would now be difficult. Lynx suggested that perhaps the Russian prisoner might know something of use, and Jules turned his attention to that prospect. The Russian responded openly, perhaps hoping to encourage leniency.

The bandaged newcomer gradually took an increased interest in the Russian prisoner, eyeing him up and down and peering closely at his face in the poor light. In a sudden flash of recognition, he started screaming in Hungarian at the prisoner, pulled a revolver out of his jacket, and fired point-blank at the Russian before anyone could intervene. The Russian clutched at his stomach and fell to his knees. The hysterical Freedom Fighter fired a second shot to the head, killing the Russian instantly. The two gunshots deafened everyone momentarily. Splattered blood covered the dead man's face, visible even in the dim light.

Lynx, revolted by the sight, thought he would be sick on the spot. The Freedom Fighter, shaking with rage, stood over the dead Russian, ready to fire again if necessary when Jules grabbed the pistol from his hand. The man turned away, his face in his hands, sobbing uncontrollably and mumbling something in Hungarian.

Jules turned to Lynx and explained that earlier that morning, the slain Russian had been party to a gang rape of the Freedom Fighter's young sister and a beating of his father, almost to the point of death. He had arrived just after this had happened, and his mother described the soldiers involved to him. One had a scar on his left cheek—the man who had just been slain. He had vowed to kill them all.

Understandable, thought Lynx, *but those gunshots have to have been heard, and we now must move quickly.*

The dead Russian had given Jules valuable intel, and he now had a plan for getting the MI-6 contingent out of the city. Just before he had been shot, the Russian had told Jules that there was a cache of six Russian tanks and an armoured troop carrier about five blocks away. Jules' plan was to capture the troop carrier and use it for getting Nomad and Lynx back to their hidden getaway car. Jules simply dismissed the execution as an act of passion. "We would have had to kill him anyway, because we take no prisoners," he said. "Forget it. Let's move on."

With that, Jules led his three men, his young brother (who grabbed the Russian's gun for himself), Lynx, and Nomad out of the cellar and towards the Russian troop carrier. Lynx carried the briefcase. They ran through alleys, over fences, and across streets with great caution, working their way towards the cache of vehicles. When they encountered troops who were searching houses door-to-door on both sides of a street that had to be crossed, the group stopped to consider their options.

They decided to detour around the area, giving it a healthy berth by going through another area that the Russians had already searched. Crossing carefully one by one—eating up valuable time but an action necessary to minimize the prospect of casualties—Jules went ahead to reconnaissance the situation. He reported back that the tanks were at the far end of a square, and the troop carrier was parked at the closer end with only one guard.

Lynx volunteered to take the guard out without a sound. He got Jules' approval, passed his carbine, .45 automatic, and briefcase to Nomad, and removed his jacket. Around the corner, Lynx saw the carrier about one hundred yards away. The guard was leaning against it totally relaxed, his back towards Lynx. Lynx watched him for a few seconds. The guard turned and glanced off to his right, then resumed looking across the square at the tanks. Lynx took off his boots and started towards the carrier and the guard, holding his knife in his right hand. He tried to keep the carrier between him and the tanks as much as possible. In a low crouch and moving slowly, he inched forward. His angle of approach put him a little to his target's left. Lynx froze when needed as he inched closer.

Lynx moved along the rear of the carrier until he was only a few feet away from the guard. Lynx had his knife ready, but suddenly found the idea of killing him nauseating. He was, however, committed. Lynx lowered the knife out of play, and with the back of his hand snapped a chop at the back of the guard's neck, rendering him unconscious but still alive. Lynx caught him before he hit the ground and dragged him out of sight. Dob's team then made a break for the troop carrier.

Jules and Lynx stripped the guard of his uniform, Jules put it on, and they took the Russian guard with them into the carrier. Nomad quickly hog-tied and gagged him. (In all probability, he was later shot, in keeping with their "Take-no-prisoners" philosophy.) Jules studied the controls, put on a headset, and started the engine while Lynx retrieved his equipment and briefcase from Nomad and started looking around the interior of the machine.

The carrier suddenly jerked forward as Jules put it into gear. He turned it to the right, away from the tanks, and gave it full throttle to gain speed. Posing as a Russian driver and speaking into his microphone, Jules informed the Russians that he was going to pick up his troops and that "orders are orders." As the carrier reached about 40 mph, Jules steered it down a main street. About two blocks along, a group of Freedom Fighters appeared ahead; one was brandishing a flaming Molotov cocktail. Jules stopped and ordered one of his men to let them pass in Hungarian. To Lynx's great surprise, they all jumped into the carrier, snuffing out the Molotov cocktail as they did so. *More reinforcements,* thought Lynx.

Jules sighted a tank ahead, spoke into his microphone in fluent Russian, and got approval to pass. Then, when his men indicated that they wanted to blow up an oncoming tank, Jules asked the approaching tank if they would like some wine. They accepted. Once stopped alongside the tank, one of Jules' men lit the wick of a Molotov cocktail, and when the Russians opened their tank hatch, one of the Freedom Fighters drove the butt of his rifle into the man's face and the Russian fell back into the tank. Jules' man then lobbed the Molotov cocktail into the open hatch, the bottle broke, and a belch of flame shot out as the cocktail ignited.

Jules floored the accelerator on the troop carrier. The gunner on the rear of the tank opened fire and bullets ricocheted everywhere, but too late—the tank blew up in an enormous explosion. Somehow, the cocktail had ignited the tank's fuel tank.

0636 hours

They resumed speed towards the stashed getaway car, now a mile and a half away. However, Jules' upbeat expression suddenly changed when he learned on the radio that the Russians were onto them as a pirated troop carrier. The Russians warned on the radio that surrender to a tank up ahead was the only condition under which they would not open fire. Jules was also able to determine from the radio chatter that Russian reinforcements had been summoned, but they were still a fair distance away.

With events unfolding rapidly, life and death decisions were being made on the fly. Jules suggested that Lynx and Nomad jump free of the troop carrier and take their chances while he, too, would take his chances at escaping with his men in the troop carrier. Lynx, thinking, *That would be suicide,* proposed using a plastic explosive to take out the tank up ahead if Jules could manoeuvre the carrier close enough for someone to get a plastic explosive under the tank. To do that, the highly manoeuvrable troop carrier would need to avoid the tank's lumbersome-but-powerful turret gun through Jules' skilful driving.

Jules agreed to give it a try. With no intention of doing so, Jules communicated his intention to surrender to the Russians while Nomad readied a plastic explosive. Jules steered the troop carrier towards the waiting Russian tank. At the last second, Jules suddenly swung the carrier to the left and started circling the tank at high speed, over curbs, through ditches, anything in its path. That manoeuvre signalled the Russian tank that Jules' indication of surrender had been a ruse. The Russian tank immediately tried to line up their big turret gun for a shot at the fast-circling troop carrier. Nomad set the explosive timer for two minutes as the troop carrier continued moving erratically to avoid the big tank gun. Then the tank started to move, making it more difficult to get the plastic explosive in place.

With the carrier moving slowly—temporarily, in order to let their man off—one of Jules' men leapt over the side, carrying the ready-to-go plastic explosive. The tail gunner on the tank opened fire, even though he could not get a clean shot at Jules' man. Nomad jumped behind the 20-mm. gun on the side of the carrier and started returning fire.

Hearing was difficult with all the gunfire. The tail gunner wounded Jules' man and he fell to the ground, still holding the bomb but fifteen feet away from the tank—not close enough to plant the explosive for full effectiveness. The troop carrier continued circling at high speed while the tank persevered to get a shot in.

The tank's tail gunner stopped shooting, probably taken out by one of Nomad's 20-mm. shots. Jules' man started crawling towards the tank to plant the explosive. Nomad's face suddenly went white, eyes agog, mouth agape as he watched Jules' man crawl under the tank, which suddenly started moving and turning at the same time. He screamed, "My God! He's crawled under the tank, and it's turning . . ."

Revolted by the sight of Jules' man being torn in two by one of the turning tank treads just as the plastic explosive ignited, Nomad was badly shaken. The bomb had blown one track completely off the tank as it continued to swivel its big gun towards the carrier. Nomad, now a driven man, jumped off the troop carrier and up onto the tank track, leapt to the hatch, opened it up, and ducked back as the Russians, trapped inside, started shooting up and out of the tank. Nomad then pointed his carbine down into the hatch and emptied his magazine into the tank interior. Bullets were heard ricocheting everywhere inside the tank.

Dead silence descended on the tank. The battle was over—for now. Jules stopped the carrier, switched it off and exited the vehicle. Nomad jumped off the tank and walked over to where Lynx and the others had assembled.

Scolded by Lynx for the danger inherent in his heroic action, Nomad simply replied, "Reflex action, man. Sometimes you have to do what you have to do." Indeed, had Nomad not wiped out the tank crew with his spectacular, carbine-emptying barrage, the battle would still be raging.

There was still no sign of Russian reinforcements arriving yet, but with all the gunfire that had just occurred and their radioing for assistance before this last exchange, they would arrive soon.

Just as they were about to part company—Lynx and Nomad to the stashed staff car, the Freedom Fighters back into the city—a pistol shot rang out. One of the Hungarians fired his rifle towards the tank. A Russian soldier, half way out of the turret, slumped down over the side of the hatch, the pistol fell from his hand and clanked down onto the tank. He had somehow survived Nomad's barrage of bullets inside the tank, but had now been taken out.

Jules was lying on the ground, blood seeping out of his trousers on one upper leg. Lynx ripped open the pant leg to inspect his wound and knew immediately that the bullet had hit a few inches below his right hip on the outside of the leg. No bone or vital artery was affected—a flesh wound only. Lynx ripped his own shirt into a bandage and dressed the wound as best he could.

Exhibiting great courage, Jules then stood up. After brief and emotional "best-of-lucks," the parties separated. Lynx and Nomad headed on foot along the road towards their Russian getaway car. Roadside cover would be needed when, once more, the Russians inevitably arrived.

After about three hundred yards, the roadside bushes thinned out and cover became more difficult. When they heard the faint whirr of a tank in the distance, they crawled into the brush. Two tanks were heading towards them at full throttle, turrets open, the upper torso of a man in each. Russian reinforcements had started arriving to help capture a runaway troop carrier, but too late—that battle was already over.

As they passed a disabled tank, Lynx got up and ran towards the next clump of roadside bushes. Nomad followed. About fifty yards farther along the road, there was another clump of bushes for cover. They made for it as the sound of tank motors in the distance got louder.

Out of nowhere, another tank appeared on the road, moving at full speed—more Russian reinforcements arriving too late—and passed the two fugitive agents. A spotter in its turret apparently had not seen them.

The next concealment possibility was about seventy-five yards away, and from then on, the roadside bushes got thicker. Lynx decided to go for it first, followed by Nomad. Then Lynx heard the sound of an approaching car. He waited until it had passed; it was carrying four Russian officers. *Plenty of supervision also arriving too late,* Lynx thought. *It looks good on them.*

Once it had passed, Lynx jumped up and ran at full tilt for a distance, dove into the bushes, his heart pounding as he waved Nomad forward. There was no sign of the old barn and broken-down house ahead yet. The roadside bushes made long-distance sighting difficult, so they advanced in short, controlled bursts a few more times. The barn finally appeared in the distance.

Lynx anticipated that the Russians might have discovered the car. Consequently, he passed the briefcase to Nomad and went ahead to determine the situation. When he got to the barn, the car was there but there was no sign of the Hungarian guard—or was there? The unmistakable feel of the muzzle of a gun in his back gave him the answer. Lynx stood motionless to avoid any unneeded excitement. The guard said something in Hungarian, and Lynx replied, "I'm English."

"Hands over your head and turn around slowly," instructed the guard.

Once face-to-face, the guard recognized Lynx immediately, smiled, lowered his gun, and inquired about Lynx's partner. Lynx called him and Nomad arrived on the run.

Then the sound of another tank could be heard approaching along the road. Lynx quickly briefed his Hungarian ally on the early morning events in the city. The guard, a Freedom Fighter at heart, announced that he was going back into the city to help his comrades-in-arms. Lynx kept three plastic explosives for themselves and gave him the rest of their supply as a contribution to the cause. The Hungarian quickly and carefully stuffed them into separate pockets—plastics in one, timers in another—expressed his gratitude, and left in haste.

Lynx and Nomad discarded any clothes they would not need, put on their jumpsuits and Russian overcoats and hats, and strapped knives onto their lower legs and automatic .45's on their waist belts. Nomad went down to the road to give Lynx a signal when to bring the car down.

Lynx started the car. On a "go" signal from Nomad, Lynx backed it out of the barn, tires spinning. He swung it into a U-turn towards the road, put it into first gear, sped down the short lane, stopped to pick up Nomad who jumped into the back seat, and they took off down the road.

0705 hours

The Austrian border was about one hundred miles away, the gas tank half full, the speed at 110 kph. Lynx, unschooled in the metric system, had no idea how fast that was.

Up ahead, Lynx could see a tank approaching. *Should I slow down*? he wondered. *No—less chance of the turret lookout seeing inside the car.*

Lynx held his speed, his eyes riveted straight ahead and looked serious as the tank passed. The soldier in the turret saluted, and Nomad saluted back. As they sped down the road, Nomad admired Lynx's driving skills—a carryover, he told Nomad, from his stock car driving days.

With the speedometer reading 165 kph, Nomad concluded incorrectly that they were doing about 60 mph—more like 100 mph!

However, both agreed the faster, the better. Without further interruptions, they should meet their 1100 hours pick-up time.

Nomad saluted another passing tank.

Calculating their ETA on the basis of Nomad's 60 mph, and with a half tank of gas, they concluded that the border was about ninety minutes away.[4]

Then Lynx sighted a roadblock ahead—a car pulled halfway across the road with a motorcycle on the other side of it. There was a four-foot gap between them.

Lynx floored the gas pedal, took a firm grip on the steering wheel and aimed the car at the four-foot gap. When the Russians at the roadblock realized that this car was not stopping, they frantically made for the side of the road just as the speeding car smashed into the roadblock. The motorcycle went flying about thirty feet into the air on the left. The car on the right was knocked into the ditch. As a result of the glancing collision with the parked car, the right side of the speeding Russian staff car went up onto two wheels for about fifty feet as it careened through the roadblock.

Once the speeding car was back on all fours, Lynx could hardly control it. The right front wheel had a severe shimmy, forcing him to slow down, but only a little; after all, that was counter to his instincts. Meantime, the soldiers back at the roadblock started shooting at the car, some bullets hitting it. One went through the rear window, smashed the rear-view mirror and exited out through the windshield—all ineffectual in terms of consequences, or so it seemed.

Nomad opened fire with four shots out the shattered rear window with his carbine, but he was unable to take an effective aim because of the car vibration.

Lynx glanced at the fuel gauge, which had suddenly dropped to a quarter tank. One or more of their shots must have hit the fuel tank.

Not only that—the shimmying right front wheel now made it nearly impossible for Lynx to steer the car.

---

4 In fact, at that speed, they would reach the Austrian border in less than an hour.

When they were well away from the Russians and thinking that it was best to assess the damage, Lynx stopped the car, got out, and observed gasoline flowing from two bullet holes in the gas tank—from the same bullet. It had gone clean through the gas tank without igniting an explosion.

Lynx willingly accepted the miracle. While Nomad held fingers over both holes, Lynx cut two small-diameter twigs, sharpened the ends, pushed them into the bullet holes in the gas tank, and hammered them in place with the butt of his .45 automatic.

While Nomad stood watch for any advancing Russian vehicles, Lynx examined the front wheels of the car. The left front wheel was toed out and bent inwards from vertical by a fifteen-degree angle to the extent that it was touching the bumper. The right front fender was so badly distorted that it was rubbing on the wheel.

Lynx spotted a slender, six-foot-long log and used it to pry the bumper and fender away from the left wheel. He then noticed that the rim was also bent, but there was no time to fix that now.

The duo jumped back into the car once they sighted a Russian car speeding towards them. Lynx started the car, floored the accelerator, and was scarcely able to control it at speeds over 80 kph.

With the car shaking badly, Nomad was unable to get a clean shot at their pursuers. Consequently, Lynx decided to make a panic stop so Nomad could shoot well. Lynx hit the brakes and Nomad emptied his magazine into the oncoming car—all ten rounds.

Once they were back at speed, Nomad gleefully reported to Lynx, who was now without a rear-view mirror, "Seems they have trouble. Had to stop. They have a few problems. Tire trouble. Rad. Windshield. Serves the bastards right."

Lynx smiled momentarily but was having a few problems of his own, not the least of which was the shaking car. Within minutes, the situation compounded when the fuel gauge suddenly read "empty" and the engine began spitting and coughing. He stopped the car and positioned it across the road, creating a roadblock.

Slipping out of the Russian coat, Lynx threw the hat onto the front seat. He slid under the rear of the car, took out his knife, placed the knifepoint under the fuel tank, rammed it through the metal and rolled out from under the car. As the little remaining fuel trickled out the hole left by the knife, he placed the big Russian coat under the trickle, soaked it well with gasoline, and then threw it onto the front seat of the car. He did the same with Nomad's Russian coat.

While Nomad blocked the car wheels with rocks, Lynx soaked another change of clothes with gasoline and shoved them under the hood of the car. Lynx gave Nomad a pack of matches, and soon both the interior and engine compartment of the car were ablaze. They threw their remaining clothes and false identification papers into the flames. Passing the matches back to Lynx, he lit one and threw it under the rear of the car. He jumped back as flames engulfed the entire vehicle.

They picked up their packs and carbines, Lynx grabbed the brief-case, and they started down the road. When they observed a long curve to the right, they consulted their map and concluded that they were about thirty miles from the Austrian border.

Using the map, Lynx set a compass course for the targeted border crossing and the two took off through the bush. They stopped briefly for some rations, trotted for a while, and then walked every few hundred yards, periodically verifying their course with the compass. They took a drink and washed their faces in the refreshing, cold water of a stream.

After covering about five miles in the first hour, they sat resting on top of a hill and chatted. They were discussing how they would relate the events of the past few hours to Mother at the debriefing, future demands and the like, when Lynx spotted something through a bush that moved in the distance. Seconds later, they sighted two men in brown Russian uniforms, followed by six men in grey uniforms, about three hundred yards away, in full pursuit.

From their vantage point, they could have taken all eight soldiers out right then and there—or at least most of them. Nomad pushed that option. Instead, in a decision that would haunt him for the rest of his life, Lynx sent Nomad ahead with the briefcase to the next knoll, while he studied their pursuers, one by one, through his carbine scope.

After looking each man over, his mother's childhood teachings of the Thou-shalt-not-kill commandment flashed through his mind, and he decided to take out their two-way radio as a first target—without a silencer. The shot echoed through the hills, striking a direct hit on the radio. All eight soldiers dove for cover.

Now, he thought to himself, *if they continue their pursuit, my next target will be human.*

As he took off on the full run to catch up to Nomad, using as many trees as possible as shields, bullets whizzed by. Lynx pointed at a tree about a quarter mile away and sent Nomad ahead with the briefcase to wait for him there.

Lynx watched their pursuers through his scope. They had now spread out in a line. He was about to wound the one on the left when he stopped, retrieved his silencer from his pack, and screwed it onto the carbine barrel. He put the chest of the man on the left in his crosshairs, hesitated, moved the crosshairs down to his side, then farther on down to his hip, took a breath, and squeezed the trigger. *Zip!* Down he went, howling in pain as another soldier ran to his aid.

Realizing that the silencer had announced to his pursuers that he was not Hungarian, he caught up with Nomad stealthily, but was still out of breath.

Justifying his decision to Nomad, Lynx reasoned that he had essentially disabled two men with one shot because one would stay behind with his wounded comrade.

0900 hours

Now only twenty-four miles from the Austrian border, they took off on the run, checking their compass frequently.

They decided to verify their ammo inventory. Nomad had five shells in his mag and a full spare mag for a total of fifteen; Lynx had eight in his carbine and a full spare mag for a total of eighteen. Satisfied that they had enough, they continued on. *Yeah! Enough. What were we going to do if we didn't*? thought Lynx.

They carefully parceled out their energy in about one-mile segments, up and down hills and across plateaux. Nevertheless, they both began to suffer the effects of prolonged lack of sleep.

To confuse their pursuers, they went off-course for a short distance to walk along a streambed—only three feet wide and five inches deep, with a gravel bottom—that would not leave any tracks. It would be very difficult for their pursuers to know where they had entered and, more importantly, where they had exited the streambed. They followed the stream for about half a mile and exited on a bank of flat rock, leaving no tracks.

Staying on the rock surface as long as they could, they made their way to a distant, heavily treed ridge where they rested.

Lynx lit a cigarette. The place was silent. They had covered a two-mile, straight-line distance since abandoning the car—three miles including the stream detour.

Looking through his scope for their pursuers, Lynx could not see any sign of them. There was *only* sixteen miles to go. The route ahead looked like rough going—quite hilly, borderline mountainous. It offered intermittent cover but featured a lot of wide-open spaces, too.

Feeling rested, they pushed on and were almost at the next hilltop when Nomad yelled, "Aircraft!"

Watching from under the trees, they sighted it—a small, two-seated, Russian spotter, its wings mounted atop the fuselage like a Piper Cub. It was heading straight for them, a hundred feet above treetop height. Definitely looking for the two fugitive agents, it flew by, climbed, and disappeared over a hill, searching but not seeing.

They discussed the possibility of disabling it with a carbine shot. Lynx decided "No" because, with their radio, airplanes—*plural*—would soon follow. They decided to sit tight on a hill up ahead with good cover and good sighting in all directions.

Lynx reasoned that, being sixty miles from Budapest, the pilot would soon run short of fuel flying back and forth, including all those climbing manoeuvres with their high-fuel consumption. And, the Russian search plane couldn't make radio contact with their ground forces. Lynx had already looked after that.

The aircraft returned from the valley, flew directly over them, circled, wiggled its wings, and then flew off towards Budapest. Lynx was right. Now Lynx and Nomad knew exactly where their pursuers were.

Off they went to the next hilltop and another rest. As they chatted, Nomad's eyes narrowed. He counted six of them coming up the hill behind them. Lynx handed Nomad the briefcase and sent him off to the next hilltop. Lynx, in the prone position, put his carbine to his shoulder and sighted them through his scope, a half mile away.

Placing his crosshairs on an officer, Lynx waited for him to be in range. With the silencer still in place, there would be no sound. He squeezed the trigger, but it did not respond. The safety was still on. Nerves. Clicking it off, he resumed his position, placed the crosshairs on the Russian officer's leg, and squeezed. *Zip!* Down he went. The bullet had hit exactly where he had aimed. While the wounded soldier's comrades rushed to his assistance, Lynx took off on the full run to catch up with Nomad.

Breathless and gasping for air when he arrived, Lynx listened as Nomad proposed the use of a plastic bomb, triggered not by a timer but by a carbine shot hitting a carefully placed rock that would cause ignition wires to short, ignite the plastic explosive, and annihilate the entire group of pursuers.

Lynx was wary of the danger that he would be placing his mission partner in, but was becoming increasingly desperate, and agreed—another decision he would regret. They selected a suitable spot with a deliberately clear trail leading to it. Lynx proceeded up the next hill while Nomad set up the booby trap, then backed away very carefully so as to not set it off accidentally.

Nomad quickly caught up to Lynx, immediately assumed the prone position, and positioned his carbine ready to fire. Four heads appeared as they proceeded towards the trap and Nomad waited for the opportune moment. The lead man pointed out the trail they had left, a conference ensued, and they moved into the clearing, appearing wary. They spread out.

Nomad concluded that this was "the moment," squeezed the trigger, and the plastic bomb exploded. When the dust had settled, only one of the pursuers had been injured. The remaining three soldiers were still capable, and all opened fire on Lynx and Nomad.

Nomad was disappointed that he had fired prematurely, but took off on the run with Lynx. Another second or so of delay in his shot and all their pursuers would have been killed.

As they reached the top of the next hill, they were both exhausted. With ten miles to go, Nomad sent Lynx on ahead to the next hilltop, claiming that it was time *he* had some fun.

1100 hours

Lynx was not quite at the top of the hill when he heard Nomad's carbine fire. Nomad then made a dash to catch up to Lynx when another shot rang out. Lynx turned to see Nomad's arms fly upwards as he toppled backwards.

As Lynx ran back to Nomad's aid, a soldier in a brown uniform raised his rifle to fire at Lynx, who instinctively pulled his own trigger four times, with no silencer. The shots echoed off into the distance. The soldier was not hit, but disappeared.

Lynx crouched by Nomad's side. He was bleeding profusely. Lynx tried to get information on where he had been hit, but the wounded man was only able to speak haltingly. Lynx felt between his pack-sack and his back, and it was wet with blood. He released Nomad's backpack straps and positioned the bag as a pillow. The bullet had hit Nomad square in the back, had gone through the pack, and had probably then gone through his spine.

Two heads appeared over the hill. In his state of emotional upheaval over Nomad's dire situation, Lynx fired three shots at them—hurriedly and without his usual aiming precision. As he continued to pull the trigger, his trusty carbine did not respond; it's magazine was empty. He picked up Nomad's carbine and fired the three remaining shells in its magazine at the top of the hill—again, hurriedly and not well aimed. He then slipped his last full magazine from his pack into his own carbine.

As Nomad lay dying, they exchanged real first names. Then Nomad asked Lynx to retrieve his cyanide pill from an inside pocket. Lynx reluctantly complied, and put it into Nomad's mouth. Between coughing spasms, Nomad coddled the pill with his tongue, being careful to not bite down on it and managed to get a few words out, "Now it's ready . . . it's not you . . . you have to . . . leave me."

When four heads appeared over the brow of the hill, all shooting at him, Lynx snapped and his training took over. Things suddenly started happening in time-dilated, slow motion as is typical for highly trained combatants.[5] He discarded the Thou-shalt-not-kill commandment that had been drilled into him as a child, that had been nagging at him ever since Sarge had told him that he was being trained as a sniper. As of that moment, he became a deadly killer.

Raging, adrenaline coursing through his system, Lynx grabbed his carbine and released two rounds at the man on the left, hitting him in the chest. The soldier in the middle stood frozen in fear, so he shot the one to his right first with two bullets. Then he finished off the middle soldier with a single shot to the chest.

His anger still white hot, Lynx started searching for the Russian officer who had shot his partner. He was nowhere to be seen.

Carefully removing Nomad's pack from under his head, Lynx put Nomad's wristwatch, papers, .45 automatic, belt, and knife into it and turned towards the dying man. Tears were running down both cheeks.

Before biting down on the cyanide pill, Nomad managed to get out a final few words of encouragement, duty on his mind until the end. "Don't worry . . . about me . . . . Get the papers out . . . . Promise."

There was still a Russian killer somewhere nearby, and Lynx was only too aware that he too was still in grave danger. He could not locate the man who had just shot his partner, but knew he wasn't far away.

---

5 Lawrence's theory is that the brain is working so fast in these circumstances that it makes things appear in slow motion. This is a commonly reported phenomenon, and he has experienced it more than once.

They exchanged knowing looks for the last time. Lynx lay his hand on Nomad's shoulder, but he could wait no longer. As his dying partner continued coughing spasmodically, carrying two packs, two carbines—one on a shoulder sling, the other in one hand—and the all-important briefcase in his other, Lynx turned his attention to getting to the Austrian border.

Then and there, Lynx vowed that, from now on, he would only go on solo missions.

Lynx plodded on, exhausted, the night in Hungary a strain, both mentally and physically. He checked his compass frequently, and the packs and carbines felt ever heavier. Stumbling across a stream, Lynx set the carbines down carefully and drank his fill. The water gave him renewed strength. He dug out some rations and ate, but the loss of his partner Nomad weighed heavily on his mind. *I'll get even, Nomad*, he vowed silently, over and over, soon finding himself saying the words out loud.

Lynx decided to reduce his load by shedding all non-essentials. He put Nomad's watch and compass into one of his pockets and put both silencers, empty magazines and a plastic explosive and timer— carefully arranged—into his own pack. He then put anything unneeded into Nomad's pack, intending to detonate it. He set the timer on an explosive for four minutes, inserted it into the plastic, put it into Nomad's pack, and gently placed it about ten feet from the stream. He picked up his own pack, strapped it onto his back along with Nomad's carbine, picked up the briefcase in one hand and the loaded carbine in the other, stubbed out his cigarette butt, and headed towards the Austrian border. Three minutes later, the plastic bomb exploded. Lynx didn't even look back to observe the devastation.

Heading across a grassy plain, his trail was obvious, but he was now not worried. No one was following him. *Nomad had been right*, he thought. *We should have taken out the whole works when the opportunity was there. Nomad would still be here if I had listened to him.*

It was thick bush and hard going. He almost fell down a steep ravine when he stumbled across it. He had to search for a way down and through it. He walked along its top edge until he found a way down—treacherous, but a way down. To free both hands for the descent, he put the briefcase on a pack strap and slung his carbine over his shoulder. He slipped a few times while inching his way down, but his plan to free two hands worked well. Finally, the slope became easier and he was able to walk and then trot, his legs limbering up as he went.

The valley floor was flat and covered with plenty of brush. For no particular reason, he looked back up the cliff and stopped abruptly. There was the shape of a man atop the cliff, silhouetted against the sky.

Lynx unslung his carbine, and through his scope, could clearly identify the man as the Russian officer who had shot Nomad. He had been following Lynx, and he, too, was now looking for a way down the cliff. The Russian set his rifle on the ground and removed his overcoat, revealing a service pistol holstered on his hip. He picked up his rifle and started down the cliff. Clearly, he did not know that Lynx was watching his every move.

Lynx found himself saying out loud, "You bastard, come and get it. I'm going to wait for you. You're a dead man."

As his pursuer descended the cliff, Lynx moved to a better spot to take a shot, intending to only wound him and make him suffer. Lynx fantasized on how to torture the son-of-a-bitch.

As the Russian reached the bottom of the cliff, he bent down looking for tracks while Lynx, lying prone, watched through his scope. Taking aim at the stock of his rifle, Lynx squeezed the trigger and hit it perfectly. With no silencer, the shot echoed down the valley. The rifle had been rendered unusable with his first shot. The Russian hit the deck and scrambled for cover. After a few minutes, he got to his knees, and then onto his feet. A second bullet hit him in the right shoulder area. He fell to the ground, this time playing dead. Lynx knew better.

The Russian pulled out his pistol and started to crawl towards Lynx, who placed a third shot near his face. *Enough cat-playing-with-mouse bullshit,* Lynx thought. *Nomad, this one's for you.*

Lynx placed his crosshairs on the Russian's head and, controlling his breathing, began the trigger-squeeze. The Russian got to his feet with his pistol still in one hand, his other hand nursing his wounded shoulder. Lynx took his finger off the trigger as his target turned and started walking away. *You arrogant bastard,* he thought. *Now you're going to get it in the back, just like you did to Nomad.*

Suddenly tears filled Lynx's eyes and he couldn't see. He blinked several times, but his vision was blurred by an incredible upwelling of emotion. Before he could clear his eyes, the Russian had disappeared into the bush. Now and again, he could see him moving away, giving up the chase but offering no opportunity for a clear shot.

Lynx thought, *What gives? What drove this man who has tried to kill me so many times to now abandon the chase?* He watched the Russian climb back up the cliff, now out of range. As he approached the top of the cliff, his pistol fell out of its holster and bounced down to the bottom of the cliff.[6] He showed no interest in retrieving it.

1215 hours

Tears still in his eyes and feeling cheated, Lynx shrugged it off, got up, and resumed his trek towards the Austrian border. With about five miles to go, he began to jog. He covered about two miles before stopping to rest and verified his location using his gridded military map.

Just as he was finishing a cigarette, he suddenly heard the sound of a heavy motor vehicle heading towards him. Quickly lying down, he saw a truck driving along the trail with Russian troops sitting in its cargo compartment. He checked his magazine and was down to two shells. The truck moved past Lynx and was soon out of sight, but he could still hear the motor running. It stopped and started up again a few minutes later—a mystery truck.

Making his way down that same trail, it was clear that more trucks had used it recently. Once into the bush on the other side of the trail, Lynx put black paste on his face and a black tuque on his head. There would be no running now because the truck had dropped off an armed guard, not far away. As a precaution, Lynx unclasped his .45

---

6 His only remaining weapon against Lynx's high-powered rifle, almost certainly why he abandoned the pursuit.

automatic holster. With only two shells left in his carbine magazine, he might need it.

He proceeded cautiously, stopped and listened frequently. He soon spotted a soldier patrolling a fence about fifty yards ahead, which he hadn't noticed before. *It has to be the border*, he thought. He took his last plastic explosive out of his pack, hid the carbines and briefcase, and inched towards the fence of barbed and rolled wire. He set the timer for one minute, inserted it into the plastic, placed the plastic as far into the barbed rolls as he could reach, and returned for the hidden carbines and briefcase.

The explosion ripped a giant hole in the fence. Wire, dirt, and rocks flew in all directions. He immediately ran through the gaping hole, now on Austrian soil. Two shots rang out immediately and bullets whizzed by. Keeping as many trees between him and the guard as he could, more shots hit several trees but he was soon out of the border guard's range.

Consulting the map, he concluded that his pick-up spot should be about a half mile ahead. He headed for it, and soon could hear the sound of an approaching Jeep. As he stepped out from behind a tree with his carbine aimed at its driver, the driver said, "I heard the explosion and gunshots and came to take a look. Are you Lynx or Nomad?"

"Lynx," he replied.

"Where's your partner?"

"He's dead," answered Lynx, as he climbed into the Jeep.

Still shaken by the past few hours of drama and trusting no one, Lynx drew his .45 automatic.

"No need for the gun, Lynx. I'll have you at the airstrip in five minutes."

As the Jeep approached the waiting aircraft, Lynx readied himself to climb aboard. He slipped his pack back on, slung one carbine onto his back, held the briefcase in one hand and cradled the other carbine on his other forearm, finger on the trigger. As soon as they turned onto the grass, the aircraft engines started. Lynx walked over to the aircraft and climbed aboard. It was mid-afternoon, November 6th, 1956.

The flight to London was uneventful. Lynx was soon walking down the hallway of a grey, stone mansion, his footsteps echoing off the hard surfaces around him. Opening the door designated by his driver—"At the end of the hall, last door on the left"—Lynx stood in the doorway, thinking momentarily about how far he had come from small-town Ontario. He looked in, and there sat Mother at the end of a long table.

Still in emotional turmoil from his harrowing escape and the death of his mission partner, Lynx stepped into the room, slammed the door behind him, and walked over to the table, glaring at Mother.

Lynx was outraged and started in. "Sarge, you bastard, you and your military officers told Nomad and me that this was just a routine milk run, a piece of cake. He's now dead, lying out there in that God-forsaken country somewhere. Why?"

Sarge, in a calm mood, asked Lynx for the briefcase, and invited him to sit down.

Lynx shoved the briefcase across the table with such force that Sarge had to intercept it to stop it from falling to the floor. Lynx continued venting his rage.

"What the hell happened to Nomad?" asked Sarge.

With full eye contact and almost spitting out the words, Lynx replied, "Shot. Shot in the back and died a few minutes later. Shot in the back by a son-of-a-bitch-of-a-Russian officer," he answered as he slumped down into a chair, tears streaming down both cheeks.

Sarge got up from the table, walked around behind Lynx, put a hand on one shoulder, and said, "Take it easy, son. It's not going to be easy, but we have to get through this debriefing."

He offered Lynx a handkerchief. Lynx accepted.

As Sarge turned on a tape recorder, Lynx started through the whole debacle—the jump, the meeting with Dob, the ride into Budapest, the teenaged Freedom Fighter, Jules, the murdered Russian prisoner, the Russian troop carrier, the Russian staff car escape, the roadblock, the pursuit.

When Lynx related that they had given explosives to the Freedom Fighters, Sarge got agitated and turned off the tape recorder. Lynx responded that anyone would have done the same thing. Sarge appeared to accept that, and simply turned the tape recorder back on.

A break was needed by the time they got to Nomad's death, as Lynx's voice began to falter.

Sarge got up, walked over to a window, and stood looking out of it when he said, "Lynx, we didn't know the Russians would move in that quickly. We thought we had at least a few more days. Believe me, the Russian officer knew from Nomad's jumpsuit that you two were intruders, picking up information. You should have killed him when the opportunity was there."

"I tried, but I couldn't see," replied Lynx, referring to the second time he had had the opportunity to kill the Russian officer. He hadn't yet related the first time.

Sarge resumed the debriefing and again was perturbed when Lynx described his cat-and-mouse treatment of the Russian officer. Sarge decided that some counselling for the rookie agent was in order and shut off the tape recorder.

"You've had a bad experience, but don't get the idea that killing just to get even is okay. It's not. That's wrong. I don't want you to get that into your blood. Wanting to kill every Russian you see is dangerous and counter-productive. Kill only when you have to—when there is no other choice. When it's either him or you. Got it?"

Lynx finished the mission debriefing, taken aback that so much action had been squeezed into so little time; it had been less than twelve hours between the jump into Hungary and his arrival at the Austrian border.

As they took another break, Sarge opened the briefcase, took out the two envelopes, and inspected their contents.

"Good job, Lynx. They're priceless. But, you know, Laddie, you've changed. There's something different about you now."

Incredulous, Lynx was unable to speak, thinking, *Well, hello? It was an action-packed twelve hours. We went through a lot of ammo and plastic explosives, and my partner—the person you made me responsible for—is dead. Wouldn't that have an effect on most people?*

Without missing a beat, Sarge picked up a phone and asked for a full-course meal to be brought in along with a bottle of brandy.

After eating, Lynx felt refreshed; the hot meal gave him renewed vitality, and the glass of brandy was the perfect top-off. He glanced at his watch: 7:30 p.m.

Lynx was unable to shake off his need to avenge the loss of his partner, and expressed to Sarge the vendetta he intended to play out with his partner's killer. Sarge was familiar with this side effect of the dangerous business he was running, so he continued to counsel Lynx.

"Our business comes first, see? Any vendettas that you create are at the bottom of my list. Get that into your head right now. I give the orders, you carry them out, and that is all there is to it." He shouted that last sentence at the top of his voice. "You are not a professional killer. You are an espionage courier, whose job is to bring valuable information from A to B whenever I decide it is needed. You have been well trained to do that, and you are in my charge. Now, have you got that?"

Shifting gears into sympathy mode, Sarge continued, "Nomad is dead and neither you nor I can do anything that will bring him back. I feel a loss, too. I've lost many brave men like this. You and I and others like you will carry on. You have to let it go."

Informing Sarge that Nomad was to be his last partner and that he wanted all future missions to be solo, Sarge agreed sympathetically. Then he switched the recorder back on and they went through the entire debriefing a second time.

Finally ending the session, Sarge informed Lynx that, "Jenny checks out just fine. A-1." With that, he passed Lynx the envelope containing his personal effects.

"What about Nomad?" inquired Lynx. "How do you explain how and why he died?"

Sarge lowered his head as he fingered Nomad's file, took out a pen, wrote "Deceased" across the file, and then looked up at Lynx.

"Yesterday, there was an air crash in western Canada. Nomad's name will be on the passenger list. His coffin will be closed. No one will ever know his fate—only you and me. That's simply how it is."

"Now," he continued, "there's a car waiting to take you to Jenny's or the Cumberland Hotel, your choice. Incidentally, as of now, my code name will revert back to Sarge."

Lynx stepped out into the huge hallway and closed the door gently behind him. Outside, the driver opened the door of the waiting black car, Lynx got in, the driver started the engine, and Lynx handed him Jenny's address.

Lynx was soon asleep, only to be awakened at Jenny's apartment. Lynx climbed the stairs to the second floor and used the key she had given him. No one was home. It was 10:00 p.m. Lynx sat on the bed and found the lingering aroma of Jenny's perfume intoxicating as it hung in the air. But Nomad's death and the elusive Russian officer still pervaded his mind. Nevertheless, he soon collapsed in sleep.

When Jenny came into the room, she shook him gently and he bolted into a sitting position, shouting. She was frightened, recoiled, and put her hand over her mouth.[7] Lynx casually passed it off as "just a nightmare."

She sat down beside him on the bed, leaned towards him, and he kissed her on the lips for the first time. Her arms suddenly encircled his neck.

Jenny was soon mixing them a drink in the kitchenette of the three-room flat. She noticed his forced and uncomfortable demeanour and inquired about his flight. Fibbing that it had been a "bad one," his mind moved uncontrollably back to Nomad and she asked him what was wrong.

"Your face just turned white and you looked awful," she remarked.

"Sorry, Jenny," he replied as he tried to regain his composure.

"My father was in the army, and he sometimes talked about men who had been in combat. The way he described them is the way you were acting just now."

"It's just fatigue, Jenny, nothing to worry about," replied Lynx, the first part being true, the second questionable.

---

7 These are early symptoms of Post-Traumatic Stress Disorder (PTSD), a term formulated years later to describe the side effects of military or other trauma.

Sipping the drink just increased Lynx's fatigue and Jenny led him into the bedroom, where he was soon fast asleep. When he awoke, she was already up, fluttering around the kitchenette. Entering the bedroom, she offered him an old-fashioned back rub, which Lynx was only too happy to accept. Instinctively, she wondered aloud why his muscles were unusually tight. Lynx passed it off as casually as he could.

On the flight back to Canada, Lynx could not shake the image of Nomad's assassin from his mind, a stream of questions racing through it for the entire flight, mostly centred around *Why?*

Chapter Three:
The Reluctant Defector

A month or so went by without any contact from Sarge. Stationed at CFB Trenton and functioning as an aeronautical engine mechanic, Lawrence went about his regular duties and activities on and off the job.

Then one afternoon, while getting ready to go over to his friend Steve's house for dinner, Lawrence was on his way to buy a pack of cigarettes and noticed an unaddressed envelope sitting on the front seat of his car.

Quickly opening it, he breathed a sigh of relief because it was not blank but written in code. That meant only a meeting with Sarge—not a mission.

While the car was warming up, he took out a pen and decoded the message, which read:

> *LYNX: MEET ME TONIGHT AT 2000 HRS*
> *JUST EAST OF THE GUARDHOUSE BESIDE*
> *THE HIGHWAY.*
>
> *SARGE*

He burned the note, picked up the cigarettes, had dinner with Steve and his wife Betty, and excused himself at 7:30 p.m. With memories of

Nomad and Budapest still fresh in his mind, anticipating what Sarge might want now was disconcerting, and he wasn't very good company over dinner.

Beside the guardhouse that night, Sarge inquired on the health of Lynx's nerves. He was not overly communicative but wanted Lynx to go for more judo training, focusing on self-defence. It started the following Monday night at a local address in Trenton.

When Lynx asked Sarge if he could find out the name of the Russian officer who had shot Nomad, Sarge exploded. He reminded Lynx what he had told him during the Budapest debriefing. Sarge shouted at him to forget about revenge and to concentrate on his training.

Lynx's judo training lasted several weeks, every Monday night under an instructor—Fred—a 160-pound Black Belt. When the subject of street fights came up, Fred related how six young "toughs" had tackled him one night in an alley. In a matter of minutes, Fred had incapacitated all six and walked out of the alley—alone.

As 1957 rolled on, Lynx made three or four operational training and cargo flights to England on North Stars, as was typical for aviation mechanics over the course of a year. Through regular correspondence with Jenny, he maintained contact and would stay at her apartment whenever overnighting in London. Being married, having children with impressive regularity back home (Carl in 1955, Larry in 1956, and Arthur on April 28, 1957), and having a secret girlfriend in a faraway apartment seemed—among the few aware—to be compatible with the high-flying military culture.

Just after Arthur was born, Lawrence went home to Midland with Elsie and the kids to enjoy some of his mother's home cooking and spend some time with family. His mother—ever the strict Baptist—forbade any drinking in the house. Consequently, Lawrence did his drinking at his sister's house with his two brothers Bill and Wally and his brother-in-law Arnie, usually over World War II stories. They had brought back some memorabilia from overseas—a German flag, a helmet, and a 9-mm. Luger—that were undoubtedly used to add colour to their recountings. Those conversations were decidedly one-sided as far as Lawrence was concerned; he could not submit anything about his MI-6 combat training or experience.

In mid-1957, Search and Rescue Squadron 102 KU came to CFB Trenton and operated temporarily out of Lawrence's hangar. It was common practice to take base staff on short test flights for the experience. One day twenty-two-year-old Lawrence was asked to go and accepted excitedly. He climbed into the big, twin-rotor Sikorski—referred to among the troops as the "Flying Banana"—and sat down. The big machine lifted off slowly and accelerated as it gained altitude. The noise aboard was deafening, making conversation almost impossible.

Thirty minutes into the flight, one of the crew sat down beside Lawrence and asked him to remove his seat belt—a surprising request, given that the helicopter was bouncing around quite a lot. He explained that the pilot was experiencing some trouble with "the bird" and that they would be making an emergency landing in downtown Bancroft, Ontario. He warned Lawrence that, once they were on the ground, he should get as far away from the helicopter as fast as he could—a scary instruction.

Once they had landed, Lawrence followed that instruction to the letter, only to witness the entire crew (including the co-pilots) on the full run right behind him. There immediately followed a loud *Swoosh!* and the helicopter burst into flames. A few hours later, they were picked up and driven back to the base. No explanation for this event was ever communicated.

As the months slipped by, Lawrence was almost beginning to think that Sarge had forgotten about him, when at last he heard from him in the summer of 1957. More parachute training had been lined up. Sarge emphasized that a minimum of a jump once a month was needed to keep his skills sharp. And just to keep the training realistic, every second jump was made into heavily treed bush.

There was also a new equipment development to keep up with. Plastic explosives technology had advanced to include the timer and plastic as a single integrated unit. Activation had also been simplified and could now be done by merely setting the timer and flipping a switch. However, once activated, the explosion was irreversibly committed—a one-way street to be walked with great care.

The following spring (1958), cargo flights to the UK resumed and Lawrence spent some time with Jenny in London, including meeting her parents. Jenny clearly had marriage on her mind, but Lawrence—already married with three children—gradually broke off the relationship by not responding to Jenny's letters. Notwithstanding, on June 4 of that year, his wife Elsie gave birth to their fourth child, a daughter June, named after her aunt.

Throughout 1958, Sarge arranged several parachute exercises for Lynx, including refreshers on line penetration. He completed all exercises successfully, keeping his perfect record intact.

However, as the year unfolded, Sarge—for his own mysterious reasons—wanted Lynx to acquire additional intrusion skills, namely picking locks and accessing the upper floors of buildings.[8] Still anxious to get to the other side of the Iron Curtain and hunt down that *son-of-a-bitch that had gunned down Nomad,* picking locks and breaking-and-entering skills did not seem to be a stepping-stone towards that goal. But then, if Sarge wanted him to do it, Lynx was game.

His lock-picking instructor was a cat burglar called Charles, an Englishman whom Sarge had sprung out of a London prison to train his agents—at least Lynx, and possibly others—in exchange for his freedom.

At first, Lynx had great difficulty understanding Charles, who spoke with a heavy Cockney accent. Explaining his arrangement with Sarge, he told Lynx, "From the 'eart of London, aye am. 'Imself tol' me that I'd be a free man if I should teach me trade. The kind sire tol' me to show you how to be a cat burglar, and I'm the best in the business, aye am." Eventually, it all came clear.

One day, Sarge watched Charles teach Lynx how to scale a three-storey building using a grappling hook on the end of a rope. He would

---

8 Sarge probably knew well before (perhaps months) initiating Lynx's next mission that lock picking and accessing upper floors of buildings would be needed.

swing it around in a giant circle before making the final upward toss, testing with a sharp tug to confirm that it was properly snagged.

"Okay, me Buck-o, up you go," he'd say.

They did this together for several successive evenings.

Lynx's final training exercise with Charles—a test that both Sarge and Charles witnessed—was to unlock a filing cabinet in a locked room on the second storey of a building. They gave Lynx a floor plan for the second floor. The easiest entry would have been through a second-storey window, as Charles and Sarge suggested. That seemed *too easy* to Lynx, whose instincts were telling him that a third storey approach to the targeted floor would be a better overall strategy. He didn't know why; he just had a hunch and suspected that Charles and Sarge had something up their sleeve.

Swinging the grappling hook in an ever-increasing circle as Charles had taught him, Lynx tossed it onto the roof, secured it, and went up the rope. From the rooftop, he went through the door leading to the third floor, took off his boots, inched his way to the stairs, and went down to the second floor, Gurkha-Jack style. He paused to listen, detected nothing, descended the stairs to the second floor, and froze. There stood an unsuspecting Charles leaning against a wall. Lynx crept up behind him soundlessly, and in a single, two-handed move, put one hand over his mouth, the other around his neck. Charles played along.

Lynx peeked around the corner and saw Sarge standing in front of the door he was supposed to open. Seconds turned into minutes and finally Sarge moved and turned away. Lynx inched towards Sarge from behind, reached out and poked him with a finger, saying, "Sarge, you have just been knifed."

Sarge wanted to know how Lynx had eluded them. "Hold that question," replied Lynx, who was not yet finished; he still had a door to unlock and a file cabinet to open in order to complete the assignment—which he did—using picks that Charles had provided and taught him how to use. Lynx then levelled with Sarge on how he had done it, including his plan change and why. Lynx explained that he had an uneasy feeling that some kind of surprise awaited him on the second floor. Sarge was impressed.

Lynx never saw Charles again.

A week or so later, there was an unaddressed envelope on the seat of Lynx's car. This time the blank page inside signalled a mission. He went to his room and carefully passed the paper over a naked light bulb. It read:

> *LYNX,*
>
> *YOU WERE SCHEDULED ON A FLIGHT TO THE UK NEXT MONTH. IT HAS BEEN MOVED TO NEXT WEEK. AS USUAL, YOU DO NOT KNOW ME. THIS IS A BIG ONE AND IMPORTANT. SEE YOU THEN.*
>
> *SARGE.*

Lynx memorized the note, burned it, and crushed the burnt paper into powder. Feeling apprehensive, that night Lynx went to the canteen and had a few drinks.

The week flew by and on the night before the mission, Lynx could not sleep, anticipating the 7:30 a.m. flight the next morning. He arrived at the aircraft before the flight crew (as was his habit) and did his usual pre-flight checks. The crew arrived, and with everything ready to go, he waited for Sarge, who was the last passenger to arrive. Sarge soon climbed aboard, this time dressed as a Squadron Leader.

Following a short hop to Montreal to pick up some freight, they went on to CFB Goose Bay, refuelled, and overnighted there. The following morning, they took off for London. Half way through the flight, Lynx got a feeling in his gut that something was wrong. Checking all gauges, he noted that the No. 4 engine was exhibiting low oil pressure. Minutes later, it started spitting and losing rpms.

The Captain ordered the No. 4 engine shut down, which left three engines still running. As a precaution, he instructed Lynx to inform the eight passengers aboard—including Sarge—that ditching-at-sea procedures were to be readied, and to explain them.

Lynx did as instructed. Surprisingly, Sarge's only concern was the possibility of a *delay*. When told that this might add an hour to the trans-Atlantic crossing, Sarge got up and followed Lynx to the cockpit. He introduced himself to the captain as Squadron Leader Conway. *Another alias*, thought Lynx.

When the Captain indicated that the arrival delay would be "an hour and a half," Sarge asked whether that could be reduced. The Captain replied, "For you, sir, we'll over-rev the engines a bit and try for an on-schedule landing in London."

Sarge left the cockpit, pleased.

The V-12 Rolls-Royce engines responded admirably, and the flight touched down in London only fifteen minutes behind schedule. Sarge proceeded directly to one of the hangars, while Lynx—now a fully qualified flight engineer, capable of repairing the engine—wondered how he would be released for Sarge's mission.

There was nothing to worry about. Sarge reappeared a few minutes later with men in white coveralls and introduced them as "Roll-Royce mechanics." They would repair the failed engine. Even the captain was impressed.

Sarge whispered to Lynx, "Tell them that Jenny is picking you up, then meet me on the other side of the hangar."

Sarge had a black car waiting behind the hangar, its door already open for Lynx. Once away, Sarge picked up the car phone, dialled, and instructed whoever came on the line: "We will be there as soon as we can. Get the Bobbies to give us an escort. Lynx is here with me." Hanging up, he turned to Lynx and asked, "Are you sure you want to go on this mission alone?"

Lynx nodded and started changing into his jump gear, which Sarge had arranged to be in the car. As he continued assembling his gear, Lynx shoved his Canadian cigarettes into one pocket—a thoughtless step that would later prove nearly disastrous.

Sarge then started into the pre-mission briefing: "We have an important scientist in Czechoslovakia who wants to defect. Your job is to get him out alive. You will not be carrying a carbine—only your .45 automatic, a small derringer, your knife, one set of civilian papers, and two sets of false papers. The briefing officer will tell you the rest." When the police escort arrived—klaxons already going—the car accelerated noticeably.

The pre-mission briefing was done at an old house. Sarge passed Lynx a balaclava to wear into the house, where six British military officers sat—different ones from the Budapest mission briefing.

Sarge simply introduced Lynx and one of the officers stood up and started in: "Lynx, this operation is code-named 'Red Comet.' A Czech scientist named Strawinski wants to come over to our side. Two flights will be needed to get to the your Jump Target. The second short flight will drop you a half-mile or so inside the Czechoslovakian border where you will be met by the Czech underground. Your contact will give you the password: 'The Red Comet flies tonight.' You will answer: 'The comet is here to stay.' You will get rid of your parachute and jumpsuit. They know that your code name is Lynx.

"On this jump, you will carry only a small pack. Change immediately into civvies, including shoes—not your jump boots, because you are to look Czech. The underground will take you to Prague where you will pick up your man. As soon as you can, the two of you will board a train south, towards Austria. We have others planted at the border to get you safely into the country."

He then pulled out a map of Czechoslovakia and Austria and spread it on the table. Pointing with a pen, he indicated the entry point, and then the exit point.

Lynx asked whether Strawinski was fit to deal with the stresses surely involved, and how eager he was to defect. The answer was evasive. "All we know is that he wants out now, and that is why we are moving with dispatch. The aircraft is ready and waiting to take you to Austria."

Dispatch? What is dispatch? So British, thought Lynx.

"Thank you, sir. I'm ready to go," replied Lynx.

Lynx was whisked to the aircraft in the car along with Sarge, who passed him an envelope with a cyanide capsule taped to it just as he was boarding. Lynx was soon strapped into the seat of a twin-engine turbojet and winging his way to Austria.

He opened the envelope and the note inside read:

> Lynx:
>
> I had hoped that you would change your mind about taking a partner on missions. I worry about you and the success of the mission because two men are simply better than one. In your small pack, you will find some new plastic explosives, which might be useful. The .45 is in a shoulder holster, but suit yourself about concealing it. There is plenty of ammunition. The small, two-shot derringer can be carried almost anywhere, and I had your knife remodelled. It is now only nine inches long, and the sheath is specially made to permit strapping it to your leg. The hilt is thinner to be less conspicuous. Put these things on before the jump. The man you are bringing out is a scientist and not used to the type of endurance we know you can handle. The underground Czech leader is 'Mike' to you; they know your code name. Use your head and that gut feeling you have when things are awry. Destroy this letter as usual.
>
> Sarge

Lynx reread the note a few times and went to the washroom to destroy it. He put the cyanide capsule in a safe pocket.

Lynx returned to his seat, opened the small pack, pulled out the .45 automatic, and stripped to the waist to put on the shoulder holster. He inspected the derringer, a .25 calibre weapon—small but deadly. He pulled the rest of the contents out of the pack—clothes, ammo, wristwatch, papers, maps, black face paste, explosives, compass, and money—and loaded the derringer. He then loaded a full clip into the .45 automatic, putting two spare clips into his inside jacket pockets, and the map and compass into one of his front trouser pockets. He put the money into his wallet, the false ID papers into a trouser pocket, and the face paste into a back pocket.

He then turned his attention to the new integrated plastic explosives. *Where and how should I store them to prevent accidental detonation—particularly for the jump?* he wondered.

He decided to wrap them in clothes in his pack. He would then increase the padding around them after the jump by further wrapping them in a small piece of chute material that he would cut off before disposing of it. Satisfied that he had it solved, he checked his wristwatch. It was 2130 hours, and he tried to get some sleep.

Two years had elapsed since his first mission, and Lynx was still obsessed with hunting down the Russian officer who had shot Nomad. He had had many nightmares—too numerous to count—in the intervening months. Some had included face-to-face contact with Nomad, and oftentimes they ended with Lynx about to be shot. He would typically wake up in a sweat.

Two hours had elapsed since their take-off, and the Austrian landing could not be far off. Lynx strapped on his small pack. He left his parachute harness slightly loose for easy access to the .45 in case of need. Then he strapped the knife sheath to his leg, just above the boot. He gently placed the explosives among clothes in his pack. He then dug out the face paste and put it on. He felt somewhat naked without his carbine, but concluded that the .45 would do.

He looked out the window at the aircraft engines and could see the running lights and the glow of the exhaust. Then, as the engine noise changed, he noticed the flaps descend and knew that landing was imminent. He strapped himself firmly into his seat, the plane banked right, and two rows of landing flares came into view. The descent was fast, and they were soon on the ground.

As soon as the aircraft had stopped, Lynx opened the door and jumped down onto the ground. A small aircraft and a contact were waiting. Lynx ran to the aircraft, got aboard, and it taxied to the end of the runway and took off immediately.

Quickly securing the parachute in place for the short flight, Lynx double-checked everything. In the end, he decided to attach his pack—containing the new, one-step design of plastic explosives—to his chute harness; that seemed least likely to be jolted on landing. The same pilot had flown Lynx on his 1956 mission into Hungary. It was indeed a small world and they reminisced briefly.

Sighting the Jump Target flare, the pilot cut the engine and Lynx jumped out of the aircraft door. He counted down then pulled the chute release as the aircraft's sound faded into the distance in the black of night.

Using the flare as a beacon, Lynx steered the chute towards it, unzipped the jumpsuit enough to access his .45, took it out, and re-zipped the jumpsuit.

The pit of his stomach tightened as he got that feeling that something was wrong. He cocked the .45 to bring the first shell up into the firing chamber and left the safety off. He steered the chute to one side of the flare and could make out two men standing beside the flare. *Why two men?* he asked himself.

As he floated towards the ground, he steered the chute well clear of the flare in case something was amiss, landed about 150-feet away, rolled onto the ground, and released the chute and harness.

The two men had not heard him land and both were still looking skyward. He wiped the black face paste off and changed clothes, keeping an eye on the two men standing beside the flare. He cut a small piece off the chute, repacked the plastics, and buried the chute, boots, and jumpsuit in the soft ground. Then he turned his attention to the two men and approached them stealthily with the .45 automatic cocked.

One of the men spotted him and said, "The Red Comet flies tonight."

It was the right password. Lynx answered, "The comet is here to stay," holding the .45 ready.

"You don't need the gun now, my friend," said one of the men, smoothly. *Too smoothly,* thought Lynx. *This guy sounds phony, somehow.*

Still not feeling safe, Lynx asked, "Where's the car?"

"Just over here," he replied, pointing out the direction as Lynx stomped out the flare.

"Lead the way," replied Lynx.

"After you," replied the man.

"I'd rather follow you, if you don't mind," replied Lynx, the .45 still in his hand but now shoved into his belt.

"If you wish," came the polite reply.

Lynx continued thinking to himself, his mind racing, *Too smooth. This guy is just too damn smooth. And too polite.* His gut was gnawing at him. *Something isn't quite right here, but what's amiss?*

The man who had not yet spoken got into the driver's seat. Lynx got into the back seat carefully after both men were already aboard. Lynx sat on the edge of his seat, his back partly facing the door. The driver started the car and turned north onto the road—north being, by Lynx's reckoning, the correct direction.

The spokesman started to make small talk as they drove along. Shortly into it, he introduced himself as Lukas, and then asked Lynx for his name.

Lynx quickly pulled the .45 out and shoved the muzzle under his chin. *He should have known my name!* he thought.

"Don't move, not even your eyelids, you son-of-a-bitch!" ordered Lynx. "Your gun. Tell me where it is."

"You're making a—."

Lynx pushed harder with the .45, saying in hushed tones, "Just whisper or I'll blow your head off. Don't move your hands! Now, once more, and once more only. Where is your gun?"

"Under my jacket on the left side. You're making a mistake. We're on your side."

Reaching his left hand gently and slowly under his jacket, Lynx pulled the gun out of its holster and dropped it on the car floor behind him.

"Put your hands on top of your head," ordered Lynx in a half-whisper. Then, he moved the .45 from under his chin to his left hand, reached the door handle with his other hand, unlatched the car door, and ordered the man to jump out. The car was going down the road at about 40 mph.

Lukas protested audibly, and the driver started getting interested. He could hear the sound of air rushing by the partially open door.

Lynx ordered Lukas to tell the driver that everything was okay and shoved the .45 back under his chin.

Lynx then forced Lukas out the door of the speeding car, pushing him out with both feet and finally kicking him in the stomach as he—in terror—tried to hold on.

In a flash, Lynx was in the front seat with his .45 at the driver's temple. Reaching in to remove his gun, Lynx discovered that the driver was left-handed. Lynx had to go to his right side to remove his weapon, which he dropped onto the car floor in the back seat.

The driver was now sweating profusely with the muzzle of Lynx's .45 still at his temple. When Lynx ordered him to jump from the car, the driver slowed down. Lynx reached over and unlatched the car door, which was forced open when he kicked the driver out of the car with both feet, taking over the controls as he did so.

A mile down the road, he spotted two men in the headlights, waving the car down. They appeared unarmed but Lynx still held his .45 at the ready.

"Do you know any good passwords?" inquired Lynx.

"The Red Comet flies tonight. Good to see you, Lynx," replied one of them.

"The comet is here to stay."

Mike, obviously the man in charge, introduced himself and his accomplice Bruno—a huge man, six foot two and three hundred pounds, most of it pure muscle—who stood silently by. Lynx quickly recounted the events since his landing, and both men got into the car. Lynx did a U-turn to go back and deal with the two men he had forced out of the car.

Mike picked up the two guns on the floor of the back seat, looked them over, and quickly concluded that they belonged to MKGB agents. They had evidently intercepted Lynx's intended contact.

A distance along the road, Lynx could see two men beside the road, almost certainly the two he had pushed out of the car. One was waving the car down, the second was lying face down on the roadside. In the headlights, Lynx immediately recognized the one standing as the driver from minutes earlier and stopped. Bruno and Mike lost no time shoving the two men into the back seat, Lukas in particular moaning with a broken arm and skull injuries. Mike asked Lynx to take them back to the flare site as Bruno shoved a gun into the driver's ribs. Bruno and Mike then began their interrogation in Russian.

Bruno asked Lukas in Russian where "our contact man" was. When Lukas hesitated to respond, Bruno smacked his broken arm with the gun barrel to help his memory.

"Over near the flare," he answered. They drove near the spot and walked the last few yards. The driver was more or less self-ambulatory, but Lukas was unable to walk. Consequently, Bruno dragged him across the grass, propped him up with the car headlights providing the lighting, and asked again, "Where is our friend?"

The question was posed a few times, and the replies came back as ever-stronger pleas for mercy. In great pain, Lukas finally mumbled, "Over there," as he pointed towards a clump of bushes.

A short hunt revealed the body of an almost unconscious and badly beaten man. Mike was aghast at the sight; the Czech's face had been pistol-whipped so badly that he was scarcely recognizable. His face was swollen and contorted.

The man was scarcely able to speak, but managed to get a few words out haltingly, "I didn't . . . tell them . . . his code name . . . I knew he'd catch on." Indeed, he had.

"Who did this?" demanded Lynx.

"Lukas did. I couldn't do something like that," shouted the driver.

Mike promptly instructed Bruno to "look after" Lukas.

Lynx cut open the driver's jacket with his knife, looked for a 30/06 shoulder scar, and found none. He had not been Nomad's assassin.

The sound of a muffled gunshot came from a short distance away and Lynx knew that Lukas had beaten his last Czech.

Bruno returned and picked the driver up by the scruff of the neck.

Mike looked up and announced, "Our friend is dead."

Bruno went berserk, slamming his huge fist into the Russian's face, beating him mercilessly until he began losing consciousness.

Finally, Mike made him stop by reminding him that they need him alive to "talk."

Bruno looked up and let go of the Russian. He went over to his dead friend, gently picked him up, and carried him to their car.

When the Russian came around, Mike asked him how they had found out about the jump. The Russian claimed that they had noticed the flare and simply stopped to investigate what was going on, insisting that there was nothing more to it than that.

Then the Russian pleaded to be let go, and Mike complied—in a way. He took the Russian's jacket off, wrapped it around his pistol, put it against the man's chest and pulled the trigger.

After Lynx had inspected his right shoulder for a 30/06 scar, he walked to Mike's car and waited for Mike and Bruno to locate the Russians' transportation. While they were gone, Lynx made a few adjustments to his pack to make it look more casual. Mike and Bruno soon returned with the Russians' car and offered their ID papers to Lynx should he wish to pose as an MKGB agent. Lynx declined; he was already well equipped in that regard.

Bruno put the two dead Russians back into their car as Mike removed four machine guns from the trunk. They moved the car closer to the road and used leafy tree branches as big brooms to sweep the area clean.

Lynx supplied the explosive, set the timer for 2.5 hours—by which time they would all be well on their way to Prague—activated the switch, placed the bomb under a seat, and locked the car doors.

With Mike and Bruno in the front seat and Lynx with their friend's corpse propped up in the back seat as a "prisoner"—a gruesome sight, but looking the part—they set off for Prague. Lynx had one submachine gun at his feet, Bruno had two at his, and there were two more in the trunk.

Mike was a talker, and it soon became clear that he was not up on espionage protocol when he started inquiring into Lynx's background. In due course and with a little coaxing, Mike relayed what he knew about Strawinski to help Lynx plan their exit from the country. The bare bones information was that Strawinski was a scholar, probably a physicist, well educated, might get nervous—possibly frightened, given the circumstances—and likely couldn't resist much Russian interrogation without spilling everything he knew.

Driving at a moderate speed to avoid attention, they met only one car in the first half hour or so. They turned on the police radio station to follow any developments and possibly extract valuable information. Mike and Bruno, who both spoke Russian, were confident they could handle any questions that might arise regarding passport checks and the like.

At the first checkpoint, about twenty well-armed soldiers plus officers were standing and waiting for the car to stop.

Planning their story, Lynx proposed that, if the questions got too bothersome, he would pretend to whisper something into Mike's ear. The ruse would be that they had an important prisoner in the back seat. Mike would show Lynx's papers, and if the papers were as good as they thought they were, they wouldn't hesitate to open up the roadblock.

Mike stopped the car at the roadblock. An officer in a brown uniform approached and saluted. The two conversed and Mike passed him Lynx's papers. Lynx leaned forward and pretended to whisper into Mike's ear. Turning back to the officer, Mike shouted arrogantly at him and the officer opened the back left door. Lynx sat looking stoically straight ahead, the officer said something in Russian, glanced at Lynx's "prisoner," and closed the door. He then said something in Russian to Mike and started shouting orders. All soldiers snapped to attention and saluted the car's occupants. The two cars obstructing the road were moved quickly out of the way.

Lynx's papers were returned, Mike started the car, and they drove away. A masterful ruse had been pulled off.

Lynx lit a cigarette and looked at his wristwatch: 3:45 a.m. Prague was about an hour away. *Sarge did a helluva job preparing my Russian papers,* he thought. *I don't know who I am, nor what rank I've got, but it sure scares the hell out Russian soldiers. Have to use that again.*

Mike passed a jacket back to Lynx so that it could be put over his "prisoner's" mutilated face.

As they approached Prague, Lynx had a now-familiar feeling that something was about to come off the rails. When they reached Mike's house—a two-storey brick structure—Lynx and Mike carried their dead contact into a bedroom while Bruno hid the car with the submachine guns still in it. Lynx took along his small pack containing the plastic explosive, a Russian pistol, and his own .45 automatic.

As they approached the house and entered with their gear, Lynx could make out three figures in the quasi-darkness of the room. Mike cautioned Lynx that no lights were to be turned on, instructed Lynx to follow him into the cellar, and the three darkened figures followed them down. The door closed at the top of the stairs, and Mike turned on a light.

Turning to see who had come down the stairs, Lynx immediately locked eyes with a young woman; standing beside her was an older woman and an old man. Guessing, Lynx put the age of the young woman in her early twenties. She was shapely, with long black hair flowing to her shoulders and down her back. Lynx shook hands with the older pair whom Mike introduced as his parents. Mike then introduced his sister Hellin, adding that, of the three, only Hellin spoke English. Hellin—oozing sex from every pore, smiling seductively and sustaining eye contact with Lynx—promptly opined in hushed tones, "You are a very good looking man."

Mike said something in Czech to his parents while Hellin joined arms with Lynx and asked in an alluring whisper, "Will you take me out with you?"

Before Lynx could answer, Mike interrupted, "Trouble, Strawinski didn't show up."

Gently removing his arm from Hellin's, Lynx replied, "Dammit, Mike. I knew something was wrong. Do you know where he is now?"

"At home. He sent a message for me to meet him tomorrow at noon in a small cafe."

Lynx asked whether they could do anything before morning, Mike said something to his mother, who went upstairs and returned with a folding table and three chairs. As Mike related the night's events to his father, Hellin sidled up to Lynx, this time whispering in his ear, "Lynx, you are a fascinating man, and very smart. Surely you could take me with you and Mr. Strawinski."

"Hellin, I would like to, but you know that I can't. I have a job to do, and it would be impossible to take you along."

"Oh, but you are wrong. I could help you a lot. And I could make the trip more interesting for you."

"Hellin, stop," interrupted Mike. "Please go and help mother."

Hellin frowned and went upstairs while Mike and Lynx sat down to figure out what to do about Strawinski. Mike started in saying that his father thought Strawinski may have changed his mind about leaving. He added that two MKGB agents had been following him everywhere, which was perhaps a factor in his decision.

Lynx simply stated, "Mr. Strawinski is coming out with me, whether he wants to or not. Those are my orders, if for no other reason than he already knows too much about Mike's underground organization, and about me. He'll soon have met me, know what I look like, and that, in itself, is enough reason." Mike agreed.

Hellin and her mother came back downstairs with some bread and cold meat. Hellin took a seat as close as she could to Lynx and gave him another seductive smile in that unmistakable way that eager women do. After having something to eat, Mike took Lynx upstairs to a second storey bedroom to get some sleep. It was 5:00 a.m. Mike left the room and Lynx decided to sleep fully clothed in case of unexpected action. He put his .45 under his pillow, lay back on the bed, took a few drags on a cigarette, stubbed it out, and dozed off.

He felt the bed move. Someone was approaching from behind and had bumped into the bed in the darkened room. Instinctively grabbing his .45 in one hand, in a swift manoeuvre, he grabbed the intruder by the hair and shoved the .45 into the face. It was Hellin—who let out a piercing scream. Lynx released her and lowered the .45.

She sat on the bed sobbing while Lynx apologized for his reflex action. Mike burst in and wanted to know what was going on. Mike scolded Hellin briefly, but Lynx offered to talk to her and explain the reality of the situation.

She was persistent, pleading with Lynx to take her out with him. Nothing would satisfy her short of a "Yes." After a few "No's," she relented somewhat with, "If you come back to our country again, would you take me with you then?"

When Lynx promised to do so full in the knowledge that a return visit was highly unlikely, she left with, "I'll wait for you. For now, have some sleep." Lynx lay on the bed for several minutes thinking, *The temptation is great, and it would be completely unfair to take advantage of her, but there would be too many complications* . . . . He finally dozed off.

The next thing he knew, Bruno was at his bedside, rousing him for breakfast. They had slept in late due to their very early morning arrival, and the sleep was badly needed. It would be a long day. As they passed the room where Lynx and Bruno had laid their dead contact the night before, Lynx saw that it was empty. Bruno had buried his friend earlier that morning.

In the kitchen, Mike, his parents, and Hellin were already eating, and there was only one unclaimed place at the table—beside her. Lynx sat down and she smiled contentedly. Breakfast was already on his plate.

Mike outlined the plan to pick up Mr. Strawinski. He suggested that Lynx leave his small satchel behind, even though he knew it contained plastic explosives. He assured Lynx that it was safe to do so, and that his parents were quite familiar with such devices.

Mike handed Lynx a Czech hat and he followed Mike and Bruno out the door. As they walked to the cafe, Mike expressed concern that the two MKGB agents that had been following Mr. Strawinski could be a problem. He also warned that with the schedule delays piling up, Lynx's pick-up team might start wondering what had happened. Lynx told him to not worry about that.

"They'll wait, " he confidently reassured Mike.

As they approached the cafe at about noon, the two MKGB agents were standing outside, dressed in civvies, blending in well, as was typical. Inside the cafe, all seats were taken except one table at the back where a lone customer sat. He was heavyset, but not fat. The hair on the side of his head had started greying. The top of his head was bald. His nervousness was obvious.

He watched as Lynx and Mike approached his table and sat down. Bruno was already sitting beside him by this time and introduced Lynx as "the man who is going to get you out." Strawinski did not respond, but when Lynx asked if he spoke English, he blurted out, his edginess palpable, "Yes, I can speak English. I have to call it off."

"Sorry, but we have to go now," replied Lynx. "We are already behind schedule, and should have been on that 9:00 a.m. train this morning."

"But, didn't you know that I am being followed everywhere I go?" he asked excitedly.

Mike intervened, "The two agents are coming in, probably to check our papers."

Lynx whispered, "Mike, as soon as I pound my fist on the table, take my papers up to them and tell them the same story you told the Russians at the roadblock last night."

Mike agreed. Lynx passed him his high-ranking papers and let out a roar as he pounded the table. The cafe suddenly went silent. The seconds ticked by as Mike ranted on in Russian. He pointed back at Lynx's table, while Lynx slowly inched his hand into his jacket, readying his .45. Bruno cautioned Lynx to not start shooting and let Mike handle the situation.

Then Strawinski interjected quietly, pleading, "Mr. Lynx, I cannot go. It's too risky. Tell your people that I am sorry, but it's better to live here than die trying to escape."

Mike had returned to the table and heard the tail end of Strawinski's statement.

"They are gone for now," reported Mike. "Those papers of yours scared the hell out of them." Then he turned to the little man who was obviously quite frightened, almost shaking visibly, and said, "So, you are not going with Lynx?"

"No. I . . . I . . . can't," came the reply as beads of sweat formed on his forehead.

"You are throwing freedom away. Don't be a fool. If I had your chance, I would jump at it. Lynx is good at his job. You have nothing to worry about," said Mike.

"I said no! And it is no!"

With that, Strawinski jumped up from the table and bolted for the door. Mike and Lynx looked at one another—poleaxed.

"Time to regroup," said Lynx. He had been contemplating the situation since the night before, when Mike's father had said he thought Strawinski would be reluctant to follow through with the plan. In hushed tones, Lynx started to outline his plan on how to proceed.

Attempting to give some context on the process of changing people's minds under duress, Lynx alluded to how American gangsters generally operate below the legal radar with rules of engagement and an honour code among themselves, including how they sometimes use blackmail to get certain things done. He implied that he might draw on such methods in bringing Strawinski around. Acknowledging that Strawinski was frightened, Lynx reassured Mike that, when he got through with Strawinski, he would be willing to come out.

When Lynx had finished outlining his plan in general terms, Mike liked it and smiled approvingly. Working together on the timing, including synchronizing with the train schedule and securing the cars and manpower needed, they went over it in fine detail when they got back to Mike's house.

When Mike left to set up the plan with Bruno, Hellin started to talk to Lynx. She, of course, wanted to be part of the plan. When Lynx disabused her of the idea, she changed tactics and started to ask about the United States, thinking that was Lynx's base. Quickly changing subjects, Lynx asked about her brother Mike.

She related how he had been married before the war to a lady called Zenovia, a beautiful woman with whom he was completely happy. Zenovia was frightened when the Germans invaded, and a year after the occupation ended, she fell ill and died. They had no children. Mike never got over losing Zenovia and he was unlikely to ever marry again. He, his father, and Bruno had all been in the Czech underground throughout the war, working tirelessly for freedom. Of course, the Communists had now been there for many years, and the populace was living under an umbrella of suspicion. Neighbourly trust was non-existent; someone might turn you in at any moment.

Bruno had lost all of his family in the war, except his brother who was once active in the underground. He left the house one day and was never seen again. They later learned that the MKGB had picked him up, and no one had any idea of his fate.

When Mike returned, he motioned Lynx to follow him into the cellar, alone. There, he related that he had gotten a message through to Lynx's base that he and Strawinski would be on the late train out of Prague that night. It was up to Lynx how he got Strawinski to the train.

Mike was intrigued by the plan, and wanted to know how Lynx was going to change Strawinski's mind. Lynx simply refused to cast any further light on the matter.

"Just leave it to me," he responded, each time the subject arose. With that, Lynx went back to bed, expecting a long night.

As he lay awake contemplating the coming hours, Hellin entered the room in the dim light, wearing a dress—fitted like a glove to her curvaceous body—with buttons all the way down the front. Several top buttons were already unfastened, revealing the enticing peripherals of her womanly assets. She offered to give Lynx a massage, he accepted, and she started with his neck and back muscles. When she indicated that there would be ". . . no strings attached" to whatever might now transpire, any residual tension from Lynx's rejection of her earlier requests quickly evaporated. He dozed off as she continued working away on his neck muscles. The next thing he knew, she had stripped naked and laid down beside him, her warm body pressed against his—still clothed from the waist down. With her help, an aroused Lynx removed his remaining clothing " . . . so quick it made [his] head spin." The ensuing euphoria was mutual and total.

When Mike knocked on the door, Lynx was already up, adjusting the straps on his shoulder holster for his .45 automatic. He quickly put on a shirt, his jacket, picked up his hat, and carrying his shoes, crossed the room towards the door. Before exiting, he took a last look at Hellin, peacefully asleep. A wave of sadness swept over him momentarily; he would have loved to help her, but he had a job to do. And he knew that Sarge would not approve of him bringing any extra defectors out with him.

Outside the bedroom door, Mike waited as Lynx put on his shoes. Dusk was descending on the city as they went outside. Mike's parents stood silently by the door, hoping for a safe return of their son. Just as the two men reached the curb, Bruno pulled up in the car. When they got in, a fourth man already sitting in the back seat spoke to Mike in Czech. They sped off.

Lynx immediately noticed the two automatic machine guns. Mike picked them up and handed one to his companion. Each checked their magazines and loaded them.

Lynx told Mike to let him off one block before Strawinski's apartment, and to meet him in the alley behind it a few minutes later. Lynx promised to return with Strawinski as planned, knowing that the two MKGB agents would be following them. He had plans for that, too.

When they got to Strawinski's apartment, Mike pointed it out on the second floor, a window facing the alley. Mike handed Lynx the hook and rope he had requested. Lynx wrapped the rope around his waist and shoved the double-pronged hook into his belt, just under his jacket. Bruno drove around the block, let Lynx out, and sped off.

The importance of success and the many lives involved weighed on Lynx's mind. *Can I do it*? he thought. *Yes, I can.*

Lynx took a pack of Canadian cigarettes out of his pocket and was about to light up when he couldn't find his matches. The matches should have been with the cigarettes, but they weren't there. He searched his pockets—nothing. He stopped walking and did another search. Still nothing.

Lynx heard footsteps and suddenly found himself face-to-face with a Russian soldier. A chill ran up his spine, and the cigarette almost fell from his lips. He was about to go for his .45 when the soldier lit his Zippo lighter and held it out, almost touching the tip of the cigarette already between Lynx's lips. Lynx took the light, the soldier smiled and lit his own cigarette.

Before any conversation could start, Lynx smiled back, put a hand up to his cap politely as a gesture of thanks, and moved on down the street. Not a word was spoken.

His heart pounding, Lynx walked casually on, expecting a command at any second from the soldier. He dared not glance back at him; no yell came. Lynx casually crossed the street and disappeared from sight.

Lynx had just had a close call. No consequence had arisen, but it had been a close call, nevertheless. If the Russian had smelled his Canadian tobacco, he would have noticed a dramatic difference from his much more pungent Turkish tobacco, and possibly have suspected something was up. *I just dodged a bullet!* Lynx thought.

A few minutes later, he was standing directly under the second-floor window to Strawinski's apartment. He quickly readied the rope and hook by coiling the rope in his left hand and tying a loop where he knew it would be needed. He gently swung the rope over his head, aiming it at the second-storey window ledge. It landed with a slight *clang* against the brick ledge. When he tugged gently on the rope, the hook gave way and almost hit him as it fell back down. He managed to catch it before it hit the street. He swung the rope and hook upward again. This time, it held.

Up the rope he went, hand over hand, just as Charles had taught him, until he reached the window ledge. Hanging by one hand, he slipped his foot into the loop he had made on the ground, struggled for balance, and then climbed onto the window ledge.

The apartment was in darkness. *Maybe he isn't here!* thought Lynx. At the open window, he tried to part the curtain as it hung inside the window. When it would not part in the middle, he simply slashed the material with his razor-sharp knife without making a sound. He climbed down into the dark room, stopped, and closed his eyes for a few seconds to accelerate their adaption to the darkness.

When he opened them, he could make out the basic features of the room as a dresser beside the bed where Strawinski was sound asleep, mouth agape. Lynx slowly drew his .45 from its holster and shook the sleeping man.

He awoke with such a start that Lynx had to cover his mouth to prevent him from crying out. Speaking calmly and quietly, he said, "Relax. It's me, Lynx. Now, I'm going to take my hand away from your mouth. If you scream, I will have to take drastic measures. Nod your head if you understand."

He nodded and Lynx took his hand away,

"Don't turn on any lights, " Lynx ordered.

"No! No! I won't," replied the shaken man. "How did you get into my bedroom?"

"Never mind that," replied Lynx. "I'm here to get you out of the country. To freedom. You have to go whether you want to or not."

"I cannot go with you. In fact, I will not."

Lynx moved his left hand quickly to the top of the .45 and cocked it, brought the first shell into the firing chamber, and placed the muzzle against Strawinski's chin.

"Mr. Strawinski, in that case, I have orders to kill you."

Strawinski's eyes widened, and beads of sweat suddenly began to appear on his forehead.

"You know my code name. You know the names of several people in the Czech underground. You know what I look like. In fact, you know way too much for me to let you live."

"You wouldn't kill me in cold blood, would you?"

"I have been trained to kill. If you don't come with me, then I will have no choice."

Lynx paused while he thought of what to say next, continuing with, "I'll make it look like a robbery, or a murder."

Pleading for time to think it over, Lynx cut him off. "I can't wait. You come now or else."

"All right, I'll come. But how are you going to get past the two agents who have been following me?"

"Leave that to me. It's what I do. Get dressed. You will take nothing with you except the clothes on your back. I will leave the way I came in. You have to leave by the front door, as calmly as you can."

"But they will follow me."

"That's exactly what I want them to do. Now, listen carefully. Fifteen minutes after I leave, you are to walk out the front door. Turn right and walk to the next street. Turn right again and just keep walking. I'll meet you farther down the street."

Shaking almost uncontrollably, the little man agreed.

"If you do not walk out of here in fifteen minutes, then I will have no choice but to follow my orders."

"I understand," he replied meekly.

Lynx looked at his wristwatch. There was just enough time to meet Mike. Lynx crossed the room, parted the curtains, and checked the alleyway. It was clear. He gave Strawinski a final glance—full eye contact—and holstered his .45.

"Remember: fifteen minutes."

Strawinski nodded. Lynx went out the window and moved hand over hand down the hanging rope to the street. He released the hook with a deft flip of the rope. Lynx caught it and he started running down the alleyway, coiling the rope as he went. As he turned the corner, the car was waiting less than forty feet away. He jumped into the back seat.

"He'll be leaving his apartment in fifteen minutes. Let's move!" said Lynx, dropping the hook and rope onto the floor.

Mike, of course, wanted to know how Lynx had persuaded him to go for freedom.

"Mike, a .45 to a person's head is always effective persuasion. I told him that if he wasn't coming with me, I had orders to kill him. My superiors will likely not be impressed, but I couldn't think of any other way."

"What if he had said no?"

"He was too afraid of dying to do that. I knew it would work."

Mike had two men waiting in the alley and let Lynx off just down the street from them. A third man had been left to wait for Strawinski at the designated meet-up location.

The three men exchanged *adieus*, Bruno stopped the car to let Lynx out, did a U-turn, and sped off. Lynx made his way towards Strawinski's meet-up location.

A man stood in the doorway at that location.

"Lynx?" he challenged.

"Yes."

"We wait here," he said simply.

Lynx pulled out a cigarette, and asked for a match. The man reached into his pocket and lit his cigarette with an annoyed expression on his face.

After lighting Lynx's cigarette, he passed Strawinski's false identification papers to Lynx and the two men continued waiting. Ten minutes had elapsed since Lynx had left Strawinski. A few minutes later, Lynx's waiting companion, too, wanted to know how Lynx had changed the scientist's mind.

When Lynx gave a vague response, the man unloaded his frustration. "First of all, he is all set to go. Then he changes his mind. He seems to have no idea how much danger he has put people in for his sake. If he falters one more time, I'll shoot the son-of-a-bitch myself."

"Look, Mr. Strawinski is my responsibility. I don't need any trouble. As for killing him, forget it," said Lynx quietly but firmly. The man glared at Lynx, and then turned his head away.

"You do your job, and I'll do mine," Lynx continued. "Your job is to get us on the train."

"I'll get you there," he answered, still looking away.

A moment later, footsteps could be heard approaching. It was a man walking on the opposite side of the street, still some distance away. He suddenly turned into an alley and disappeared. *Good,* thought Lynx. *We don't need any witnesses.* Another look up the street and Lynx recognized Strawinski's walk as he hurried towards them. The two ever-present MKGB agents were following him, walking briskly but a good distance behind him.

Lynx readied his .45 as a car, its headlights out, proceeded slowly down the street, suddenly accelerated, and screeched to a halt beside the two agents. Two Czechs, their rifle butts held high, jumped out of the car and deftly smashed the two agent's heads.

Strawinski turned to take a look as the car doors flew open. The MKGB agents were dragged into the back seat of the car. The two Czechs jumped into the front seat and, tires squealing, took off, speeding past the waiting triumvirate of Lynx, his train-connection contact, and Strawinski.

Lynx took charge of Strawinski, and the three started towards their waiting car, walking briskly.

Not far down the street, they stepped into an alley as Strawinski panted for breath. They reached the parked car, got in, and the driver drove them away carefully to avoid drawing attention.

A few blocks later, a car appeared behind them. *Probably a tail*, thought Lynx. Lynx instructed the driver to turn at the next street to see if they were being followed while he readied his .45 automatic.

They turned and the car followed.

Lynx decided to try to lose the tail and put Strawinski on the floor in case shooting started. He had his driver floor the accelerator and they made a turn onto another street. Lynx aimed his .45 out the back window at the speeding car, its tires also squealing with each turn. The tail was in hot pursuit, but it wasn't navigating the turns as well as Lynx's driver. Their tail was bouncing off curbs and onto the sidewalk for significant distances at a time, then skidding back into the street, all of which was costing time. The effect was cumulative.

Lynx's driver was steadily losing the tail. A few turns later, no one was in pursuit. They had shaken their pursuer.

Lynx was perplexed as to how the tail had arisen. *Did they have a leak?* he pondered. He decided that the best course of action was to go to the safe house and wait for the train there. Lynx instructed his driver to take them to the safe house, which was located a block past the train station, and he drove straight to it.

The three men walked up to the door. The driver gave a few knocks and it opened. Strawinski entered, but the driver just stood there.

"After you, Lynx," he said in the same sarcastic manner he had used throughout their thirty-minute relationship. Lynx was not about to turn his back on him, and was now a little suspicious. He motioned to the driver with his .45 and ordered him into the house.

The house was a two-storey structure, and the host led them into the kitchen. On the way, Lynx noticed two children watching from the stairs in their pyjamas. All the lights in the house were turned out except for an oil lamp burning feebly in the kitchen. The host and his wife were young, but spoke no English. They motioned for their three guests to sit down, Strawinski on Lynx's right, their driver on his left.

Turning to his driver, Lynx snapped at him, "What time does the train leave?"

"11:45 p.m.," he replied, looking off into space, straight ahead.

"What about tickets?"

"I'll go and get them now, " he replied.

"Here," said Lynx, handing him a wad of Czech bills. "Will that cover it?"

"That is more than enough," replied the driver, sarcasm dripping from each word. "You have a big gun, lots of money, and sound like a real tough guy. But I don't think you're so tough. Probably got no guts."

Lynx resisted the temptation of being drawn into a battle of egos, and struggled to remain calm. Lynx defused him with, "Just get the tickets, and let's not worry about who is tougher than who. Okay?"

Without further discussion, the driver got up and walked out the door to buy the tickets at the train station.

Strawinski could now see that a healthy Lynx was clearly critical to his successful escape from the country, and that some abrasion had developed between Lynx and their driver. He would be left high and dry if anything happened to Lynx. Strawinski wondered aloud whether Lynx, by far the smaller of the two, would be able to handle himself should they come to blows.

Lynx reassured him that agility trumps size, the smaller man has the advantage in hand-to-hand combat, and to rest assured that there would be no problem.

Strawinski, of course, was also curious about Lynx and North America, where his future lay. He began probing Lynx for information—not a suitable avenue of questioning, but he simply couldn't help himself. Lynx was evasive and tossed them off nonchalantly. As soon as he could, without offending his naïve charge, Lynx simply changed the subject.

At about 10:00 p.m., still more than ninety minutes before the train would depart, Lynx decided the best waiting place would be the cellar.

Strawinski asked their host in Czech where the entrance to the cellar was, and he pointed at the cellar's entrance door. They continued chatting, and ten minutes later, their driver still had not returned with the tickets.

Lynx got up, checked the back of the house, and looked outside through the rear door. He was becoming increasingly mistrustful of the driver, and wanted to check out the rear exit in case it was needed in haste. All appeared to be clear.

When he came back into the kitchen, the driver had returned. He was shouting at Strawinski and pointing a gun at him. Lynx was only three feet from the driver when the driver finally noticed that Lynx had returned from his backyard reconnaissance inspection. Lynx's .45 automatic was now pointed at the driver's head.

"Put the gun down now. Any quick moves and I'll blow your brains out. I mean it!"

The driver placed his gun gently onto the table, still glaring at the frightened scientist.

"What the hell is going on?" asked Lynx.

"Lynx, don't do anything in front of the children," pleaded Strawinski.

The driver's pent-up frustration suddenly surfaced, and he shouted at Strawinski, "You're a traitor. I should have killed you. You have probably already informed on all of us."

"Shut up and step back from the table, " ordered Lynx.

He did, and Lynx reached over and picked up his gun off the table.

Concerned that the ruckus—albeit all inside the house—may have attracted some attention, Lynx instructed Strawinski to ask their host to see if anyone was outside, which he did in Czech. The host moved across the room and went to the front door. He returned and signalled negative with a headshake.

A goodly hour or more passed in silence as the parties eyed each other up and down, which killed some time. That was fine with Lynx; they needed to pass the time somehow. Their 11:45 p.m. train departure had been a long way off. Perhaps it would have been better to wait in the basement, but that was now in the past.

As Lynx mulled things over in his mind, the driver's earlier comments on his capabilities were eating at him, and he decided to teach his driver a lesson. Suddenly trusting Strawinski with something for which he was totally unsuited, Lynx put both his .45 and his driver's pistol on the table side by side and told Strawinski, "Keep an eye on the guns. We'll be back in a few minutes."

Lynx stood beside the entrance to the cellar and motioned the driver to join him in the cellar. The two men descended the stairs, Lynx behind the driver.

Face to face in the cellar, the driver started snarling threatening remarks at Lynx. "I'll tear you apart," he shouted and lunged at Lynx. That was precisely the wrong manoeuvre. Lynx's combat training kicked in instinctively. He grabbed one of the driver's arms, spun around, and easily put him into a shoulder throw. He slammed down on the floor, hard, sending a table crashing across the room. Lynx took the dazed man by the neck in a submission hold that, with a bit of pressure applied, would cut off the blood circulation to his brain.

"Had enough, big mouth?" Lynx said into his ear.

As the driver continued to struggle, the hold got tighter.

"If you keep this up, big man, you're going to get a little sleep. If I put a little more pressure on, you'll be out in seconds."

"All right! All right!" said the driver as he succumbed.

Lynx released him and backed away. The driver sat dazed for a moment, then got to his feet. He stared at Lynx, his face getting redder by the second. Lynx knew that he would charge again and was ready. When he did, Lynx deftly turned ninety degrees, bent forward, balanced on one foot, and kicked him square in the jaw with the other foot. Down he went a second time. But this time, Lynx turned him over onto his stomach and bent one arm up behind his back. He reached into his leg holster for his derringer and placed the weapon where his victim could see it.

"Now then, you big-mouthed son-of-a-bitch, just who are you working for? The underground, or the MKGB? This little gun makes hardly any sound, but it would make a nice, clean hole in your forehead."

"Okay, Lynx. I don't work for the MKGB. I didn't think you could do your job, but you're better at handling yourself than I thought."

Accepting his word, Lynx added a warning that another false move and he would crack his skull. Lynx released him and the driver stood up, rubbing his arm.

"Train time is not far off, so we'd better get ready to go," said Lynx and followed him up the stairs, back into the kitchen.

Taking Strawinski aside in another room, Lynx asked a favour of the scientist, who readily agreed. Lynx quietly instructed him to get the host alone and have him contact Mike to let him know two things: there had been a tail and how their driver had behaved. Acknowledging that he could be wrong, Lynx wanted Mike to know that he had a strong suspicion that they could have an informer in their underground organization.

Lynx took the driver to the front of the house to ensure nothing was amiss. Strawinski was left alone with the host in the kitchen so he could pass on the message.

They walked out the front door and looked up and down the street. All was still, and no one was lurking in the shadows.

The driver, impressed with Lynx's hand-to-hand combat skills, was now eager to "hang out" with Lynx. His sarcasm had disappeared, but Lynx was still wary. Back in the kitchen, the host and Strawinski were still deep in conversation when Lynx entered the room. Lynx announced it was "Time to go," they said their "Goodbyes," and headed out the front door. Strawinski and Lynx hurriedly headed for the train station, the driver to his car.

As they walked briskly to the station, Strawinski confirmed that he had asked their host to contact Mike with Lynx's message.

As they approached the station, Lynx could see a man standing near the entrance to the platform. Strawinski indicated that he was probably checking papers, and told Lynx to "follow me." Strawinski instructed Lynx to deal with his inability to speak Czech by playing dumb—after all, he was posing as a "highly-placed Russian." Strawinski was confident that this would be just "routine."

As they approached the train car entrance, Lynx knew that the uniformed soldier was looking at him and Strawinski. Strawinski gave him his ticket and showed him his papers. The young soldier examined them, handed them back, and Strawinski boarded the train.

Lynx was feeling nervous and trying his best to hide it. He passed the man his ticket and his papers, the man said nothing and passed them back. Lynx said nothing and stepped onto the train. Turning into the same car that Strawinski had entered, Lynx cast a quick glance back at the uniformed man and he was paying no attention to Lynx. Breathing a sigh of relief, he wondered, *Is there any limit to how far I can push my false ID papers?*

Thank you, Sarge, he thought as he sat down beside a smiling Strawinski.

Moving to an empty compartment, Lynx immediately pulled down the shades on both the inside wall and outside windows. Until the train was in motion, he continued to check outside periodically by opening a crack in the window blind in case some excitement was brewing.

Lynx finally settled into a seat facing Strawinski, his small satchel containing the plastic bomb—should it be needed—sitting on the floor at his feet.

Strawinski eyed the bag curiously, asking, "What are you carrying in there?"

Looking at him for a moment, Lynx decided it would do no harm if he knew and responded, matter-of-factly, "I've got a bomb in there."

"A bomb!" exclaimed Strawinski in subdued tones. "What are you going to do with it?"

"Hopefully nothing. It's very powerful, but not as it currently sits. It's quite harmless as it is now. I had two when I landed, and have already had to use one. Let's hope I don't have to use this one. But if I do, I will."

After the adrenalin rush of the past few hours, Lynx was feeling like he needed a nap and dozed off while Strawinski stood guard over his satchel. The train was gaining speed, and Lynx found the *clickety-clack* of the train on the track soothing.

The train trip would be just three hours. It had pulled out on time at 11:45 p.m., which made their ETA at the Austrian border about 3:00 a.m., say 3:30 a.m. at the latest for the mission to be complete.

Unable to sleep, Lynx began thinking about the possible eventualities. *Here I am, in a foreign country,* he thought. *If caught, I could put up a fight or take the cyanide capsule. But what about Strawinski? Could I put a gun to his head if the occasion demanded it? Hell, I've already done that! He simply knows too much, and certainly wouldn't be able to withstand any heavy questioning. The slightest amount of torture would have him singing like a stool pigeon. So that leaves me only one option: kill him if necessary.*

He opened his eyes, not wide enough for anyone to know, and looked at Strawinski to see if he was watching. He had opened the window blind and was staring blankly out into the darkness.

Lynx finally dozed off, confident that they had clear sailing from here on in. He glanced at his watch when he awoke and noted the time as 12:20 a.m. He hadn't had much sleep, but felt well rested.

Strawinski was now watching him in a fixed stare. They engaged in some small talk.

Strawinski was a non-smoker but carried matches. He handed some to Lynx so he could light a cigarette.

Then, as Strawinski attempted to probe into his background, Lynx quickly drew the line with, "Mr. Strawinski, must I remind you that my life, my age, my country of origin, my training, and anything else about me is to be kept secret? How about we talk about you? How old are you?"

"Middle forties," he replied. "I was born in a small town near the Polish border. Never married. I was engaged once, but that was a long time ago. During the German occupation, I was forced to work with them . . . . "

Lynx jumped in. "Please don't tell me anything about your line of work. I know you are a scientist, but that's all. And in a way, that's enough."

Determined to share something with Lynx, Strawinski continued, "I was born on a farm, the youngest of five children. My father was a very strong man, physically, very strong. He pushed my education and worked hard to make sure that I got good schooling. He wanted at least one of his sons to not be a farmer. Farm work is so hard—exhausting, really."

As Strawinski went on, Lynx noticed that the train was slowing down, and then it came to a complete stop. He looked out the window and could see nothing but total darkness. In a few minutes, another train sped by them in the opposite direction, a blur, its wheels rumbling and clattering as it went by. Lynx breathed a sigh of relief when their train started moving again. Strawinski had stopped talking when the train had stopped, but now resumed his monologue.

"My father died a few years ago from overwork. My mother died shortly after. He had no way of knowing, but the education that he wanted so badly for me has become a curse. Now, here I am fleeing my home and country because of it."

"The free world is not so bad," interjected Lynx.

"That's true, but I love my country," he sighed sadly.

Lynx checked his watch: 1:20 a.m., and all was quiet but for the sound of the train.

Strawinski dozed off—or so Lynx thought.

To kill time and just stay on top of things, Lynx took his .45 out of its holster, removed the magazine, and ejected the shell out of the firing chamber. He checked the slide for dirt, and satisfied that all was well, replaced the ejected shell into the magazine and inserted the magazine into the gun butt. When he looked up, Strawinski was watching him.

When Strawinski expressed a dislike of even seeing weapons, Lynx put his .45 back into its shoulder holster and promised that he wouldn't take it out again—unless he had to, that is. Theirs was a clash of cultures in that respect, to be sure.

At 2:00 a.m., Lynx noticed the train slowing down again and the lights of a town came into view. He quickly closed the window blind. Then that gut feeling hit him in the stomach that something was about to go awry.

When Strawinski wanted to know why he had closed the blind, evidently forgetting (or not knowing) the dire consequences that being a defecting scientist lay himself vulnerable to—a firing squad, perhaps—Lynx snapped at him, "Because I want to make sure no one looks in."

As the train finally came to a halt, Lynx pulled the blind aside a crack, looked out, and could see two men boarding the train. One was elderly, the other much younger. And something about the younger one made Lynx feel uneasy. His gut feeling persisted.

When Lynx asked Strawinski if he recognized either of the two men getting aboard the train, Strawinski didn't make it to the cracked blind in time to see either of them.

"He has a long black coat and hat, twenty-five or thirty years old."

Lynx tossed it off as likely inconsequential in order to avoid alarming Strawinski, but he still had an uneasy feeling, particularly about the younger of the two. Lynx lit a cigarette and tried to appear calm.

Strawinski noticed a change in Lynx's demeanour.

"Tell me more about your life," Lynx invited his charge, attempting to keep him talking and move his mind onto something else.

But the gut feeling intensified. Then he remembered that he hadn't brought up the shell into the firing chamber of his .45—which could cost precious seconds if it was needed in a hurry. If he took the gun out now, Strawinski would know that something was wrong. It would have to wait. So he decided to split his hearing—one ear listening to Strawinski drone on about his life, and one ear aimed at the corridor outside the compartment door.

Suddenly, hearing something in the corridor, Lynx motioned Strawinski to be quiet. He pulled the .45 out of its holster and cocked the weapon. Now the gun was ready to fire. He slowly turned the knob of the compartment door and cracked it open. He could see no one in one direction. He opened the door and looked down the corridor. He could see the old man who had boarded the train at the last town coming down the aisle towards him.

Lynx was not worried about the old man; it was his younger companion that gave him the willies. *Where is he?* he wondered.

Lynx closed the door and sat down to think things over.

Strawinski wanted a report. Lynx gave him a totally innocuous one, but Strawinski sensed that Lynx was concerned about something.

When Lynx asked him how many towns there were between where they were now and the border, Strawinski replied "Only a few, just one larger one." Lynx pulled the map out of his satchel and laid it on the seat beside him. He had Strawinski point out their current location and the larger town. There would be a few small villages in between. On the right—to the east, their intended direction—was a road that ran all the way to the border.

When Strawinski indicated that he had to go to the washroom, Lynx volunteered to accompany him to "stretch his legs." The real reason was that Strawinski could not be allowed out of his sight. Lynx opened the compartment door, looked both ways, and the coast was clear. Lynx followed Strawinski to the front of the car. As Strawinski went into the washroom, Lynx told him, "I'll wait for you here."

A rush of moving air greeted Lynx as he opened the door between cars. The noise was almost deafening as the train was charging down the tracks, in startling contrast to the silence inside the compartment and corridor. Lynx was leaning against the door—relaxing—when Strawinski reappeared in the coach door coming from the washroom, heading back to their compartment. He looked as white as a sheet and obviously shaken.

"He's at our compartment door and he saw me!" he exclaimed in a frightened but subdued voice.

"Who?" inquired Lynx.

"The man you saw in the black coat that got aboard at that last stop! He's obviously MKGB, I'm sure of it." Lynx caught a glimpse of the man as he closed the door at the other end of the car.

He instructed Strawinski to walk back to their compartment as calmly as possible, and he (Lynx) would follow in about a minute.

Strawinski was worried that he would be arrested. Lynx reassured him that no one was going to arrest him. Besides, he told the shaken man, in less than a minute, he would be there to sort things out, should any complications arise.

Strawinski opened the door, walked back to their compartment, and went in. Lynx watched him through the door window. Lynx waited for about a minute and walked to the empty compartment just before the one Strawinski was now in—theirs. He entered the compartment, pulled down the door blind, and left the door slightly ajar.

He took out his .45 from its holster and waited a few minutes. The man in the black coat appeared in the corridor, walking towards him. Lynx thought he would go right past Strawinski's compartment but, when he reached it, he turned and flattened himself against the wall. Through a small crack in the open door, Lynx watched him intently as he bent over and listened at Strawinski's door. The young officer's back was towards Lynx who quietly opened his door and moved silently towards him, stopping only a foot or so away.

The young officer suspected nothing and straightened up. As his left hand slowly reached for the doorknob into Strawinski's compartment, his right hand went inside his coat for a weapon.

Gun in hand, Lynx raised his right arm and brought its barrel crashing down onto the back of the Russian's neck. He slumped to the floor like a sack of potatoes. Lynx quickly dragged the unconscious man into their compartment.

"You've killed him," exclaimed Strawinski in hushed tones.

"He's just taking a nap. He's not dead—yet," replied Lynx with a smirk on his face. "Close the door."

Strawinski stood drop-jawed, looking at the man on the floor for a few moments while Lynx re-holstered his .45.

"Give me a hand to get him up onto the seat," he ordered Strawinski.

Lynx felt for a pulse and detected one. He reached into the unconscious man's coat, removed the pistol from his shoulder holster, pulled out the magazine, and ejected the shell from the firing chamber. Taking all of the cartridges out of the magazine, he opened the window and tossed them out. He then installed the empty magazine into the weapon and placed it back into the man's shoulder holster.

Lynx emptied all the agent's pockets onto the seat beside him, checked his wallet, and found his MKGB identification. The rest of his belongings were of no interest, so he replaced them into the pockets that they had come from. Lynx checked his holster for a spare shell pocket, found a loaded magazine, and tossed it out the window.

Lynx opened the unconscious man's coat and jacket and pulled them down to expose his right shoulder—his "Nomad mission." He pulled his knife from its sheath on his leg, cut the shirt open, and there was no sign of a 30/06 wound.

Someone has to be informing the MKGB of our every move, Lynx thought quietly. *There was the high-speed car chase. Now these two appeared on the train—unlikely coincidences.*

Lynx calmly turned his attention to the precarious situation he and his important charge—now a trembling weakling—were in. *The guy might not be the most courageous soldier of fortune,* he thought, *but his brains are apparently packed with some real, valuable shit.*

Wondering aloud to Strawinski, and referring to the still-unconscious Russian agent slumped on the seat across from him, Lynx asked, "Now, what do we do with this garbage?"

"Where there is one, there are more," stated Strawinski, referring to his nemeses, the MKGB agents.

Lynx decided it was time to air his latest idea, namely bringing liquor into the picture. He asked Strawinski to somehow beg, steal, borrow, or buy a bottle of liquor and handed him a wad of Czech money. Knowing that the MKGB agent wouldn't be coming around any time soon, Lynx and Strawinski exited their compartment with Strawinski leading the way. Lynx brought along his satchel containing the plastic bomb, slung over one shoulder.

They proceeded from compartment to compartment as Strawinski inquired in Czech whether anyone had any hard liquor they would care to part with—at a goodly price, of course.

Near the end of the train car, Strawinski started to talk to someone in a compartment, some laughter was heard, then more conversation, when Strawinski reappeared, a bottle in hand.

They returned to their own compartment and Strawinski handed the bottle to Lynx. He tilted their unconscious visitor's head back and poured a goodly slosh into his mouth. When he let his head go, liquor dribbled back out of his mouth onto his shirt. Then he spilled more onto his shirt, propped the bottle up between his hands in his lap and stepped back.

"Now then, doesn't he look like he just drank too much and fell asleep?" he asked Strawinski, as he admired his masterwork of deception.

"Well, he does smell drunk. But so what? What are we going to do now?"

Lynx had been hesitant to tell his important charge his latest thinking, but decided, *Hell with it,* paused, and simply said, "Mr. Strawinski, we are going to jump off this Midnight Express."

"You've got to be crazy," came the expected reply from the already terrified scientist. "We'll both be killed!"

"Look. It's 2:50 a.m., and in a few minutes, the train will be slowing down for the next village. That's when we make our move. Sure, it's risky, but you, yourself, have already said, 'Where there is one, there are more.' The other agent that boarded the train with our 'friend' here is still prowling around somewhere. It's our best chance. Trust me."

Whether Strawinski liked it or not, Lynx had decided and that's how it would be. Packing as much cushioning around the plastic explosive in the satchel as he could, the two moved out of the compartment and stepped between the cars. The train had already started to slow down and Lynx opened the gate. He took a look at the ground and it appeared suitable, not overly treacherous. One had to accept imperfection given the circumstances. *My plan should work*, he thought.

As the train started to make its way up a slight grade, Lynx reasoned that it would slow down a little quicker as it went uphill. The opportune moment of minimum speed should be imminent.

"Get ready. You're going first," announced Lynx.

Lynx didn't trust that Strawinski would follow him. He was hesitant, of course, and got ready, anticipating the worst.

"Okay, now! Jump!" yelled Lynx.

Strawinski jumped clear. Lynx wondered what condition he would find him in. For Lynx, this was a normal parachute jump—except that he did have a plastic bomb under one arm. Hoping for the best, he braced himself and leapt as clear of the slow-moving train as he could.

Lynx hadn't realized that the tracks were raised above the grade by about three feet; that made for a higher jump than he had anticipated. Also, in a parachute jump, it is usually straight down unless there is an unusual wind, in which case some compensation is advisable.

In this jump, as his heels hit the ground, the sideways motion of the moving train caused him to spin into a full three-sixty before he could regain control. Rolling and tumbling down the bank, he remained as "loose as possible" to minimize the likelihood of injury, and finally slid to a halt on his back, head first on the ground. Slowly sitting up, he checked immediately for any injuries or broken bones. All appeared in order; he could feel a few bruises here and there, but he could feel no localized pain.

Suddenly remembering the bomb under his arm, he opened the satchel and checked the switch. It was still set in the "Off" position, and the timer was set at "0." Greatly relieved, he set out to find Strawinski.

He backtracked to where he estimated the jump point to be and felt his way along in the darkness. He finally heard Strawinski moaning somewhere not far ahead. He called out for him in hushed tones and got only another moan in response.

Lynx found him a few minutes later, but the darkness prevented him from getting a good look at Strawinski's condition. He was curled up in a fetal position, moaning continually and obviously in pain.

Lynx crouched at his side and instructed him to stay still until he had checked him over for injuries. Speaking feebly, the man said he felt like "every bone in my body is broken."

"Just lie still," instructed Lynx as he went through the procedure.

Lynx checked his legs, his arms, and his ribs and found no bone breaks. His head had no bleeding or bumps. Lynx concluded that he had been only badly bruised by the jump.

"Good news—no broken bones," he said. "Now, try and sit up,"

Lynx helped him into a sitting position. The two sat there for a few minutes, both feeling a little stiff and bruised. They had survived with little consequence.

Despite Lynx's section-by-section assessment of the state of his anatomy, Strawinski remained convinced that he must have some broken bones. Surprised that a scientist would be so oblivious to the facts of an examination, Lynx simply said, "Look. I've checked you over from head to toe. There are no broken bones. All 206 are intact," he said, citing one of the few skeletal facts he knew about the human body. "So, let's get ourselves into the best frame of mind we can to get out of here. We are by no means out-of-the-woods yet. We have a long way to go. Just relax for a few minutes and we'll press on."

"We'll never make it," he answered. "The MKGB will catch us now, for sure."

"No they won't. They are not going to catch us now. They think we're still on the train and have no idea where we are. Even the one in the black coat is out of the picture. I could have thrown him out of the train window, you know. And I did consider that option. So don't you think I didn't."

That shook him a little. "You what?" he exclaimed.

"That's right, my friend. Now, I'll help you to your feet, and let's try walking," said Lynx, hoping that he was physically fit to travel, albeit slowly. *Perhaps we'll get some transportation assistance as we go,* thought Lynx as his mind brainstormed options. *Hijack a car or truck? Hitchhike? No, hitchhiking is out. Steal a car or truck; now there's a real possibility.*

His ability to come up with options might be challenged, but he could improvise—that was something he had demonstrated, time and again—one reason Sarge had such confidence in him.

With a lot of moaning and groaning, the little man struggled to his feet and Lynx helped him take a few steps. He had been badly shaken in the jump from the train, but they had to press on.

"Lynx, my whole body hurts. I don't think I can make it," complained Strawinski.

"I understand," replied Lynx sympathetically. "After all, you've never jumped from a train before, have you?"

"No."

Doing his best to restore the man's confidence, Lynx related how he had been terrified in his first parachute jump, but that fear had eventually passed—as would his. "In a few minutes, you'll be as good as new," he reassured his companion.

"If this is how you feel when you land after a parachute jump, remind me never to try it," he replied.

Lynx took that as a sign of progress. The man was regaining his sense of humour. He had been helping him walk, and with that remark, decided to let him walk on his own. He seemed to do well, if limping slightly.

They had been proceeding in the same direction as the train, parallel to the tracks. They took a right-hand turn—away from the tracks—into the bushes towards a road that, according to the map, was a quarter mile away and would lead to the border.

The going was tough, and about halfway to the road, Strawinski was pleading with Lynx to stop for a rest. Lynx now knew that their walking progress would be an uphill battle.

After a few minutes of rest, Strawinski offered the view, that, "On the train, we had a chance. But, this way, we'll be caught for sure."

"Look, Mr. Strawinski, we're not going to be caught. Trust me. We'll get there." A few minutes later, they were making their way through the bush again, Lynx leading the way, groping his way through the darkness. Finding it hard slogging himself, he knew that his companion was finding it that much harder.

They took another rest. Lynx pulled out his compass, lit a match so he could read it, and verified that they were on the right course. Lynx reassured himself with the thought that, once they get to the road, the going will be easier.

Strawinski started complaining about pains in his legs, asking the question repeatedly, "How much farther?" like a kid on a motor trip.

When Strawinski stubbed a toe or was hit by a branch in the face as he followed Lynx, it became the focus of his complaints. He whined continually like a spoiled child, unable to endure any hardship.

When he accused Lynx of getting them lost, Lynx's patience evaporated and he snapped at the scientist. Little did Strawinski know the level of orienteering achievement that his rescuer had attained—not that Lynx was about to elaborate on that.

Nevertheless, Lynx rechecked the compass course, and again confirmed that they were on course.

"Lynx, they will surely be searching for us by now, don't you think?" asked the exhausted scientist.

"No. I don't think so," responded Lynx. "The train will just be getting to the border about now, but the MKGB agent will still be out cold. By the time they find him, they will think he has been drinking on-the-job. He will get a severe reaming out, and they will be confused, for sure, as to what has happened or where we are. Certainly, when they find their agent the way we left him, they won't believe a word he has to say. Whatever he tells them, he won't know what happened, or where we are. No one will. That all buys us time.

"So you see, Mr. Strawinski, there is nothing to worry about. By the time they get organized to track us down, we will be across the border."

Reassured, they resumed their trek through the bush and finally reached the road. Strawinski was jubilant.

They managed to get a few miles down the road and Strawinski began to falter again. Lynx knew that they had about ten miles to walk in rolling countryside, and the hills would make frequent rest stops necessary. Strawinski's poor physical condition made for slow going. Alone, Lynx would probably have been across the border by now.

They had covered about five miles overall, half the distance to the border. The going was so slow that Lynx wondered if daybreak might not be upon them by the time they made the border.

Just ahead, Lynx could hear running water, and the thought of a cool drink gave him renewed energy. That meant they had reached a stream that was shown on the map, only about two miles from the border. The water break also seemed to rejuvenate Strawinski.

The bad news was that the sky was getting brighter. They had failed to beat daylight, and had now forfeited the cover of darkness.

Lynx checked the time as 6:00 a.m. Strawinski was now exhausted beyond complaining, a development that Lynx quietly welcomed.

Lynx was the first to sight the border barricade as they came around a long curve. Lynx quickly grabbed Strawinski, pulled him out of sight, and dragged him into the bushes.

When Lynx told him what he had seen, Strawinski hadn't noticed a thing—not that one might expect him to. That was not his line of work—but it was Lynx's.

"You stay here and rest. I'll go ahead and scout things out," instructed Lynx. That was fine with Strawinski. Even though he didn't like the idea of staying there alone, he welcomed the opportunity to rest.

Lynx crept off into the bush, heading for a spot about 200 yards to one side of the barricade. About 150 yards from the border, he froze. Soldiers were patrolling a wire fence set back from the border. The fence consisted of three separate strands of coiled, barbed wire, raised slightly off the ground by short posts, ending at the guardhouse. *No chance of penetration there,* thought Lynx.

Lynx moved parallel to the fence towards the road, only to find two soldiers armed with machine guns. A heavy wooden barricade blocked the road where it crossed the border, with a wooden structure—about six feet square in cross-section—to one side of the barricade.

Lynx then noticed a transformer connected to the fence. It was electrified. *That explains why it's up off the ground,* he thought. Chances of crossing the border looked grim. Outside help would be needed, but that wasn't available.

Lynx made his way back to Strawinski and explained the situation. Totally discouraged, Strawinski was ready to give up.

And do what? thought Lynx. He, on the other hand, had come up with a plan. "I think that our best option," he went on, "is that I cause a distraction while you get across to the Austrian side. I'll use a bomb to blow a hole in the fence away from the guardhouse. When the guards arrive, I'll engage them with gunfire while you make a run for it through the abandoned barricade."

"Why are you so sure that the guards will leave the barricade?" asked Strawinski.

"Because I will take the guards along the fence out of the fight first. Then, once I shoot at the guards at the guardhouse, they will follow. That's when you take off to the Austrian side."

"I don't like it. They will shoot you and then me. There must be another way."

"If there is another way, I don't know what it is," replied Lynx. He was adamant.

Lynx, of course, had no intention of getting killed. It might happen, but only if things were not well thought through. He had plenty of tricks up his sleeve that he had no intention of disclosing to Strawinski. However, when it came to fire power, armed only with his .45 automatic, he was grossly underpowered relative to the opposition. Great pistol marksmanship, which he possessed, would be needed to take out the guards before they could take him out—his plan's biggest drawback. The derringer was there, an asset as such, but not a great asset per se. *I could go for using two pistols at once,* he thought, *but then, my left hand is a little rusty.*

Then, suddenly, there was the sound of a truck approaching in the distance. Lynx could see the truck heading towards them. *Probably carrying more soldiers looking for us,* he thought.

As the truck got closer, it became clear that it was not carrying soldiers. It was carrying a load of cargo. Lynx instructed Strawinski to get up onto the road, and one way or another, get it stopped. "Get up there and wave it down. Feign being wounded. Do whatever you have to do. You're Czech. I'll wait in here," he said, pointing at the bushes.

"I don't understand, but all right," replied Strawinski.

As the truck approached, Strawinski stood on the road, frantically waving his arms. At first, it looked like the driver wasn't going to stop, but then the big truck slowed down. There was only a driver, and no one else in the cab. Lynx had the advantage.

Lynx wondered, *Why would a truck carrying freight be crossing the border? Whatever the reason, it's a Godsend. Just what we need.*

As the truck stopped, Strawinski engaged the driver in conversation, and Lynx slipped out of hiding on the other side of the truck. He tried the passenger side door handle and found it locked. He knew that going around the back of the truck was out of the question, because of the rear-view mirrors. Crouching low, he crept around the front of the truck and along the left fender. In a single, cat-like leap, he was up onto the running board of the truck with the muzzle of his .45 stuck under the driver's chin.

That move was becoming a habit. He had executed the exact same one only hours earlier to bring a reluctant defector around to his point of view—not to mention his car ride with the now-deceased MKGB reception committee at the Jump Target.

The truck driver's face blanched, his eyes widened, and he threw both hands up in the air in surrender.

"Tell him to get out of the truck fast. If he doesn't, tell him I'll blow his brains out," Lynx instructed Strawinski.

Strawinski spoke to the driver in Czech and the driver did as instructed. Lynx stepped down from the running board and opened the truck door. The driver stepped out of the cab with his hands still up. Lynx motioned with his .45 for him to go to the other side of the truck. He obeyed, his eyes riveted on Lynx's pistol, a terrified expression on his face. Lynx reached down, lifted up one pant leg, and drew his knife out of its sheath.

“Here,” he said to Strawinski. “Cut two pieces of rope from the tarp hold-downs so we can tie him up.”

Strawinski took the knife, climbed up onto the truck, cut two pieces of rope, and handed them to Lynx, along with the knife.

“Tell him to sit down with his hands behind him,” ordered Lynx.

He did as Strawinski requested.

“Lynx, please remember that he is not our enemy, only a hard-working Czech citizen,” requested the former-farm-boy-turned-scientist.

Lynx walked around behind their captive and started to tie the man’s wrists with one hand. Once he was confident that he couldn’t move them, he holstered his .45 automatic and used both hands to tie them securely.

Strawinski stood talking in Czech with the driver who was sitting on the ground. Lynx tied his feet together.

Lynx stood up, stepped up onto the running board, unlocked the passenger door through the open window, and opened the door.

“Come on,” Lynx said to Strawinski, who was still talking to the driver. ”Get in. Let’s get the hell out of here!”

Without another word, Strawinski climbed up into the truck and closed the door.

“Can you drive this?” he asked.

“I think so,” replied Lynx playing with the gearshift to get the feel of it. He selected a low gear and the truck nearly stalled with its heavy load as he released the clutch. He immediately pressed the clutch back to the floor to prevent the engine from stalling, selected a lower gear, and released the clutch slowly. The truck started moving forward.

“The driver told me that the border guards know him. He runs goods to the border, someone from the other side picks them up, and the guards are paid off,” reported Strawinski.

‘That’s good,” replied Lynx. “They won’t suspect anything when they see the truck, then.”

Lynx soon had the truck moving well along the road, an curve towards the border was just ahead. He ordered Strawinski to lie down on the floor until they were through the border. Strawinski voiced his doubts one final time on the success of the coming border crossing; this time his reason was the guards being too heavily armed. *We'll see about that,* thought Lynx.

Expecting gunfire imminently, Lynx gave him a final briefing. "Listen. We're going to smash through the gate. So just stay down there and be careful to not touch any metal parts of the truck. Remember, the fence is electrified and there could be some short-circuiting going on when we break through." *Not to mention bullets flying,* he thought.

As they rounded the curve, the soldiers could hear the truck coming and expected it to stop. Moving along at good speed, Lynx put the gearshift into neutral, leaving the clutch out. The truck was coasting towards the barrier. He purposely ground the lower gear to make it sound like he was having difficulty getting it into gear. The soldiers watched, their guns tucked comfortably under their arms, suspecting nothing. *Good,* thought Lynx.

The big truck was rapidly closing the gap between it and the barrier, still coasting freely in neutral. Just at the right moment, Lynx shoved the gearshift into the proper gear for their speed and floored the gas pedal. The truck lurched forward, accelerating rapidly. Lynx lined up—in effect, aimed—the truck at the barrier's weakest point for a head-on crash. He set the wheels in the straight-ahead position so that no steering adjustments would be needed in the coming collision. Then, keeping one hand firmly on the steering wheel to maintain its position and one foot still hard on the gas pedal, he laid down on the seat.

Just before disappearing from view below the windshield, he caught a glimpse of two soldiers waving frantically for him to stop.

Within seconds, two machine guns opened fire on the truck. Broken glass was flying everywhere in the cab. Strawinski shouted something but was drowned out by the sound of the speeding truck and the blazing guns.

Then came a terrific crash at the barrier. The truck shook but did not falter, holding its course as barrier parts went flying out of its path, left and right. Lynx held the steering wheel in place as steady as he could and waited for a few seconds before he popped his head up.

"We're through!" exclaimed an elated Strawinski over the din of gunfire from behind, bullets whizzing by on both sides, some hitting the truck, its cab now shielded by the cargo behind it. Evidently none had hit the tires. "I'm free! You did it! You got me out!"

"Yes, sir," Lynx answered, "You *are* free now," as he picked shards of glass from his hair like nits. After a few minutes, he slowed the truck down and stopped by the side of the road. He, too, was feeling great relief.

Lynx pulled the map out of his satchel to see if there was a road to where his pick-up team was waiting, and located a spot not far away from the train station that looked like a good possibility. He stepped out of the truck and continued brushing remnants of glass from his clothing, arms, and face, and then checked the tires and fuel tanks. All were okay.

Relieved, he got back into the cab and started putting on black face paste.

When Strawinski wanted to know what he was doing, he explained that he was simply concealing his identity. There could be people at the pick-up spot who must not see his face. "My identity is secret, and always must remain so," he reminded Strawinski.

Strawinski continued looking at Lynx incredulously for several minutes until they drove off towards the planned rendezvous with Lynx's support team. Lynx turned into the small town, located the train station, and pulled the big truck to a stop within a few hundred feet of two black, parked cars.

Lynx immediately recognized Sarge standing beside one of the cars. Even Sarge didn't recognize Lynx, as he watched the truck approach and Lynx shut off the motor.

Lynx pointed out Sarge to Strawinski and sent him over to introduce himself. Strawinski thanked Lynx profusely and proceeded over to meet Sarge. Lynx sat watching the two men chatting for a few minutes. Sarge opened a car door for Strawinski, he got in, and Sarge closed the door behind him.

Sarge then proceeded rather briskly towards Lynx who was still sitting in the truck. "Where the hell have you been?" he asked Lynx.

"Here," said Lynx, tossing him his last plastic bomb. Sarge caught it easily but was not amused. "Are you ever going to set up one of these missions for me that goes right?" asked Lynx, as he sat with both arms braced on the steering wheel.

"Well, Laddie-Buck, looks like another ringer-of-a-job! We got a message that Strawinski had changed his mind about coming out. Apparently you managed to reverse that. Good work. You can tell me about it later," said Sarge.

"You'll never believe me, " replied Lynx, smiling.

"Looks like you hijacked a truck," said Sarge, "and not a very good one at that. It doesn't have any damn windows. Come on, Laddie. The car's waiting. We watched them carry some bloke off the train. For a minute, I thought it might be you. Glad you made it, Laddie-Buck."

With Sarge driving and only the two of them in the car, Sarge invited Lynx to wipe the black paste off his "ugly puss." Lynx obliged. As they drove along, Lynx began wondering when his luck would run out. With two missions completed and so many things gone wrong in both, he was starting to harbour skeptical thoughts.

"Who was the bloke they carried dead off the train?" inquired Sarge.

"MKGB."

"You kill him?"

"Nope. I busted his head with the barrel of my .45, though. He was still alive when I last saw him, but it sounds like he didn't make it."

"Did he see your face?" he asked sharply.

"No. He was too busy looking the other way." *Besides,* thought Lynx, *what if he did see my face? The guy is dead!*

"Well, just make sure you know the rules, Laddie. If one does, make sure he doesn't live to talk about it," he said in a rather stern manner, looking straight ahead. Then, surprisingly, he asked, "Did you find your Russian officer?"

"No," replied Lynx, realizing immediately that he was admitting that he had looked for him.

That brought an icy stare from Sarge, who followed on with, "I told you to forget about him, didn't I? Remember, no vendettas!"

The rest of the trip to the plane passed in silence. They turned onto a grass airstrip and were just about to get out of the car when Sarge passed Lynx a balaclava to wear "until we're aboard. Can't take any chances."

Lynx wore the hood as they walked to the plane, climbed aboard, and were airborne before Sarge spoke again. "Mike got word to us that things were delayed. Strawinski didn't want to leave or something?"

"He didn't at first," replied Lynx.

"What changed his mind?"

Lynx thought, *Do I tell him now? Why not? Better sooner than later*, and responded, "Well, I crept into his room last night, woke him up. We had a brief conversation about my mission and his willingness to participate. He continued to hesitate about coming out. So I put my .45 under his chin and told him that he either came with me right then and there, or I would have no choice but follow orders and kill him."

"You what!" exclaimed Sarge.

Lynx had had it with Sarge's sometimes-simplistic viewpoint and started in, pumped. He decided to unload his rationale in a single, full-blown blitz. "Listen, you sawed off little son-of-a-bitch, you heard me. I put my gun to his head and threatened him. It was the only way I could think of to get him to change his mind—and quickly. We didn't have much time, remember? I didn't want to give him the option of not coming. He had seen my face, obviously knew a lot of Czech underground—too many, in fact—and he was scared shitless in the circumstances. He is not strong-minded when it comes to this kind of stuff, and would sing like a canary if the Russians ever decided to bring him in—a not unlikely proposition, given the way they were following him night and day. They had to have some reason to be doing that. Finally, for your information, I passed a message through a safe channel back to Mike that he has a leak in his organization. They seemed to know our every move."

Sarge's demeanour suggested that he accepted that explanation, but he did not respond verbally.

As the plane made its way towards London, Lynx washed up with soap and a towel, changed into his RCAF uniform, and put the clothes he had been wearing into a suitcase, followed by both guns—the .45 and derringer—and his knife.

Lynx sat down across the aisle from Sarge, he turned on the tape recorder, and the debriefing began. "Let's start with the jump," stated Sarge.

Lynx proceeded to relate the sequence of events, leaving nothing out except inspecting the shoulder of each of the two Russian agents at the Jump Target. Sarge took particular interest in the exploding of their car. The Czech underground reported to him that they had heard the explosion.

When Lynx related how he had taken the driver down into the cellar to teach him a lesson, Sarge was slightly perturbed and shut off the tape recorder. "He had been asking for it," replied Lynx, "So I decided I'd throw him around a bit to give him a message. I know it was a little reckless, but it felt good."

Sarge wanted reassurance that no living Russian agents had actually seen Lynx's face when he and Strawinski had gone out of their compartment to the washroom. Lynx reassured him at length that was the case.

Just as the aircraft was about to land in London, Sarge pushed the "Off" button on the tape recorder and the debriefing was over. A car awaited them and drove them to a similar house that his last debriefing had been held in. Once inside, Sarge re-taped Lynx's entire account of the mission's events.

Later, over drinks and a meal, Sarge admitted that he would likely have done the same thing to help Strawinski make up his mind. And Sarge admitted to Lynx that leaving the train had been a smart move. The MKGB had had about twenty men waiting for Lynx at the station.

Lynx proceeded to a waiting car, knowing that his baggage was waiting at the Cumberland Hotel. He went straight to Jenny's apartment. He still had the key and found it empty, totally stripped of furniture.

Still enjoying a buzz from drinks he had shared with Sarge before departing, he walked to her parents' nearby address, but hesitated about knocking on the door. He decided to think things over, and sat on a park bench as he reassessed the situation. After all, it had been some time since he had seen her and letters hadn't been exchanged in months.

Within an hour, he spotted Jenny holding hands with a male friend as they walked up the street. Her demeanour signalled that she was happy, perhaps even in love. Lynx watched as they entered her parents' apartment building.

Saddened, Lynx decided that there was no point in staying there any longer. He flicked his cigarette into the gutter and made his way towards the Cumberland Hotel. An empty feeling descended as he contemplated how his life was unfolding along two parallel but distinctly different paths—one a normal existence, if normal was the word, the other, the lonely existence of an espionage courier, code name Lynx.

Chapter Four:
A Favour, then Into Poland

In late 1958, Lynx drove eight Saturday mornings to the Yonge and Bloor intersection in Toronto from CFB Trenton to a dance studio for karate lessons from a Japanese instructor named Yamoto. Sarge, of course, made the arrangements. Although Yamoto was only in his sixties, Lawrence remembered him as an "old man" with long white hair to his shoulders, sporting a pointy white beard.

When Lawrence arrived for his first lesson, he walked into the room that adjoined the main dance floor. He found Yamoto standing and looking out the window, wearing a dark floor-length robe trimmed with colourful Japanese symbols—some white, others bright yellow.

Lawrence didn't think he had heard him enter the room, so he spoke his name, "Mr. Yamoto?"

The renowned karate instructor slowly turned his head towards Lawrence. His eyes glared as he looked right through the young soldier. He said in perfect English, "Mr. Lynx, you will address me as Master Yamoto at all times. I am to teach you how to kill with your hands." He paused and then continued. "We begin now."

He bowed from the waist in a typical Japanese gesture, then straightened to his full five-foot height.

Appearing almost feeble at times, Master Yamoto was a killing machine in disguise. He was a Level 10 Dan Black Belt in karate,[9], a Master of Martial Arts, in possession of four lethal weapons at all times—two hands and two feet. For the next two months, Lawrence would spend every Saturday morning with him. There were no coffee breaks, no smoke breaks—no breaks of any kind. It was all business.

Lynx followed Yamoto's instruction with great interest and honed his karate skills to a new level. Never knowing what Sarge's assignments might require him to do, he took maximum advantage of the opportunity. In the eight instructional sessions, Master Yamoto brought Lynx to the bare-hand-killing level of competence that Sarge had requested.

While this instruction was going on, Sarge contacted Lynx once again, this time exhibiting a peculiar nervousness that Lynx had not seen before. Sarge was distracted, and seemed uncertain about something. As usual, there were no answers to any of Lynx's questions. Sarge practised the culture of "know only what is needed to execute your role, nothing more," a rigorous mantra that probably pervaded the entire MI-6 operation. He did, however, allow that this next "job" was one that, in his judgment, "his" Lynx could execute "better than" any of his agents.

It began with a visit to the local bar. As usual, Sarge abstained while Lynx sipped on a glass of rum and 7-Up. After a few drinks, Lynx had agreed to accompany Sarge to Switzerland "right away," but still had no idea for what purpose. Their pattern of interaction was now undeniably clear: Sarge dominated the relationship.

At Toronto's Pearson International Airport, Sarge produced the tickets that he had already purchased. That's how sure he was that Lynx would accept his "proposal"—not that Sarge referred to it as an "assignment," a "mission," an "order," or any such thing. He never referred to it as anything in particular. His behaviour suggested that a "favour" would probably fit the situation well.

---

9 The top level.

Sarge had continued to be the mystery man in Lynx's life, always showing up furtively at what seemed like random times. Answers to questions were few, and typically consisted of a half dozen words or less. Small talk only—nothing substantive—was typical.

On the overseas flight, Sarge had so little to say that Lynx slept for almost the entire time.

In Switzerland, Lynx loaded the baggage into a taxi. He noticed that their baggage had somehow multiplied in both weight and volume from what they had checked on departure. He has never understood how Sarge managed to do that.

When Lynx asked where the additional baggage had come from, Sarge simply replied, "Well, you know, Laddie-Buck, it's equipment we need for the job"—as usual, an evasive answer.

They were driven to a small town in the Alps that had two large hotels, more or less across the street from one another, both buildings set well back from the street. Lynx remained puzzled as to what they were doing there, and Sarge offered no explanation.

Lynx struggled to get the bags into the elevator while Sarge got in with ease, carrying his briefcase. When they reached their room, Sarge motioned Lynx to check the room out, as if there could be someone inside—his penchant for paranoia at work. Once Lynx had verified the safety of the room, Sarge came in and sat down.

"Laddie, your carbine is in that case. Go ahead and assemble it," he said, as if everything was copacetic.

Surprised, Lynx nevertheless obliged, and once his carbine—the Sterling Arms SAS prototype that he had used many times—was assembled, Sarge passed him a tripod to fix to the rifle. Lynx had never used a tripod.

Sarge then said, "Laddie-Buck, the Russian officer that killed Nomad will be coming into one of the hotel rooms across the street."

Lynx was shocked. Sarge most definitely now had his full attention.

"How do you know it's him?" asked Lynx.

"He's a Russian MKGB agent, and I know who he is."

He moved over to the window and pointed at the other hotel, about 150 yards away.

"We're on the fifth floor, he will be on the fourth, five windows from the left corner of the building. He will be coming into that room, but I don't know exactly when. He will be your target. This is your chance to get even for Nomad, Laddie."

Here was Sarge assigning Lynx an action that he had, several times, forbidden.

Without uttering a word, Lynx picked up the rifle, attached it to the tripod, adjusted the tripod to the right height so that he could wait sitting down comfortably, and adjusted the scope. The silencer had already been installed.

All set, Lynx lit a cigarette, took a puff, and put his eye to the scope. It was early afternoon and there was plenty of light flooding into the room. The scope was one of the best—the image was crystal clear. He would be able to count the whiskers on his target's chin.

I can't miss, thought Lynx. *This will be a routine 150-yard shot.*

It wasn't his first choice. He had promised himself that he would make the bastard suffer; but that was a minor consideration. *At least this way*, he thought, *I'll settle the score here and now. Then we'll be even.*

While Sarge left the room to get some food, Lynx was so focused on his assignment that he didn't even hear him leave. When Sarge re-entered the room, Lynx was almost startled by the closing of the door as he continued looking intently through the scope.

Lynx refused at first to eat, but when Sarge said there was "lots of time," Lynx got agitated.

"Whaddaya mean, lots of time? You mean you know his schedule?"

"It's my job to know, Laddie."

"How did you get his schedule? You know his name, too? What's his name?" Lynx almost shouted at him.

Sarge tried to shift the focus away from Nomad's assassin by getting Lynx to sit down and have something to eat. That just raised Lynx's blood pressure even higher.

"I said, I'm not hungry," he snapped. "Sarge! What the hell is going on? You have already ordered me more than once to forget any vendettas! Now you say he's coming through that door down there! Now it's suddenly okay to kill him?"

"Now, now, Laddie. Settle down. Take it easy. You have a job to do. Kill the bastard. For Nomad."

Sarge knew how to pull Lynx's strings, to manipulate his feelings, to get him to do whatever he wanted. Whenever Lynx was in Europe on an assignment from Sarge, a metamorphosis would set in that transformed him into a cold-blooded killer. That persona was in stark contrast to his home-in-Canada self, where he was a model citizen in most every way. Haunted by the Thou-shalt-not-kill commandment, killing was something he was still uncomfortable with—and always would be. Sarge knew it, but was now openly preying on the killer facet of his make-up.

Lynx was upset and went into the bathroom, tossed his cigarette into the toilet, and lit another. Sarge's eyes followed his every move. Lynx walked to the table and grabbed a coffee, added a spoonful of sugar, no milk, walked over to the mounted gun, sat down, took a sip of the coffee and a long drag on his cigarette.

The two sat there for hours without speaking—Sarge on the sofa reading papers scattered on the coffee table while Lynx watched through the scope. Sarge didn't appear to notice that Lynx's field of view included keeping an eye on him.

Lynx finally broke the silence. "How did you find out his name?"

Without looking up and continuing to sort through his papers, Sarge replied, "You forget that I have a network of agents, and one of them got me his name."

"Sarge, you never saw him. So how could you find out his name?"

"You described him to me. Five-foot-eleven, dark hair, heavy set, about thirty to thirty-five years old," he answered again, still not looking up. He was attempting to imply that Lynx's description had been ample data from which to identify the man.

Lynx wasn't having it. "From that little shit-assed description, you got a name?" he asked.

"Yes," came Sarge's reply, still not looking up.

His temper was approaching boiling point as Lynx shouted, "Bullshit! Who's coming through that door?"

Finally making eye contact with Lynx, Sarge looked up and said, "Now, look, Laddie. A Russian officer shot your partner. You had your sights on him. You got emotional and didn't take him out. I'm telling you that that same Russian is coming through that door, any minute now." His eyes suddenly widened as he finished with, "Kill him! I know you want to!"

Lynx stood helpless insofar as any further information from Sarge was concerned. Reluctantly, he sat down behind the scope while Sarge resumed working on his papers.

The light outside was dimming as the evening wore on. That meant that the "target" room would be lit even better, making the shot easier.

Hours passed as Lynx sat awaiting his target. He and Sarge had not spoken since their shouting match. Sarge was winding him up like a toy soldier to kill the next person who walked into that hotel room—yet he lay sound asleep on the hotel room couch, evidently without a care in the world. Lynx looked at him, his fingers interlocked on his chest, his legs outstretched, blissfully asleep.

Lynx glanced at his watch: 6:00 a.m. He had spent the night poised for a kill, nerves on edge, ready to squeeze the trigger of a state-of-the-art, high-powered rifle on cue, and now—nothing.

Had he really set him up to take out Nomad's assassin? Perhaps a discovered double agent who had either outlived his usefulness or double-crossed Sarge would walk through that door and have his justly deserved comeuppance, he thought.

When Sarge awoke and announced that he was leaving to use a telephone, Lynx pointed out that there was already a telephone beside the bed.

"No," replied Sarge. "I need a secure one."

Sarge was gone for at least an hour. When he returned, he promptly announced, "Okay, Laddie. Pack everything up. He's a no-show. We're leaving." He started jamming his papers into his briefcase.

When asked how he knew that they had a no-show, without even looking up, Sarge replied, "Because my sources tell me he's not coming here. Let's go. Pack 'er up."

They had been in the hotel room for almost eighteen hours. The flight back to Canada was uneventful, except for Lynx rolling over the possible explanations in his mind. The only one that made any sense was that one of Sarge's charges had been exposed as a double agent and had either double-crossed him, or outlived his usefulness.

Months passed without any contact from Sarge, and Lawrence went about his routine engine maintenance and overhaul duties at CFB Trenton. Then, in the late summer of 1959, there was a note from Sarge sitting on the front seat of his car, directing him to a meeting outside the Sergeants' Mess at the base.

When Lynx arrived, Sarge was waiting for him in a rental car, all smiles—out of character, to be sure. He told Lynx that he had just received a "wee promotion."[10]

"What's up, Sarge?" asked Lynx.

The smiles suddenly evaporated as he instructed Lynx to pick up his .45 in the back seat and strap it on.

"I've got some pictures and film to show you," he said to Lynx, "but I'm being followed."

Driving to a nearby motel, Sarge had rented Room 5, but pulled up in front of Room 4. Unexpectedly, Sarge drew a gun and motioned Lynx to draw his. After unlocking the door to Room 5, Sarge flattened himself against the building wall and nodded to Lynx to enter. Sarge's paranoia was at work again.

Lynx checked out the bedroom and bathroom, found them safe, and lowered his gun. Sarge, however, continued to hold his gun—a smaller pistol than Lynx's .45 automatic—at the ready. When Lynx asked if he could examine Sarge's weapon, he passed it to Lynx—a

---

10 This "promotion" was almost certainly Sarge's appointment as a SIS representative in Washington (a post once held by Kim Philby) to cultivate relations with the CIA. He held the post for four years.

9-mm. Beretta, a much lighter weapon to carry than the three-pound .45 automatic.

"It's yours, Laddie," he said—just like that, making Lynx the new owner of the Beretta—which, as the future unfolded, he would make extensive use of.

With that, Sarge announced that Lynx was now to go on a propeller course, to get an understanding of how propellers are like a gearshift on a car; varying the pitch changes the rate of "air bite," which is, of course, directly related to aircraft speed. That was fine with Lynx.

Once that piece of business was agreed, Sarge pulled out some photographs of Russian military installations—ICBM launching sites and the like—including a facial snapshot of a highly ranked Russian officer.[11] Sarge told Lynx that the officer pictured was one of his prime spies in the Russian military, and that he had just sent out some valuable "stuff"—namely, the snapshots they had just been examining.

To this day, Lawrence has no idea why Sarge showed him those photographs; it was a completely out-of-character move that was totally inconsistent with his obsession with secrecy.

Sarge gathered up the photos and told Lynx that he now wanted him to learn the basics of how to read blueprints for their authenticity, particularly those with Russian electrical, chemical, atomic, and other symbols. He had already arranged a trip to a United States military installation to create that capability.

Proceeding immediately to Toronto International Airport in a typical impromptu move that would simply add to Lawrence's growing marital strife, they boarded a plane for Phoenix, Arizona. Lynx was wearing the freshly gifted Beretta in a shoulder holster, including a pocket on the holster for a silencer. The whole ensemble was much more comfortable than his .45 automatic, even including the silencer.[12]

The flight was uneventful—except for one small incident. Lynx went to the washroom about half way through the flight. When he

---

11 This was Lynx's first look at the husband of Susan, his future (1965) mission-travelling companion.

12 This, of course, was a long time before 9/11 and current airport security requirements.

returned to his seat, there was a man sitting in it whom he did not know. Lynx froze. For a good half minute, he stood watching them, and Sarge was looking worried—or so Lynx thought. Concerned, Lynx returned to the washroom, removed his jacket, and wrapped it around the Beretta, carelessly dropping the shoulder harness on the washroom floor. He then moved back down the aisle to a point just behind the man sitting beside Sarge, pushed the muzzle of the gun touching the back of the man's head, and snarled, "Don't make any sudden moves!"

Sarge had heard him and rather nervously said, "Laddie, it's okay. Don't fire the gun. We're at 30,000 feet and the bullet could go through the fuselage. That could be a problem. He's Secret Service."

Lynx backed off, and Sarge introduced him to their visitor, "Agent. Turner, this is my aide, Robert Hammond."

The US Secret Service had sent Turner to protect Sarge while in the USA. While the two men continued to converse, Lynx returned to the washroom to retrieve his shoulder harness, embarrassed at his carelessness.

Turner walked Sarge and Lynx through customs to a rental car kiosk, at which point Sarge informed Turner that "Mr. Hammond" was the only bodyguard he needed. Lynx drove Sarge out of the airport in a rental car, and soon noticed a car following them in the rear-view mirror.

Trained to be wary if anyone follows for more than three or four blocks and turns whenever you do, whether driving or walking down the street, Lynx alerted Sarge that there was a blue Chevy following them. Lynx floored the pedal of their Ford rental to gauge the tail's reaction, and their car accelerated. The Chevy followed suit.

At the next crossroad, Lynx swerved right onto a gravel road. The Ford rental skidded sideways as it negotiated the turn—gravel flying off the front wheels in a nicely carved bow wave. As he straightened out the steering wheel, Lynx glanced at the rear-view mirror and the Chevy was definitely keeping up.

Sarge got excited, yelling, "They're onto us, Laddie!" Lynx instructed him to "Hang on!" and he floored the gas pedal. They gained a little on that manoeuvre. Lynx was in his element, driving like a Steve McQueen in the 1968 movie *Bullitt*. He was reliving his stock car days—but this time, Sarge was on board.

Lynx reassured his usually stoic passenger that he "knew what he was doing," and was soon rocketing down the gravel road—60, 70, 80 mph. Flying stones were hitting the bottom of the car in a continuous barrage. Then Lynx negotiated another corner—a "drifter" this time. The rear wheels grazed the shoulder at the end of the turn, but he kept the vehicle under control. He was gaining on the Chevy with each manoeuvre.

Then, as the Chevy attempted to negotiate one of its turns, it disappeared in a cloud of dust. When it reappeared in Lynx's rear-view mirror, it was rolling over, well off the road.

Sarge, now visibly shaken with this "bloody dangerous" business, wanted "urgently" to get to a telephone. He was nevertheless smiling that his "bodyguard" had shaken their "tail" so quickly.

Lynx got back onto the highway to a phone booth at a gas station and Sarge made a telephone call. When he hung up, he told Lynx that the blue Chevy would be "taken care of."

Sarge pulled out a map of the area and had soon navigated them to a deserted house. It was sitting in the middle of nowhere, fitted with a rather obvious "No Trespassing: Department of National Defence" sign.

Lynx had no idea where they were, but apparently Sarge did. He took a key out of his briefcase, unlocked the door, and motioned Lynx to follow him into the ramshackle house. Once inside, Sarge closed the door and they appeared to be standing in an elevator. Sarge pressed a button on a panel, and the floor started sinking. They *were* on an elevator, descending to the sound of a barely discernible hum, a distance of about ten floors below the desert surface.

The elevator lurched to a stop and the door opened. Standing there were four men dressed in white smocks, apparently *expecting* their arrival.

Sarge introduced Lynx as Robert Hammond once again to a Dr. Alan Bowen, who was to teach him the Russian symbols and their significance on electrical, mechanical, and atomic drawings.

They were inside of what amounted to an enormous, subterranean city. It included amenities needed for all aspects of underground living, both on and off the job—working, playing, sleeping, and eating.

Sarge and Lynx stayed there for a week and worked intensively every day for as long as they could. Lynx crammed as much training in reading Russian blueprints as he could. Then, as unceremoniously as they had arrived, they departed.

On the return flight to Toronto, for the first time in their six-year-old relationship, Sarge and Lynx conversed, touching on personal matters, particularly Sarge's early life. The two men genuinely bonded for the first time. Sarge was not "highborn," as the British expression goes. His parents had died when he was six; he was raised in an orphanage and joined the army at seventeen. In World War II, his fiancée had been killed in an air raid and he never married. He had risen to the rank of Regimental Sergeant Major (RSM) before the war ended. After the war, he had entered the Military Intelligence arm, excelling in the Secret Service. He now had a network of people reporting to him that spanned the globe.

The month Nomad had died, he had lost eight good men.[13] The Cold War with Russia was taking its toll.

Lynx discovered that Sarge had a warm, approachable side that he liked very much. In the course of the extended conversation, Sarge assured Lynx that he would always be there for him. At least now Lynx knew that there was another side to the distant Sarge.

Lynx shared his loneliness on all matters MI-6 with Sarge and pointed out that he—Sarge—had several people with whom to converse on the subject. By comparison, Lynx had *no one*. That, in a nutshell, was the loneliness that only Secret Service agents can know.

As the flight neared its end, Sarge closed the conversation with his acknowledgement that Lynx was developing into one of his best

13 This was November 1956.

agents, distinguished by his innate ability to sense when things were about to go awry. That Sixth Sense that kicked in when "something was not right" was unique. Sarge claimed that it was rare, and could not be taught. Many agents were great marksman, capable combatants and excelled at the mechanical skills, but few possessed that innate ability to just *know* when things weren't right. It made the difference between life and death, success and failure. Only Lynx had it among his current operatives—as far as he knew. At least, no one else had volunteered an awareness to the extent that Lynx had.

As he looked Lynx full in the eyes, Sarge said, "Whenever you want to talk, I'll give you a secret number to reach me at any hour of the day or night."

Finally, thought Lynx.

Lynx subsequently contacted Sarge's 1-900-xxx-xxxx number from time to time. The procedure was to ask for "the Man," and Sarge would either promptly get back to him or, depending on the urgency, appear in person a day or so later.

In 1958, Lawrence's enthusiasm for airplanes had spread into model planes and he started a club for CFB Trenton teenagers in his basement. Six youngsters were regularly there working on the models. The cost of an airplane kit was sixty-one cents, and the engine was an additional $5.50. All were painted blue—from a single can of paint—to minimize costs. Soon the base had supplied a clubhouse.

One of the teenagers had designs on Lawrence's wife, Elsie. He took advantage of Lawrence's absences, knowing when Lawrence would be out of town because Lawrence was flying with his father. Elsie responded in kind and started wearing alluring, black-patterned stockings and the like. That was a signal that Lawrence noticed, but did not fully comprehend, nor act on.

Sarge had counselled Lawrence early to not get attached to anyone, but Lawrence had followed his instincts. Married since 1954, and by this time with four children, Lawrence had told Sarge nothing about his marriage—a part of his life that he considered private.

Lawrence's sudden, unexplained absences on MI-6 training and mission assignments certainly hadn't helped the health of his marriage. Cumulatively, they were mounting up. An up-front spousal trust pact had never been set up—nor had even been discussed—in the marriage. Without that as a base to buttress mutual trust, most marriages would not tolerate extended, unexplained disappearances by the husband—or by either spouse, for that matter. Then, when asked to account for whereabouts on returning when no truthful explanation could be given, a faltered relationship would almost certainly result. That was Lawrence's MI-6 marital dilemma.

In an attempt to save the marriage, Lawrence was granted a compassionate transfer to CFB Namao, near Edmonton. It was 1960.

Their initial months in Edmonton were happy ones. The young couple settled into life anew. Then one night in December 1961, when Lawrence got home earlier than expected, he found the children with a babysitter. He paid the babysitter and sent her home while he awaited his wife's arrival. When she got home, she had a boyfriend in tow.

As Elsie walked past Lawrence into the house, her boyfriend took a swing at Lawrence. Being taller and heavier than Lawrence but unaware of Lawrence's hand-to-hand combat prowess, the next thing the boyfriend knew, he was picking himself up off the floor. Thinking he would improve his chances with a weapon, the boyfriend pulled out a knife. Lawrence grabbed a handy weapon of his own—a shotgun—and fired at the knife from the hip. His gifted hand–eye coordination, of course, came into play and the blast knocked the knife out of the boyfriend's hand[14]—without damaging the hand. The blast did, however, leave a sizeable hole in a door behind the target.

Uninjured, Elsie's boyfriend took off and disappeared for several months. The Edmonton police promptly charged Lynx with Attempted Murder and locked him up in the municipal jail. When they were unable to find his wife's boyfriend—whom they suspected Lawrence

---

14 This was from thirteen feet away, as measured afterwards by the police.

had murdered and disposed of the body—they warned Lawrence that they expected to be soon charging him with murder.[15]

On Lawrence's second day in jail, the attendant announced that his "lawyer" had arrived. There was Sarge sitting in the small waiting room, briefcase in hand, looking rather stern.

Sarge had a few questions: "When were you going to tell me about the wife and kids? Whaddaya think you are doing, busting up the locals? My God, Laddie-Buck, they've got you charged with attempted murder. Have you told your wife anything about your [MI-6] life?"

Lawrence apologized for not telling Sarge about his marriage and children, and reassured Sarge that he hadn't mentioned a word about his MI-6 work—to anyone. When Lawrence asked what he was doing there, Sarge replied that he was there to help. The story of the shooting was all over the news, and he presumed that Lawrence would need a lawyer.

"I guess I had better get one," Lawrence acknowledged. Almost before he could say "Jack Robinson," a lawyer appeared later that day, courtesy of Sarge. His name was Mr. Edwards, who immediately bailed Lawrence out of jail. His one instruction to Lawrence was, "Don't say one more word!"

The court case dragged on for nine months (December '61 to September '62) and included five appearances by Lawrence. One nightmare episode included him being assigned to a psychiatric unit for evaluation. It included a week in an asylum and sitting naked for several hours in a padded cell, probably under surveillance with hidden cameras. Lawrence privately concluded that the lunatics were running the asylum. One "inmate" named Dale, who had not spoken to anyone for twenty years, came out of his shell and started speaking when Lawrence befriended him. After a week of this nonsense, Lawrence was decreed normal and released.

In the midst of all this turmoil and continuing martial strife, Elsie delivered child number five on February 26, 1962, a son Wayne—a little brother for Carl, Larry, Arthur, and June.

15 In fact, her boyfriend had left town. His next known appearance was in Uranium City, nine months later, in jail.

The string of character witnesses that lined up to testify on Lawrence's behalf was impressive and convincing. It included several First Nations folk who testified unanimously to Lawrence's upstanding character. Finally, Sarge and Mr. Edwards approached the bench one day, a short three-way conversation ensued, and a plea bargain was reached. In exchange for pleading guilty to common assault, Lawrence would be placed on a year's probation—to which he readily agreed—and the case ended (September 25, 1962). Three months later, the probation officer terminated the probation.

A few days after Wayne's birth, Sarge made contact with Lawrence and expressed concern about his drinking. When Lawrence convinced him that he "could handle it," apparently that was all the reassurance Sarge needed. He then outlined the immediate need for an urgent mission into Poland to bring out the family of a "highly-ranked" civilian, a Mr. Petroff.[16] He was in danger of imminent arrest in the early stirrings of the Solidarity Movement. The father, probably a close associate of Lech Walesa, was refusing to come out until his wife Marina, thirteen-year-old son Edward, and six-year-old daughter Sophie had safely made their exit. Sarge was turning to Lynx as a reliable accomplice to bring them out. The intention was that Petroff would come out with another courier a month or so later.

Sarge had already presumed Lynx would accept the assignment, even though the court case was still proceeding and Lawrence was not supposed to leave the country. Sarge was evidently prepared to push the envelope when it suited his purposes.

The mission—fly to the UK, board a British submarine bound for a designated Polish landing spot, secure the family, bring them back to the submarine, and thence back into the UK—was ready to go as soon as Lynx was ready.

Lawrence let Elsie know he would be gone for up to two weeks, and left the children in her care. Later that same day, Sarge and Lynx flew Edmonton to Toronto, then Toronto to London—commercially. They were immediately driven to the docks, where several submarines

---

16 Not his real name.

were moored. All the gear needed was already in the car except his carbine, which Sarge had decided he would not need for this assignment. However, the new lightweight 9-mm. Beretta—complete with silencer, shoulder holster, and spare magazines—was there, to Lynx's great delight.

Sarge and Lynx walked to the submarine together from the car, Lynx with his pack slung over one shoulder; the time was about 3:00 a.m. There was no one around, and Sarge started into his usual last-minute instructions: "You have three days to get into Warsaw, and three days to get back to the submarine. Your contact man goes by the name of Karvarski. He will meet you after you leave the submarine. They tell me it will be after midnight when you land. The Polish underground has everything set up, including a meeting place in Warsaw and a car to take you into and out of the country."

"What could go wrong?" Lynx asked him, an obtuse reference to the fact that both of his MI-6 missions had included several surprises.

Sarge wished his emissary the best of luck, patted Lynx on the back, they shook hands, and Lynx proceeded down the gangplank onto the deck of the submarine. Lynx and a few crewmembers stood watching as Sarge returned to his car. Lynx pensively relived some of their moments together, which by then had become almost encyclopaedic. They went below as the vessel slowly moved away from the dock and made its way off into the black of night.

Lynx entered a hatch near the front of the conning tower and followed a sailor down into the vessel. From there, they descended into the submarine proper and he was shown to his bunk. He stowed his pack.

Sarge had counselled Lynx to minimize contact with the crew. Consequently, once he knew where the galley was, he knew all he had to know. Under the impression that British submariners would drink tea as the beverage of choice, Lynx was pleasantly surprised to find that coffee in fact had that label of distinction.

Provided he didn't get in the way, Lynx was allowed up on the conning tower. He found the captain and officers cordial, and had some interesting conversations without getting personal. They, however, surely wondered who their special passenger was—a lone wolf who had to have extra-ordinary capabilities for whatever special assignment he was about to undertake. They nevertheless respected the confidentiality aspect and didn't probe—just followed orders.

The submarine sailed on the surface to the mouth of the Thames River and then submerged. It was time for bed.

Sleep was evasive for Lynx who had been experiencing recurring nightmares, reliving Nomad's assassination with innumerable variations and endings. In different versions of the nightmare, he was being shot point-blank by the Russian officer, only to awake screaming as the trigger was about to be pulled. He repeatedly imagined how it *could* have turned out, had one or two variables been set down differently.

Sure enough, Lynx had dozed off, a typical nightmare had occurred, and someone was shaking him awake, reassuring him that, "It's okay. It's okay, Laddie. Have a bad dream?"

"Yeah, I did," admitted Lynx sheepishly.

Lynx went to sleep, this time without any nightmares, and spent the next twenty-four hours in his bunk. A trip up to the conning tower whenever the vessel was on the surface was a good diversion. He returned to his bunk for more rest whenever it seemed convenient.

They were back on the surface again, and he went back to the conning tower. This time the captain told him that they would be at their target jumping-off destination at 12:45 a.m.

Lynx went to his bunk to get ready. Disconcertingly, he was nursing a churning feeling in his gut that something was not unfolding according to plan. His Sixth Sense kicked into high gear, putting him on ultrasensitive alert.

Once the submarine was safely anchored, a four-man rubber raft with a small outboard motor was used for the short trip ashore. The sailors bid Lynx "Farewell, and good luck" and pushed off, back to the sub. They quickly disappeared from Lynx's view into the darkness.

Now alone once again, he dug into his pack for the holstered Beretta, his knife, which he strapped to the inside of his left leg, and the derringer .25, which he strapped in its holster to his right leg.

Slinging the pack over one shoulder, he trudged along the beach for a short distance, and then turned inland.

He hadn't gone far when he spotted a car. His gut feelings intensified as he approached it. His Sixth Sense was screaming, "danger ahead!"

Two figures—*Two?* thought Lynx. *These guys aren't my contact*—were standing beside a car, talking. Lynx realized that they hadn't heard him yet. He stopped to listen to the language and it was clearly Russian. To avoid any trouble, Lynx moved to his left to give them a wide berth. In the darkness, he stubbed his boot against a rock, which made an audible sound.

One of the men heard the sound, turned on a flashlight, and shouted something first in Polish, and then in Russian. Lynx knew that he was being told to stop, and he could now make out a large automatic pistol in one hand behind the flashlight.

Thinking, *If I make a move to draw my Beretta, he will surely shoot,* Lynx played dumb and raised his hands up to about the level of his ears. He signalled that he couldn't hear what the man was saying by cupping one hand over one ear. As his mind raced to improvise a method of distracting them, Lynx motioned to his right shoe and bent down to tie its lace, now only a few feet from the two men.

The man holding the flashlight turned and spoke to the other, whom Lynx had noticed was unarmed. Both men were now at close range. As he continued talking to Lynx, the armed one's head turned away momentarily. With a single motion executed at blazing speed, Lynx pulled the derringer out of his leg holster and fired it into the armed man's face. The bullet travelled only about three feet. He then immediately delivered a karate drop kick to the face of the second man.

The dazed recipient fell back against the car. Like a cat possessed for the kill, Lynx leapt onto him, grabbed his head with his left hand, his jaw with his right, and in a single snap, broke his neck. The crack was audible and sickening, but effective. The man went limp. Master Yamoto had taught him well.

Lynx had dropped the derringer just before he had kicked the Russian. He looked around for a few seconds and found it. Then he started wondering, *Where is my contact Karvarski?*

"Lynx?" came a voice out of the darkness. Now fully alert in case of more trouble, Lynx sprang into a karate stance for best response.

"Yes. Who's that?" he answered.

A figure, about five-foot-eight and heavy set, stepped out of the darkness and approached. He answered in good English, "What happened? I saw you momentarily in the flashlight beam, and then you moved so fast, I couldn't believe it. Are they both dead?"

"Yes," replied Lynx. "Are you Karvarski?"

"Yes. But what are you going to do with them?" he asked, his voice shaking.

"Help me get them into the back seat," requested Lynx. "Have you got a place we could hide them? If the authorities find them, we could be in trouble."

"I have a friend," replied Karvarski, "who will know what to do."

With the two dead Russians in the back seat, Karvarski driving, and Lynx sitting in the front passenger seat, they drove to a small town nearby. They pulled up to a house with all the lights out. Karvarski knocked twice on the door, it opened, and there stood a small, stout, middle-aged woman.

They exchanged a few sentences back and forth in Polish. The woman disappeared into the house and a man appeared. He was introduced to Lynx as Mr. Parwicki, who asked Lynx to call him "Al."

When Al spotted the two dead Russians in the back seat of the car, he and Karvarski had a brief conversation in Polish and Al turned to Lynx.

"Karvarski tells me that you killed them, and that you are a very dangerous man."

"What can I say?" replied Lynx. "We checked their identification, and they are Russian Secret Police. I don't like Russians generally—Russian Secret Police in particular."

Al smiled and said, "I don't like them either."

He turned to Karvarski and they spoke in Polish. Karvarski nodded and motioned Lynx to follow him to another car that was parked in the street. Karvarski told Lynx that Parwicki and his friends would look after disposing of the Russian car and its occupants. He also told

Lynx that Parwicki would contact the submarine the following night and let them know that Lynx had safely made contact.

The time was about 2:00 a.m. and Warsaw was still a long way off. Karvarski told Lynx that the plan was that they would drive until daybreak and stop for the day to get some sleep at a safe house. It was in a small town ahead where he had friends waiting.

As they drove along, Lynx learned that Karvarski's first name was Steve, and they exchanged stories—within limits—as they drove through the night. For example, Lynx let Steve know how he had acquired his karate skills, including the deadliness of Master Yamoto's skill level, believing that there was no harm in sharing that. As the day started dawning, Lynx noticed that the first light was coming from his left, which meant that they must have been heading in a southerly direction.

"The town is just ahead, so we'll soon be there," said Steve. A few minutes later, they pulled up in front of a bungalow, their first safe house. Steve got out of the car, approached the front door, knocked, and a man appeared in the doorway. They talked for a few minutes and he motioned Lynx to come into the house. Steve introduced Lynx to their host. His name in English was George.

A beautiful woman in her mid-to-late twenties entered the room wearing a blue housecoat, open in the front, exhibiting some alluring cleavage, her bra and panties visible—obviously trolling for action. Steve seemed surprised to see her. She was introduced as Anna and spoke English.

"Are you English, Mr. Lynx?" she said in a seductive voice with a slight accent.

"Yes.

"Perhaps we should get to know each other a little better," she said, eyeing an embarrassed Lynx up and down. "Of course, we don't know each other at all yet, so we have a lot of ground cover. Maybe we should get started sooner, rather than later, don't you think?" To his relief, neither Steve nor George had heard the remark.

It was 6:30 a.m., and their host began preparing breakfast for their guests as Anna walked off down the hall to the other end of the house.

After breakfast, Steve took one sofa, Lynx the other to get some rest. Feeling quite safe, Lynx left his Beretta in his shoulder holster and dozed off. A light sleeper, he jumped to his feet as Anna entered the room and gasped. Steve, a deep sleeper, heard nothing, but turned over on the sofa.

When Lynx told her that it was not a good idea to enter a room unannounced like that, she looked at him, now clad only in her bra and panties, holding a drink in one hand, swaying off-balance slightly, and replied, "Why don't you come and sleep in my bed?"

Evidently drinking vodka, perhaps to gain the courage to confront him, Lynx decided that she was beyond herself as she continued, "Come on, Mr. Lynx. I won't hurt you. You like girls, don't you?"

"Yes, I do, but right now, I have to get some sleep," replied Lynx.

She continued with a smile, "Mr. Lynx, I am offering myself to you—free of charge. Just for the fun of it."

"I know that," replied Lynx, "But you are George's wife, and it just wouldn't be right to sleep with you."

"Who is going to sleep?" she replied. "Sleeping is a waste of time when we could be doing other things. And I'm not George's wife."

Now getting annoyed, Lynx replied, "It doesn't matter, Anna. I have to get some rest."

She muttered something in Polish and walked away. At about 2:00 p.m., Lynx had to use the washroom and passed her bedroom, its door ajar. She was lying naked on the bed, passed out.

George got back to the house at about 6:00 p.m., Steve warmed up some stew, and the three men ate together. Steve and George conversed in Polish, the two laughing frequently while Lynx ate in silence. Anna was still asleep—or passed out. He didn't know which. Lynx never saw her again.

George brought in a five-gallon can of gasoline to top up the gas tank. The underground didn't want them to stop any more than necessary en route to the pick-up. They made some sandwiches to bring along for the trip, and at 7:00 p.m., all was ready to go. Steve and Lynx shook hands with George and headed down the road, continuing south.

Lynx and Steve talked through the night as they drove, mostly small talk. Lynx avoided any discussion about his background, the mission, and such. They snacked on the sandwiches. After a few hours, Lynx dozed off and suddenly awoke with a start. His Sixth Sense was screaming something to him; he did not know what, but there it was.

There could be trouble ahead, and he went into full alert.

After a few minutes, Lynx convinced Steve to pull onto the shoulder while he thought things over. They did so easily, as the shoulder was quite wide.

Lynx thought for a few minutes, and came up empty. Consequently, they started on down the road again, but at a slower speed, proceeding with caution. Not far along, they could make out a roadblock in the distance. Steve hit the brakes, doused the lights, and picked up the map while Lynx cupped his hands over the flashlight beam to prevent light from emanating from the car. Lynx found their position and noticed a side road just up ahead—a way to avoid the roadblock.

They proceeded to the crossroad, turned right for about a mile to another intersection, and turned left, now proceeding parallel to the highway. A half-mile down the road, they could see the lights of the roadblock off in the distance. Steve again doused the car headlights and they moved forward at a slow speed until they came to the next intersection, where they turned left again and were soon back at the highway, the roadblock now behind them. They turned right and continued along the highway, resuming their journey south.

Steve asked Lynx about that gut feeling he would get when things were about to go wrong, either immediately or sometime in the near future. Lynx simply couldn't explain it to him, Sarge, or anyone else. It was just there. It had already saved his life more than once.

They drove on in silence, passing through several small villages and towns. As dawn approached, they stopped at a village and drove on to their second safe house.

Steve told Lynx that they would be spending the day there. It was his favourite uncle's house, but he spoke no English. At the door, Steve's uncle embraced him. Lynx was introduced and the man's grip was like a vise—powerful and calloused, a workingman's hand.

They had a breakfast of bacon, eggs, and toast while Steve and his uncle conversed in Polish. His uncle told him that the roadblock that they had detoured around was intended for a prisoner escaped from the local jail. Lynx took that as a good sign, namely that the local police did not know that he was there.

The day passed without incident. Both men slept well into the afternoon. After dinner, Steve's uncle gave him a can of gasoline that he used to top up the tank. They bid their *Adieus* and were soon off on the final, inbound leg—next stop, Warsaw.

Before long, they had reached the outskirts of Warsaw, notable by the growing urban sprawl. They pulled up in front of a huge house. It was 4:00 a.m.

The owner appeared in the doorway, a man of at least three hundred pounds, aged about forty years, by the name of Gregor. His wife Olga was standing beside him. She was the other extreme—a tiny, lean, stick lady. They were pleased to see their guests, particularly someone with whom they could practise their English—Gregor spoke it well, Olga, not so much. While Olga prepared breakfast, Gregor showed their visiting travellers to their sleeping quarters. They had bacon, eggs, and toast for the second day in a row. *That must be popular breakfast fare in Poland,* thought Lynx.

Lynx was so exhausted that he was almost asleep before his head hit the pillow. When he awoke, Gregor informed him that Steve had already left to gas up the car and pick up their passengers—Marina, Sophie, and Edward.

Hours dragged by with no sign of Steve. Gregor started pacing the floor, nervous and visibly worried. After a while, Gregor left to find out what had happened to Steve, promising that he would not be gone long.

Lynx had a premonition that something had gone awry because he, once again, had that churning gut sensation. Besides, Steve had been gone away too long.

About ninety minutes later, Gregor returned with the information that Steve had had a car accident. It was not his fault, but he was nevertheless being held by the police. He explained that in Poland, one is guilty until proven innocent—the opposite of typical North American or British practice. When the investigation was finished, they would release him, but for the moment and perhaps for some time, he was in jail.

Now there is something that even Sarge couldn't have anticipated, thought Lynx.

Gregor was flummoxed as to what to do. Lynx suggested calling Marina's husband, who was probably well connected. That gave Gregor an idea. He picked up the telephone and made a short call in Polish.

Unusual, thought Lynx. *Underground rarely use their own telephones, because of the possibility of authorities tapping their lines.*

Off the phone, Gregor turned to Lynx, excited but a little nervous, and announced, "Lynx, we have another car. Someone is going to pick up Marina and the kids and bring them here."

At about 10:00 p.m., Marina Petroff and her two children arrived. The driver spoke to Gregor. They exchanged a few words in Polish while the driver pointed rather excitedly at Lynx and promptly left.

Gregor explained the situation to Lynx, saying, "Steve was supposed to be the driver for the Petroff family to the Baltic Sea. But, as you know, he is in jail. The man that just delivered the car does not want to have anything to do with you, Lynx. He is afraid that he might get caught with a spy and be shot. He will not drive you. My friend, we have no driver."

Eager to keep things moving forward, Lynx immediately offered to drive the car himself, with Marina navigating—provided she was agreeable. When Gregor posed the question, Marina started sobbing. Even Lynx, who spoke scarcely a word of Polish, detected mostly negatives interspersed between her sobs. Gregor took that as a "No." Her six-year-old daughter Sophie immediately started sobbing in harmony, a pattern that was to recur repeatedly. Her thirteen-year-old brother Edward, in stark contrast to the other two, looked very calm and mature for his age.

When his mother declined the job of navigator, he readily volunteered, saying, "I can," in perfect English.

Gregor interjected his objection on the basis of his age, but Lynx cut him off short and took charge.

"Edward," he said, "It's nearly four hundred miles. How can you be so sure you can do it?"

"I've been to Gdansk many times with my father," he replied confidently.

"Will you be able to find your way to two safe houses in two different towns?" asked Lynx.

"Yes. I've been to most of our safe houses at one time or another," he replied.

Turning to Gregor, Lynx simply said, "He's our man," as Edward sat there, smiling.

Still not convinced but prepared to go along with Lynx's assessment, Gregor acquiesced.

Lynx showed the boy the map and they started studying it together. Gregor indicated the two safe house locations, and Lynx showed him the submarine pick-up spot. Edward was sure he could find those three locations and the four prepared to leave. Knowing that if Edward could get them somewhere in the neighbourhood of the submarine pick-up spot, Lynx believed he would recognize *something* in the area, and they would make their pick-up connection just fine.

The car was an older one than Steve's, and Lynx was assured it would get them to the Baltic. Whenever Marina cried, Sophie chimed in—and that was pretty much constantly. He remained concerned about Sophie and Marina's weak attitude, but not Edward's. He was a trooper.

It was going to be a long four hundred miles, but by midnight the three passengers had been loaded into the car. With Lynx at the wheel, they drove off into the cold, dark night. The temperature was almost at the freezing point.

Except for Marina and Sophie's incessant sobbing, the first part of the journey was uneventful. The mother and daughter sat in the back seat while Edward rode in the front passenger seat, navigating. Lynx and Edward talked as they made their way through the night. Edward warned Lynx whenever something was about to appear long before it came up.

The car was old and running well, but started to backfire at one point. Lynx fixed it, and they made their first safe house without incident. But then, on the second night at about 3:30 a.m., the engine quit completely. Lynx lifted the hood and could smell gasoline. It was dripping from the carburetor. Lynx concluded that the float in the carburetor was probably stuck. He found a large screwdriver in the car, tapped the side of the carburetor gently, and the dripping gas stopped.

He got back into the car and signalled to Edward by crossing his fingers for good luck. Lynx turned the ignition key, and *presto*—it started, and off they went again. Even though the fuel gauge was unreliable, Lynx was sure they had enough fuel to make it to the next safe house—but not much to spare.

Conversing with the boy made the hours pass quickly, and Lynx was enjoying his company. Edward wanted to pursue a trade in the aircraft industry. He was enthralled with Lynx's stock car racing stories. They became fast friends.

By 5:00 a.m., they were searching for their second safe house, which would hopefully mark their last day in Poland. Snow was falling gently in large flakes, but melting as soon as it hit the ground.

They managed to locate their second—and final—safe house, and slept there throughout the day. After dinner, Edward helped Lynx pour a can of gasoline into the car's fuel tank. Lynx put the empty can into the trunk of the car. Once Marina and Sophie were in the back seat, they were off again. It had snowed all day, and there were about two inches of snow on the ground. By then, Marina and Sophie had settled down and had stopped crying. Lynx could not detect any problems as he reviewed the situation.

Glancing at the fuel gauge, it read a quarter tank. Thinking that could not be correct, he tapped the gauge and it went to half full. *Just stuck,* he thought

As the snow continued, it got heavier and the windshield wipers couldn't handle the volume. Ice was forming on the wiper blades and Lynx stopped and knocked it off. When he got back into the car, the fuel gauge was again reading one quarter full, and he tapped the gauge. This time it went to empty and stayed there. With over fifty miles to go, if the gauge was correct, they were facing a serious problem.

Meantime, the weather had deteriorated into a blizzard of heavy, blowing snow. When Marina asked Edward what was happening and didn't like his answer, she started sobbing again. Sophie, of course, joined in on cue.

Within a few minutes, it was snowing so hard that Lynx simply couldn't see the road. Lynx stopped the car and got out to clear the wiper blades with the engine idling when it suddenly quit. He got back into the car and tried to restart the engine—to no avail. The situation was going from bad to worse with each passing minute.

Lynx managed to locate a set of spanners in the trunk and removed the fuel line from the carburetor. When Edward turned the engine over for him, no fuel squirted out of the fuel line. They were out of gasoline. Here they were, fifty miles from their destination in the middle of nowhere. Contemplating the situation but coming up empty, Lynx secured the fuel line and closed the engine hood.

The temperature was dropping, but it had stopped snowing. Then Edward motioned Lynx to look back down the road. In the distance he could make out an army truck, stopped about three hundred feet down the road. Its driver was standing to its left, facing away from them.

His mind racing, Lynx quickly developed a plan. He motioned Edward to get out of the car and described his plan. He had Edward inform his mother to "stay in the car with Sophie" and that they would be right back.

While Edward engaged the driver in conversation, Lynx approached silently on the other side of the truck, a gas can and a short section of hose in hand. He prepared to siphon gasoline from the truck's passenger side-saddle tank.

Lynx removed the tank cap quietly and smelled its contents to confirm that it was gasoline—not diesel. While Edward talked up a storm with the driver on the other side of the truck, Lynx put the end of the hose into his mouth and took a good, long drag. As the gasoline arrived at his mouth, he suppressed his coughing and spitting as quietly as he could and quickly directed the end of the hose into the gas can.

As the gasoline level rose in the can, he was concerned that perhaps the driver had heard something. Fortunately, he hadn't. With the gasoline can partially full and in hand, Lynx proceeded back to their waiting car as inconspicuously as he could in the poor light.

By the time Edward had returned, Lynx was still emptying the gas into their gas tank. After a few revolutions of the engine, it started and they were off down the road again.

At 4:00 a.m., they reached Mr. Parwicki's house. He immediately got on a short-wave radio and had made contact with the submarine about five minutes later. The captain instructed them to proceed to the landing spot immediately. He wanted them aboard the submarine before daylight.

Parwicki pulled Lynx aside and told him that they had already disposed of the Russian car and its "reception committee" contents.

"How?" inquired Lynx.

"Buried the whole shebang with a big earth-moving machine," he replied with a smile.

By 5:00 a.m., they had reached the shore where a small inflatable raft was waiting. Lynx helped Marina and Sophie into the raft. To avoid overloading the inflatable, Lynx and Edward waited for a second ferrying to the submarine. Once aboard the submarine, Edward was awestruck with the vessel. An alert and pleasant boy, he quickly made friends with the crew.

Many hours later, the submarine surfaced in the North Sea. A high-speed Navy boat arrived, it pulled alongside the sub, and Lynx and the rescued family were transferred to the surface boat.

As the submarine crew watched, the Navy boat lifted its bow, turned, and sped off towards England at a good thirty knots, knifing its way through the flat, calm sea.

They arrived at a small coastal town in short order, and cars were waiting on the dock. The captain had been in contact with MI-6, and all parties had been informed of the success of the mission.

As Lynx helped Marina off the Navy craft, she stopped, turned, looked at him, and embraced him tightly, saying "*Dobsha*," and then walked away.[17] Sophie smiled and waved; Sarge was holding her other hand.

Edward shook Lynx's hand. They hugged and he went to join his mother. They would meet again—but not for several years.[18]

Lynx stood watching as a large black car drove them off to freedom.

The next thing Lynx knew, Sarge tapped him on the shoulder. Lynx turned around and there he was, grinning from ear to ear, obviously feeling proud of his young agent's success.

There would be no taped debrief on this mission—only a discussion with Sarge. Consequently, when Sarge asked him how it had gone, Lynx immediately referenced his penchant for attracting trouble, and how this mission had been no different than the previous two. Many unexpected situations had arisen. However, he quickly went into his main observational concern that Sarge *had* to be apprised of: there was a leak somewhere in the MI-6 operation—to wit, the two Russian agents awaiting his arrival as soon as he had gotten ashore at the start of the mission.

After careful thought, Sarge's viewpoint was that the leak must be in the Polish underground, because ". . . not too many people on my end knew that you were going into Poland."

"Sarge," said Lynx, "wasn't it a little strange to have two Russian agents waiting almost exactly where the submarine put me ashore? Was that coincidence? I don't think so."

---

17 Meaning "Thank you" in English.

18 In 1967, five years later, Lawrence bumped into eighteen-year-old Edward at the De Havilland plant in Toronto, where he was also then working. Lawrence immediately notified Sarge on his 1-900 number, Sarge came quickly, and "Eddie" invited Lawrence and Sarge to his parents' St. Clair Ave., Toronto home, where they met his father for the first time. They marked the occasion by polishing off a fine bottle of vodka together. "You drink it like I drink it: straight," the father informed Lawrence. Sarge, of course, abstained, but immediately made moves to redeploy Lawrence to a new job at Douglas Aircraft the following week to avoid complications with their MI-6 operation.

Sarge agreed that it was strange, and undertook to pursue the issue. He, and only he, knew precisely who those "... not too many people" were, and would have been well advised to eliminate them through systematic investigation—one by one.

It would be almost five years before Sarge would find the spy in his organization. That delay would almost cost Lynx his life.

Steer's White Rose gas station, 1930, site of Lawrence's first job at age 8.

The Fox family, 1946. Left to right, standing back: Grace (mother), Reginald (father), Jean Fourdice, William (brother, Sea cadet, Korean veteran) Mid-foreground: Lawrence. Foreground: Walter (brother).

King St., Midland Ontario, looking north, circa 1950. The Roxy Theatre (discernable on left, now the Midland Cultural Centre) where Lawrence worked for Al Perkins in 1951.

The Fox family, 1963. Left to right: Walter (brother), Lawrence, Grace (mother), Reginald (father), June (sister), William (brother).

Maurice Oldfield (1915–1981). The manipulative MI-6 recruiter who directed Lawrence Fox's trainig and missions behind the Iron Curtain in the 1950s and 1960s. He became head of MI-6 in 1973.

The Canadian-built, twin-engined, STOL, the Buffalo, a favorite De Havilland aircraft of Lawrence's. It could clear a 50-foot obstacle in just 1200 feet of runway taking off, loaded at 41,000 lbs.

Lawrence Fox, master aircraft model builder in the mid-1990s with one of his Lancasters that featured four gasoline engines; upper left, a Lancaster model aloft.

Chapter Five: **To Russia With Love**

In November 1962, Lawrence was still stationed at the Edmonton base and was given an honourable discharge from the RCAF. Sarge had almost immediately arranged a job for him at the de Havilland Aircraft Corporation in Ontario. He clearly wanted Lawrence to continue providing services to MI-6.

Lawrence and his family moved back to Ontario in December 1962. No longer formally in the military per se, he started work as a riveter at de Havilland in Downsview the following month. Soon he was moved to the Experimental Department, exploring and developing new and improved aircraft designs. This was an exciting area of work for him, and clearly a career highlight. Things were unfolding badly in his private life but his work at de Havilland sat on the opposite side of the ledger—a source of motivation, pride, and satisfaction.

A good example was the Buffalo project[19]—a favourite aircraft of Lawrence's—along with the Caribou, which was deployed extensively

---

19 The Buffalo could be steered on the ground with the nose wheel, the brakes, or the engines. It could also take off in a short distance (STOL), could climb at forty-five degrees, and even take off with one engine—an incredible, Canadian-made aircraft.

into Vietnam.[20] "The Buffalo Project" had just been launched when Lawrence started at de Havilland, and he witnessed the first fully built unit came off the production line one Saturday morning in March 1963.

When the new Buffalo was taken outside to operate the engines for the first time, the Auxiliary Power Unit (APU) was unable to start either engine. The aircraft had to be towed back into the hangar and engine specialists—of which Lawrence was the sole designated man on his shift—began the engine disassembly to diagnose the problem.

It was an exciting time for some in the Canadian aeronautical industry, which was still staggering from the blow three years earlier when the Diefenbaker government ruthlessly cancelled the Avro CF-105 Arrow. De Havilland had soldiered on, building fine Canadian aircraft, and Lawrence was right in the middle of it—loving every on-the-job minute.

Off the job was another matter. As 1964 unfolded, Lawrence's mood swings and PTSD nightmares persisted. He did manage to slow down his drinking, perhaps a result of regular lectures from both Sarge and his parents. His marriage to Elsie remained as tempestuous as ever, and in August, they agreed to separate. A custody battle over the children started immediately and raged on for almost a year.

Early in the proceedings, Elsie shouted at the judge who threatened her with contempt. As the issues emerged in full view of the provincial legal system, Elsie eventually forfeited custody of the children and the legal system took them into its care. They became crown wards under the care of the province, and were assigned to a foster home in Wyevale, Ontario, where they stayed for eighteen months. Lawrence was torn apart by the situation. He could not disclose his MI-6 obligations to either the judge or his parents, all of whom, of course, were seeking the best possible arrangement for the children.

---

20 The Caribou was de Havilland's first STOL aircraft powered by two engines. It only required a 1200-foot runway and became a phenomenal military cargo workhorse.

One-on-one discussions between Lawrence and the judge—a learned and balanced woman—went on almost daily for months. In the end, they agreed that the best interests of the children would be served in an adopted home, kept together as a unit. Lawrence knew this was the case, but was nevertheless devastated. To this day, it remains his greatest heartache.

The children's adopted home was in Oakville, Ontario, where they lived for seven years. One day in 1974, two of them—Larry and Arthur, now strapping young men—appeared in Lawrence's driveway one evening just as he was returning home from their cottage with his second wife, Georgette. After making sure they were speaking to the right person, they greeted a drop-jawed Lawrence with, "Hi, dad."

The 1963-64 period was thus a low point in Lawrence's personal life. Loose behaviour was included—one-night-stands with fast women and lots of them. Canadian balladeer Gordon Lightfoot was undoubtedly reflecting on a similar period in his life when he wrote the graphic lyrics of his tune *For Lovin' Me*:

> I've had a hundred more like you,
> So don't be blue,
> I'll have a thousand 'fore I'm through.

That typified Lawrence's approach to life during this brief time. He was living in the fast lane for today—because a lot of the time, he felt like there may not be a tomorrow. Easily provoked into barroom fights, many an unsuspecting opponent had no idea how lethal Lawrence's bare hands could be. Somehow, he managed to control himself. There were no fatalities arising—but there easily could have been.

His rationality was being blurred by a complicated haze through which he was viewing life. Sarge appeared from time to time and repeatedly made his case as to why this lifestyle was a "foolish way to throw [your] life away." Living in his own world, Lawrence was calling his own tune, feeling all alone, with no one on his side—not even Sarge. The one highlight in his life seemed to be his work at de Havilland—and it likely preserved his sanity.

At one stage, Sarge developed serious concerns about Lynx's ability to carry out further espionage missions. In an attempt to rescue him, Sarge even took Lawrence camping in the bush country north of Marmora for two weeks to dry him out. He had Lawrence running with a pack on his back, yelling at him to ". . . go faster, you freakin' pussy," pushing him to purge the toxins from his body and get into shape. Sarge was generally pleased with the results.

Back in civilization, Sarge enrolled him in more karate training at Dufferin and Finch in Toronto for two hours a week. The workouts were beneficial, and things seemed to be moving back onto an even keel. Lawrence could feel his old self returning.

Sarge was well connected in the corporate world, especially those that supplied the military and he used those connections for his purposes effectively. In mid-1965, he made contact with Lawrence, having already arranged a two-week leave of absence from de Havilland through his Hawker Siddeley network. A ". . . highly important mission" was in the works ". . . for immediate execution." Once he was notified, Lynx was quickly on a commercial flight, heading to London.

Only he and Sarge knew his identity. Just to be sure it stayed that way, Lynx wore a hood into the pre-mission briefing. There, six army officers sat at a large table without any briefing papers in front of them, facing Sarge and Lynx—sitting side by side.

The meeting had scarcely started and someone mentioned that Paris was the mission starting location. Then, out of the blue, one of the officers asked Lynx, "Why do you think you are competent to go to Russia and retrieve this data?"

Before Lynx could answer, Sarge was on his feet. He was screaming at the officer in the most derogatory of terms. Incensed to the bone, he ranted on that a ". . . run-of-the-mill, second-rate officer who does nothing but push pencils and count paper clips all day would question my judgment at selecting Lynx for this job."

Lynx had never seen him so enraged. All those who were present recoiled in shock, including the officer who asked the question. The room suddenly descended into silence. A dropped pin would have sounded like an anvil.

All sat back down to regroup and one of the officers simply declared the meeting adjourned. The only information that had been imparted before Sarge's spectacular outburst was that the mission was to start in Paris. Before the group could disperse, the officer who had questioned Lynx's competence apologized to Sarge and then asked how Lynx was getting out of the country.

"Don't worry, Major Austin.[21] He'll pick up a car at the French border and drive to Orly [Airport]," replied Sarge.

"A French car?" he wanted to know.

"One of our cars from our embassy in Paris," Sarge answered.

Sarge was fed up with what he considered to be useless prattle and motioned Lynx to follow him out of the room.

As they left, Sarge quietly briefed Lynx on the plan, which was to take a military aircraft to Paris—despite the slightly different version of the mission launch he had given at the meeting—and board a train there with a female accomplice.

Has Sarge forgotten my vow of only solo missions after Nomad was shot? wondered Lynx. So he told Sarge, "You know better than that, Sarge. No partners. Remember?"

"She's not a partner, Lynx. She's a travelling companion," replied Sarge, smiling broadly.

Such an unusual facial gesture for the normally staid Sarge. Why would Sarge be smiling? Lynx wondered.

Sarge accompanied Lynx to Paris. When they arrived, there it was in all of its summer glory: the City of Lights, bathed in moonlight by night, in dappled sunlight by day, warm winds wafting the aroma of that irresistible French cuisine across the olfactory senses of every passer-by.

Sarge and Lynx sat, waiting in an outdoor patio restaurant. Lynx was sipping a coffee while they talked. Suddenly the question occurred to Lynx, *Why are we waiting, and for what?*

When Lynx asked Sarge that question, he replied that they were waiting to meet his travelling companion.

---

21 Not his real name.

As they continued talking, a few minutes later Lynx could not help but notice a stunningly beautiful woman in her mid-twenties with long, flowing blonde hair approach their table.

Sarge obviously recognized her. He stood up to greet her, saying simply, "Susan."

"Maurice. So nice to see you," she replied in a low, sexy voice.

Turning to Lynx, Sarge introduced him to Susan as Robert Hammond.

She gently extended her hand towards Lynx, only allowing him to touch it ever-so-lightly before immediately withdrawing it.

Sarge invited her to have a seat and she promptly accepted, her tight-fitting, short, dark blue skirt struggling to conceal her shapely upper thighs as she did so, her loose white blouse gently caressing her upper torso contours which were now seductively discernable through the translucent material. Her black heels emphasized the toned shape of her lower legs for maximum allure as she tucked them neatly together, angled slightly to one side.

As Lynx stood there admiring all this beauty of human form, attempting as sophisticatedly as possible to *not stare*, Sarge jerked him back to reality by pulling on one sleeve. Sarge politely asked him to "please, sit down."

It registered with Lynx why Sarge had smiled so broadly when he had clarified the matter of a "travelling companion" a few hours earlier.

Starting in, Sarge addressed his first remark towards her, saying, "Susan, on this mission, Robert here will be posing as a Russian Secret Service agent, and you will be posing as his aide. He has top-notch clearance papers, but speaks no Russian. You, on the other hand, speak Russian fluently."

"Doesn't that pose danger for both of us?" she asked.

"I don't think so, Susan," replied Sarge. "His papers are so highly ranked, they will almost be unable to resist kissing his feet."

He continued, "I planned it this way to get him across the Ukrainian frontier only. At that point, Lynx will change identities, and you two will part company. Susan, you will continue on to Moscow to pick up your microfilm." Turning to Lynx, he continued, "Robert, you will meet a Polish agent by the name of Mr. Pasloski who will travel with you to Beslan for your microfilm pickup and return with you on the train, again until you are safely across the border. [22] You will continue on the train to a small town about twenty miles outside Paris where a room and a car have been set up for you to change clothes, drop your gear, and drive to Orly [Airport] for pickup. All the needed information is in your pack."

He similarly passed instructions to Susan for her Moscow leg of the trip. Susan then asked if that was everything needed for this meeting. When Sarge said it was, Susan stood up, shook his hand, and started to walk away. Sarge quickly shook Lynx's hand and told him that there, indeed, were no further instructions for him either. Lynx joined Susan—Lynx carrying his small kit bag, and Susan carrying a purse and a medium-sized overnight bag.

They caught a taxi to a Paris train station and boarded an eastbound train. When they were finally settled into a compartment, Susan sat eyeing Lynx up and down, probably trying to place him in the hierarchy of the espionage business. She decided to start with his name.

"Robert Hammond. Is that your real name?" she inquired.

"No."

"What name will I call you?" she asked.

"Call me Robert, or Bob."

"Okay, Robert," she said as she smiled, her restrained demeanour starting to thaw but still signalling distance—a signal that Lynx missed in his pseudo-euphoric state.

Now it was Lynx's turn. "Is Susan your real name?" he asked.

"That's what it says on my passport."

That non-answer was, of course, correct, but *Hey, we're both in the hush-hush game. Everybody has a fake name on their passport,* thought Lynx. He interpreted her response erroneously as an invitation to advance relations. Consequently, feeling secure in the privacy of their

---

22 Beslan is a small city of about 30,000 in the Ukraine, situated halfway across the isthmus between the Black Sea and the Caspian Sea, approximately a 3,600 km train ride from Paris, making the return trip 7,200 km.

compartment, he moved across to her side of the compartment seating and gently placed one hand on the bare skin of her upper leg.

"You know, Susan, I think we should get better acquainted, since we are going to share this compartment. It's going to be a long train ride."

"Take your hand off my leg," she snarled.

Then, without hesitating for even a second, she grabbed Lynx's thumb and quickly bent it backwards. She suddenly had Lynx on his knees in pain, yelling in muffled tones for relief. She had clearly demonstrated the advantage of deftly executed surprise against an accomplished martial arts practitioner.

After several seconds, her eyes burning laser beams at his, she let go. Mustering the sexiest voice she could—simply for reverse emphasis as to what was *not* going to happen—she then ordered Lynx back to his own side of the compartment.

After several minutes of awkward silence, Lynx decided to make another attempt at starting a conversation and asked her, "I take it that you are with Her Majesty's Secret Service?"

"Yes, I am," she replied cordially. "Do you have a code name?"

"Yes, I do."

"Should I just call you Robert?" she asked.

"Fine," replied Lynx, nursing his thumb.

Thinking over his hasty move of putting his hand on her leg, Lynx started wondering to himself why he had done it. *That is not something I would normally do,* he thought. *I am usually a gentleman—who treats women with respect. Sure, she's a beautiful woman, but why would I behave like such a jerk around such a stunning chick? Look at her now. She's upset with me, and she should be. Her mood has changed completely because of my stupidity.*

As she sat there staring out the window for several minutes, Lynx suddenly blurted out without any preamble, "Susan, I'm sorry, and apologize for my action."

In a complete surprise reaction to his apology, she suddenly looked at Lynx, put her hand over her mouth, and burst into tears.

"It's not your fault, Robert. I'm in turmoil because my husband has just been shot. They shot him," she sobbed, almost uncontrollably.

"Who shot him?"

"The Russians. He was in the Russian military, acting as a spy for the British, and somebody squealed on him," she replied as she dug a photograph of him out of her purse and passed it to Lynx.

One glance at the photograph and Lynx recognized him immediately. In 1959, in a motel room in Trenton, Sarge had shown him a picture of a highly ranked Russian officer and had told Lynx that he was Sarge's top man in the Russian army.

Stunned at this revelation, all Lynx could think to ask was, "When did this happen?"

"A month ago. They didn't even know that he was British. They tried him for treason as a Russian and had him shot by a firing squad," she said, dabbing the tears from her eyes.

To break the mood, Lynx proposed that they go to the dining car for a drink and something to eat. She accepted. Turning to him as she exited the compartment, she said, "Robert, I shouldn't have grabbed your thumb like that. I'm sorry."

He followed her towards the dining car. "That's okay," he replied. "I deserved it," and smiled at her.

In the dining car, Lynx ordered some wine to sip while their dinner order was being prepared. She started to let her hair down a little, volunteering some peripherals on her situation. "I work at one of the MI-6 offices in London. I took this assignment to retrieve microfilm that my husband secured some time ago. He wrote me letters, and we had a code that we used just between the two of us. The film is well hidden."

As Lynx tuned into the mood of the conversation, quite out of character, he volunteered, "As you have probably guessed, I'm a courier. This is my fourth mission."

As she sipped her wine, she looked up from the glass without raising her head, her eyes levelled at his, and she said, "Robert, don't tell me your code name. I would probably recognize your missions. Your fourth, you say? You must be either lucky, or highly skilled—or possibly both. Usually couriers don't make it past three."

Continuing this confession—which it seemed it was—to this beautiful travelling companion, he continued, "I get a strange feeling in my stomach when something is about to happen, or when something is not quite right, which alerts me to be extra careful. I tense up and go into a state of full vigilance. I can't explain it, but it has happened several times on every mission so far. It's kind of a Sixth Sense."

"I have never heard of that before," she replied, looking into his eyes with an almost hypnotic allure. "Have you killed?"

"Yes."

"Are you married?"

"Yes, but separated."

"Not divorced?"

"Not yet," answered Lynx. The particulars of their respective marital situations were on the table.

"No chance of a reconciliation?"

"Susan, why all these questions?"

"Oh, no particular reason. Just getting to know my travelling companion," she smiled, reaching across the table and taking his hand in hers. "Could you order me another glass of wine, Robert? Those French wines are so interesting and so complex—like many people's lives."

"Why surely, Susan," said Lynx, signalling the waiter.

They continued chatting. Lynx told her about how Nomad had been killed, and his vow to get the Russian that did it. He probed subtly about her background, and she was surprisingly forthcoming—twenty-eight years old, and knew that she was a fetching woman. Men were constantly hitting on her because of her good looks. She had come to consider her looks a curse—essentially why she had been so careful when shaking hands for the first time. However, as the conversation proceeded, she openly admitted that she was enjoying his company.

She had another glass of wine while Lynx continued nursing his preferred drink: rum.

The conversation stretched on for two hours amid a slow crescendo of increased handholding intensity across the table. Some sort of chemistry was at work. Perhaps it was a tension release from the danger inherent in their impending mission.

Then Susan suggested that they return to the privacy of their compartment. Lynx found the thought of what that invitation might hold intoxicating.

When he opened the door to their compartment for her, he found the aroma of her perfume brought on a momentary delirium as she brushed past him into the tiny room.

She walked the few steps across the compartment and stood beside the windowpane, no shade drawn. She stood looking into the darkness outside for a few moments. Then she suddenly wheeled around, threw her arms around Lynx's neck, and pressed her body against his.

Lynx kissed her gently. As he did so, she reached her hands up to the back of his head and pressed it against her lips. He could hardly breathe. He almost forgot that there are nostrils for such emergencies.

After the extended kiss, she moaned, "Robert, you are so wonderful. I need you."

Now fully under her spell, Lynx reached for the light switch and turned the light off.

For the next hour, the couple engaged in a mutual watershed of tension release. For that brief, blissful interlude, as the train sped on through the night, all the cares of the world were gone.

Much later, as he sat in the small compartment, Lynx started thinking over their actions. *Was this just another one-night stand*, he asked himself, *like the dozens of the past few months? She is a beautiful woman, but there is more to it than that. We're both agents, in the same business. She would comprehend the loneliness like no one I have ever met. She knows what my life is like, because hers has to be the same; we have the same pressures, the same conflicts, and the same tensions.*

Lynx's mind was racing. The attraction to this woman was irresistible. It had depth and seemed like it had the potential to last a lifetime—the rest of his lifetime. *Have I finally met the woman of my dreams?* he wondered.

When she returned from the washroom, she opened the compartment door, smiled broadly, bent over, kissed Lynx tenderly, and asked, "Are you all right?"

"I'm just fine," he replied. "Just deep in thought. About us, actually. How are *you* feeling about us?"

"Just great," she replied, still smiling.

"I don't want to take advantage of you," he said.

"Don't worry, Robert. You didn't. I started it. So I guess you could say it was my idea. But you had been thinking similar thoughts, by the way you responded. Remember, it takes two to tango," she replied, as she sat down on his knee.

They talked in near-whispers, exchanging tender puppy-love kisses between sweet-nothing verbal exchanges for several minutes. Susan eventually fell asleep on Lynx's shoulder, lulled off by the gentle rocking of the train. Soon Lynx, too, had dozed off and his mind drifted into yet another PTSD nightmare of the Nomad death scene. The imagery was vivid. He could see the Russian soldiers closing in on him, beating him with their fists, and then standing triumphantly over him and his dying partner. An officer walked up and placed a pistol at the back of Lynx's head. Lynx waited for the gun to go off, then suddenly, *boom!*

Lynx awoke with a start, yelling. Susan jumped to her feet, startled.

"Robert! Robert! What is it?" she asked, alarmed.

Lynx knew immediately what had happened, and apologized to her for reacting to a ". . . bad dream. They come often these days, an effect of some of the trauma I've been through on my missions. I've been having them regularly. I'm not sure what triggers them, but the general theme is more or less the same."

He recounted how the Russian officer had taken Nomad down, and the whole sequence of events. When he had finished the story, he felt better for it. *Now at least one person other than Sarge knows that story,* he thought to himself.

Having listened attentively to his tale, Susan began expressing her concern for his long-term welfare. With three missions to his credit, her considered opinion was that he was pushing his luck. Her experience was that couriers typically execute three missions and resign from the Service.

"Robert," she said, "I think you should quit. They're clearly starting to get to you. If you keep this up, you'll almost certainly have a nervous breakdown."

Noting a few landmarks out the window of the train, Lynx concluded that the border was not far away, and that they should get ready for the coming manoeuvres.

Her comment indicated that things were moving quickly emotionally for her, too. She had been having thoughts lately about her own long-term plan after a life in espionage, and seemed to like the idea of finding someone who, like Lynx, could understand and sympathize with the realities of espionage work.

They agreed to rendezvous back in London after the mission. Lynx let her know that he would be staying at the Cumberland Hotel, registered under the name of Robert Hammond.

"Robert," she said, "I can't wait. That would be wonderful!"

Lynx was not certain whether Susan felt the same commitment towards him, because she had hinted at it but had never said so in so many words. He had, however, already decided that—if she was game—she was the one he could spend the rest of his life with.

Now having crossed the borders of Italy and Austria, the Ukraine and the Iron Curtain were not far away. At the Ukrainian border, Susan and Lynx stayed in their compartment to maintain as low a profile as possible.

When the train stopped, they could hear voices in the corridor outside their door. A young Russian army officer suddenly opened the door and demanded to examine their travel and identification papers

Susan jumped to her feet, passports in hand, and spoke to him in Russian. The neck of her blouse was already loosened enough to exhibit just the right amount of cleavage. She gently handed him their two passports.

Obviously distracted, the Russian officer's eyes dropped down to her chest. He was dazzled by her beauty and paid very little attention to the passports.

Susan snapped something at him in Russian and his attitude changed into that of a chastised minion. He handed the passports back to her after only a cursory glance at them, saluted, and closed the door. When Lynx asked her what she had said to the officer, she indicated that any mention of a Siberian assignment to a Russian soldier always got a fearful reaction. "Remember Maurice's kiss-your-feet remark? Well, your high rank gives you the authority of arrest. I simply reminded the soldier of that."

A few moments later, the train lurched a few times and started to move. They had crossed the Iron Curtain and were now in hostile territory.

As a precautionary measure, Lynx took his knife and Beretta out of his packsack and installed them in their customary places—the sheathed knife onto his leg, the Beretta in its shoulder holster—while Susan watched.

She was jubilant and excited about dining in celebration of making it easily across to the east side of the "Curtain." Lynx, on the other hand, raised his antennae and cautioned her about being over-confident. He made a few remarks about how the tough part was just beginning and reminded her that the danger would be omnipresent from here on until they were safely back into friendly territory.

Lynx also mentioned that her own husband, as knowledgeable as he was, had probably made a single, minor slip and had paid the price. "You need to remember where you are, and what could happen if you get caught. Never lose sight of that," her told her, his romantic relationship with her now taking second seat to their mutual survival. "We need to be careful on how we're seen and make it look like we are arm's length travelling companions. Nothing more."

"Thank you for reminding me, Robert. That's agreed," she replied.

Lynx also reminded her that the Russian army was still on the train. He pressed her against him, they kissed, and he said, "Okay. Let's go eat."

They talked over dinner. Susan worked her way through two glasses of wine and the conversation, once again, turned to how they would see each other after the mission. They agreed that this would be Lynx's last mission, that she would quit the Secret Service and come to Canada. Lynx committed to telling Sarge of their agreement when he got back.

After dinner, they walked hand in hand—dangerously forgetting their pact on public deportment—back to their compartment and Lynx left her there alone while he went to the washroom.

Lynx took his time in the washroom, feeling no urgency, humming a tune as he washed his hands. He started leisurely back to their little love nest—having been gone less than ten minutes.

When he arrived back at their compartment door, he could hear a male voice inside, speaking in Russian and laughing. Switching immediately into full alert, Lynx silently opened the door a crack.

The scene inside made his blood run cold. Susan was on her knees with her hands tied behind her and her skirt pulled up onto her back. A young Russian officer—his pants dropped to the floor and laying in a clump about his feet—was standing behind her, obviously intending to commit an aggressive sexual act. He was facing into the compartment, away from Lynx.

Lynx closed the door without making a sound and reached down to unsheathe his knife. He quickly glanced up and down the corridor to make sure no one was coming. What was about to happen would not be pretty.

He slowly opened the door enough to permit entry, and in a single swift movement, clamped his left hand over the soldier's mouth while he slid the knife deep into his starboard quarter, precisely between the optimal pair of ribs for best results.

Without making a sound, the soldier stiffened. Lynx sliced his double-sided blade from side to side to sever the main arteries to the heart for maximum efficiency in such matters. In two seconds, the Russian officer collapsed to the floor—dead.

Lynx quickly closed the door and cut Susan's hands free, his knife still dripping with blood. She got onto her feet, pulled her skirt back into place, kicked the dead Russian lying on the floor, and uttered a profanity under her breath as she did so.

"That son-of-a-bitch was going to rape me. He pulled a gun on me and I had no chance. Thank heaven you came back when you did," she said, as she started sobbing. Lynx put his arms around her, hugged her tenderly, and she had soon stopped crying.

Now came the issue of body disposal. Lynx looked out the window and immediately had the answer. He lowered the window as far as it would go and, between the two of them, they dragged the slain officer across the floor. They managed to lift him up enough to get him started out the window. The farther he went out the window, the easier it was to push him out more. He finally fell down onto the side of the tracks as the train sped on through the night.

Lynx stepped back from the window, saw the Russian's hat lying on the floor, and threw it out the window. Then he quickly went to the washroom and got some paper towels to wipe up the blood on the seats and floor. They, too, went out the window.

Lynx closed the window and sat down on one of the compartment seats beside Susan.

"You killed for me," she said, looking gratefully into his eyes.

"Only protecting my travelling companion," he said lightly.

"You were right. Never lower your guard."

"You got that right, sweetheart," he said as he kissed and held her.

As the train continued on down the tracks, the steady cadence of the rhythmical sound put them into a deep silence for a few minutes. Lynx rolled over the events of the past few hours in his mind. *I am so taken with Susan, an agent in the same business*, he thought. *She is beautiful, smart—the perfect soul mate for me, however many years I might have left. She is someone who knows the loneliness of a secret agent. We are the perfect match.*

His thoughts continued: *But here we are, going across the Ukraine on a train. In a few hours, we will be going our separate ways to complete our respective missions, she to a Moscow suburb to pick up a highly valued microfilm for Sarge, me to Beslan to do the same.*

Shaking himself back to reality, Lynx reminded her that, as much as they now were experiencing the pleasures of new love, they would have to be careful. No walking hand-in-hand in public, as they had just done. No kissing where anyone could see them. No drawing attention to themselves in any way, especially whenever any soldiers were in sight. She was to be his aide, and would have to give every appearance of being so—nothing more—at all times.

With the lights out in the compartment, they settled in for what they both knew could be their last moments on this journey together, snuggling cozily.

Then, with unexpected openness, she turned to Lynx, looked him squarely in the eyes in the dim light of the room, her face only a few inches from his, and told him that she could feel herself falling helplessly in love with him. Lynx kissed her gently on the lips, and tears welling up in his eyes, managed to get a few words out, "Susan, I love you, too. I've known that for several hours now."

What is this? he thought. *A tough guy like me going all soft over a woman. But what a woman! But, yeah, what the hell? That's how I feel!*

They kissed tenderly several times in romantic small talk, knowing that in less than two hours' time, their parting would come. Neither wanted that moment to happen, but duty was calling.

They forced themselves into the agreed modus operandi—no handholding, and a mutual, professional aloofness evident in every mannerism. They left the relative safety of the compartment and started walking to the dining car for something to eat. About halfway there, they saw a Russian army officer with two soldiers coming towards them. The officer spoke to Susan in Russian.

How could they know she speaks Russian? was the first thought that flashed through Lynx's mind. He instinctively readied himself into full alert. Just in case, he placed his first two fingers just touching the edge of the automatic in his shoulder holster as surreptitiously as possible, feigning that he was soothing his upper chest in some medicinal way.

Later, Susan translated the conversation for him:

Officer: Excuse me, madam. Have you seen a young officer? He would be the one who checked your travel papers.

Susan: No. You're the first officer I've talked to since our papers were checked.

Officer: Thank you, madam. If you see him, please inform me.

Susan: I will.

With that, the two parties continued on their ways. Once in the next car, Susan turned to Lynx and asked, "What are we to do now?"

"Nothing. They won't find his body, at least not for a long time. There were plenty of small trees and brush beside the tracks where we dumped him out the window in the middle of nowhere. I'd guess it'd be a several days before anyone finds him."

Over dinner, they talked quietly about their possible future together—what they would do, where they would live, she asking questions about Canada, he answering as fetchingly as he could.

As the conversation went on, and before they were ready for the eventuality, they suddenly became aware that the train was slowing down. No firm, long-term plans had been agreed. Lynx felt he was on the edge of nowhere.

They began making their way out of the dining car and back to their compartment. Susan was carrying her purse and travel bag as the train slowly decelerated. The two newly minted lovers were standing between two cars looking into each other's eyes—again in violation of their pact. They spoke not a word as the train came to a full stop.

They went into their compartment and quickly said their good-byes in private. Lynx watched a tear trickle down her cheek. She said nothing, exited the compartment, stepped down onto the platform, and started to walk away while he stood on the train, watching her go. Ten paces away, she turned, smiled once, and resumed walking, swallowed up by the crowd on the platform.

It was to be the last time Lynx would see her alive.

As he stood there, fraught with emotion, the train suddenly jerked into motion and resumed its journey. Lynx was shaken back to reality. His immediate priority was to focus on making contact with Pasloski, his contact who—hopefully—had gotten on the train at this stop.

About the only thing he could guarantee: This travelling companion would not be as pretty as his last—and the sooner this mission was over, the better. Then a new life could begin.

Returning to their compartment, Lynx quickly opened his kit bag and changed passports. He selected the most credible option from the four that Sarge had given him. He sat, thinking pensively for several minutes, about the unfolding situation. Then he headed to the dining car.

An hour later, Lynx was still sitting at a table and twice had postponed making a dinner order by waving the waiter off. He was waiting for his contact.

Several people were coming and going. Lynx played it cool whenever a new person entered the car. Just when he was starting to wonder whether Pasloski could be a "no show," a man came in and sat down at the next table, facing Lynx.

Lynx made eye contact and immediately noticed a red ribbon tied onto the left collar of his jacket, the agreed signal. Lynx saluted with two fingers, the man got up and moved to Lynx's table.

"May I join you?" he asked.

"Please do," replied Lynx. "Pasloski?" he asked.

"Yes. You are Lynx?" replied the man.

"Yes. Here comes the waiter. Order us something."

Sarge had given him minimal information on Ivan Pasloski, who was to travel with him to Beslan and then back to the border. Lynx was pleased with what he saw: good English, albeit with an accent (to be expected) about five foot eight, 175 to 185 pounds, broad at the shoulders, strong and muscular, a powerful man, and a good ally should any hand-to-hand ensue. *A good thing for our side, the way these things seem to go*, thought Lynx.

When Lynx related his "encounter" with his previous travelling companion's "problem" and his quick-fix "solution," Pasloski simply shrugged his shoulders and smiled.

"One less Russian son-of-a-bitch to worry about," he whispered below his breath.

As the two agents ate, they also talked. Ivan socked back several straight vodkas in the course of the conversation. Simply put, Ivan hated the Russians. His job was straightforward—to get Lynx to Beslan, pick up the microfilm, and get him back to the border.

When the meal was over, the two agents went back to Lynx's compartment where they knew that their passports would be checked at least once. Ivan spoke Russian so he would be their spokesman.

They didn't have long to wait. Five minutes after they arrived at the compartment, a Russian army officer—not the same one who had spoken to Lynx and Susan previously—opened the door and demanded to see their passports.

Ivan, putting on a congenial act, talked and laughed with the officer who responded in kind. He was backed up by four soldiers standing in the aisle of the car with what looked like AK-47s held at the ready, trigger fingers in place and all.

Once the officer had gone over their passports, he passed them back to Ivan and closed the compartment door.

Ivan quietly relayed their conversation to Lynx. The officer had asked whether they had seen a young officer recently. Ivan told him that he hadn't, and speculated that he had probably gotten off the train somewhere along the way with some good-looking woman, a bottle of vodka, and checked into a cheap hotel. And that the two of them were likely lying drunk and naked somewhere, even as they now spoke.

Funnily enough, the officer had agreed with Ivan. He said that, indeed, that seemed highly likely, knowing the young officer as he did.

Serves the bastard right, thought Lynx.

By this time, Lynx had been on the train almost two and a half days. In two hours, they would be in Beslan.

Sure enough, they pulled into the station on time, late at night. Ivan and Lynx stood between cars as the train came to a stop. They stepped down onto the platform, walked to the edge of the station, and Ivan flagged a taxi. He gave the driver an address and settled down in silence as the cab driver made his way there. The two agents deliberately did not speak; the driver was thus unaware that there was an English-speaking passenger aboard. The "Trust no one" agent mantra was fully in play.

At the designated destination, Ivan got out of the taxi, paid the fare, and the two agents walked along the sidewalk. As they did so, Lynx took out a cigarette and lit it with a paper match.

As he was about to put the matchbook back into his pocket, he dropped the small booklet and bent down to pick it up while Ivan continued walking. As he was picking up the booklet, someone walked past him, going at a much faster pace. By this time, Ivan was about ten or fifteen feet ahead of Lynx. Lynx's gut took a now-familiar, something-is-wrong jump.

As the man proceeded towards Ivan, who continued on outwardly unawares, he slowed his pace. However, in agent code, Ivan's not turning around signalled to Lynx that he was aware of the man's presence.

To see if the man was tailing him, Ivan turned left into a church and went up the steps. His tail followed and Lynx continued bringing up the rear as the three men entered the church. Ivan proceeded up the centre aisle about half way to the altar and sat down in one of the pews. The man sat down in the pew immediately behind Ivan, leaned forward, and whispered something to Ivan as he drew a pistol.

With no time to fit the silencer to his Berretta, Lynx drew it out of his shoulder holster and looked around to see whether there was anyone else in the church. Seeing no one else present, Lynx moved quietly alongside the man who hadn't noticed that he was there. He looked up at Lynx.

The man said something to Lynx in Russian and started to move the muzzle of his pistol towards him. As Sarge's instruction of "If they see your face, you have no choice but to kill them" flashed through his mind, Lynx fired the Beretta from point-blank range, the shot echoed throughout the church like a cannon, the bullet travelled eighteen inches, a small hole—gushing blood—appeared in the man's forehead, and he slumped over onto his side, his hand still holding his pistol.

Ivan quickly got up from his pew, took the gun from the dead man's hand, and removed his wallet and watch.

"This way, it'll look like he was robbed," said Ivan as he smiled and took Lynx by the arm. The two agents proceeded post haste for the church door.

By this time, a shocked but excited priest was standing just to the left of the door. Ivan spoke briefly to him in Russian, telling him to feel free to administer the last rites to the dead man and call the police. The priest responded that he would and waved the two agents on.

Once they were clear of the church, Ivan opened the wallet and found the man's identity as that of a Russian army officer, obviously not in uniform. Just before he was shot, the dead man had whispered to Ivan that he had recognized him from the last time he was in Beslan, when Ivan had killed his partner.

As they proceeded down the sidewalk, Ivan tossed the Russian's pistol, wallet, and watch into a garbage can.

Lynx was not upset. In fact, he was calm. He had done what he had to do. After all, his last mission would soon be over. He already had two dead Russians in his rear-view mirror. Both had been necessary actions that he could easily justify to Sarge when he got back.

At the same time, he started wondering about himself, *What have I become? A heartless, cold-blooded killer? Has taking a life become too easy? I'm just a small-town kid that wanted to become a qualified aeronautical mechanic. Those guys likely have wives and kids, too. But they're in this game, knowing the risks, just like me. I had no choice.*

As the two walked briskly away from the church, they made a few turns at street corners, alternately lefts and rights and eventually arrived at a large red brick house. By this time, it was after midnight. The front door was unlocked and they walked in. All was dark and quiet, but they could discern the outline of doorways and the like.

Inside the house, they turned into the living room where there were two sofas. Ivan motioned Lynx to sit down on one while he sat on the other. Exhausted, Lynx put his kit bag down on the floor, sat down, and was soon fast asleep.

He awoke with a start when Ivan called in whispered tones, "Lynx! Lynx! Come into the kitchen! I want you to meet the doctor."

Checking his watch, Lynx read the time as 6:30 a.m. He got up and followed Ivan into the kitchen, where he was introduced to two people—first, the doctor: a small man of slight build, five foot six in height, no taller, about 140 pounds, wearing rimless glasses, about thirty-five years old. Ivan introduced him as Dr. Pete. Lynx was to later learn that he was a noted surgeon.

Standing beside him was his nurse whom Lynx was then introduced to, a woman in her early twenties, no name given.

"Come, Mr. Lynx," said Dr. Pete in English with only the slightest trace of an accent, laughing quietly as he spoke. "We are going to make a mould of your face and give you a completely new look. No one will recognize you. I guarantee it."

"What kind of look?" inquired Lynx.

Still chuckling to himself, the doctor replied, "Well, the look of an old woman—say, in her late eighties."

"And how are you going to do that?" inquired Lynx, feeling slightly apprehensive at the prospect.

"It's something new that we have here," replied Dr. Pete. "First, I make a mould of your face and, from the mould, I create a new face for you. We attach it to your face and, before you know it, you are an old woman in a wheelchair." He pointed to a wheelchair sitting in the corner of the room.

The procedure was to start after Lynx and Ivan had breakfasted. While they ate, Dr. Pete mixed a white paste-like material in a sizeable bowl and set it aside at the ready.

When their meal was finished, Dr. Pete's nurse led Lynx to a table where he lay down on his back. She inserted a plug into each nostril and a straw into his mouth. Dr. Pete then spread the white paste over his face and neck and instructed him to lie still for an hour while the paste solidified.

In fact, it was an hour, but it seemed like much longer. Finally, Dr. Pete and his nurse carefully lifted the mould from his face and disappeared into another room. Lynx cleaned his face with some cream and then wiped it with a towel.

Several hours went by while Lynx and Ivan chatted. Ivan outlined the plan for exiting the country. Lynx's delivery package was to be microfilm in a small vial, about an inch in diameter and two inches long. The vial design included a small, internal compartment filled with acid. If the vial was tampered with, the acid would drain into the main compartment and destroy the film. A special tool was needed to open the vial—properly.

Once Dr. Pete started installing Lynx's disguise face, Ivan would pick up the vial, return to pick up Lynx, and the two would board the train heading to the border.

The disguise procedure was soon under way, and Ivan left to pick up the microfilm. He returned an hour later, but Dr. Pete needed more time to complete the look. When he had finally finished, Lynx was amazed at the result. Just as Dr. Pete had promised, there he was, standing in front of a mirror, looking at an old woman who was well into her eighties.

Lynx then put on a long dress that almost touched the floor and sat in the wheelchair. Dr. Pete's nurse added padding around his legs and feet so that they would look swollen. A grey wig was added, then a scarf and a shawl. His shoulder holster was too bulky in its normal location, so he held the Beretta—fully loaded, silencer installed—under his shawl. Lynx was ready.

He and Ivan arrived at the train station in the late afternoon. Ivan pushed the wheelchair towards the checkpoint where two soldiers were checking papers. There were five people standing in line.

When their turn for checking papers arrived, Lynx avoided eye contact with the soldier. Dressed in a Russian military uniform, the soldier spoke in Russian to Ivan who answered in kind. He waved at two soldiers standing near the train, barked some orders, and asked the next person in line for their papers.

The two soldiers came over to the wheelchair, moved it closer to the train, and then lifted it onto the platform between two cars. As one held the car door open, Ivan pushed the wheelchair with Lynx aboard into one of the cars and then into a compartment.

Ivan was chuckling to himself. "Russians are so heartless," he said. "When I told him that my grandmother was going to die, his reply was, 'One less mouth to feed.' That's what that stupid Russian son-of-a-bitch said!"

While Ivan raged on about the Russians in whispered frustration, Lynx quietly harboured his thoughts as he sat in the wheelchair. He contemplated how powerful Ivan was and how happy he was to have him as his travelling companion. He thought, *Ivan could put two or three of those Russians into the hospital with his bare hands in hand-to-hand—or worse—if he wanted to.*

A few minutes later, Ivan had calmed down. The train jerked into action and started to move slowly. Lynx told Ivan that his face was uncomfortable and getting itchy, and Ivan chuckled quietly. His remark lowered the tension.

Then Ivan inexplicably descended into a sullen mood. The two agents did not speak for a good two hours as the train sped down the tracks towards the border.

Finally breaking the silence, Lynx asked Ivan about the man in the church. "He said you killed his partner?"

"Yes. It was about a year ago. My partner and I were chased by the guy we killed last night and another agent. We split up and his partner came after me when I ran into an alley. I hid and waited for him with this," said Ivan, pulling out a nine-inch, double-bladed knife from its sheath, the same as Lynx carried. "Some people call it a stiletto but I call it a death-maker. Now he's with his partner. Good riddance."

Lynx eventually reached the point where he could no longer tolerate the itchiness of the mask. He told Ivan that the mask was just too itchy, and he'd have to take it off.

"Okay, my friend," Ivan said with a smile. Lynx got out of the wheelchair and Ivan said, "I'll get rid of it." He folded up the wheelchair and exited the compartment with it under one arm.

Taking the mask off was no easy task, but Lynx managed to remove it. Then the dress came off, then the padding on his legs. He dug into his kit for a pair of pants and a shirt and changed passports. He opened the window and tossed the mask, the lady's clothes, and the matching passport out the window of the speeding train—now clearly his preferred repository for unwanted garbage. Then he sat down on the compartment seat. A few minutes later, the door opened.

Lynx thought that it was Ivan returning from disposing of the wheelchair. But the face of a Russian soldier wearing a big grin appeared in the door. He had surprised Lynx, and the look on his face telegraphed that message.

The Russian grunted something that Lynx did not understand, but knew instinctively that he was being asked for his passport. Lynx reached into his breast pocket, produced his passport, and still sitting, handed it to him. The Russian officer studied it page by page, and then went back to the first page. His hand slowly went down to his holster.

Before Lynx could react, the Russian had opened the flap on his holster, drawn his pistol, and was pointing it at Lynx, yelling orders in Russian.

Again, not understanding a word but clearly getting the gist of the tirade, Lynx stood up. His mind was racing, running through his options. If he reached for his Beretta, he would be shot. If he tried the "undone shoelace" routine, that too would likely get him shot.

As the officer continued yelling, Ivan appeared behind him in the doorway with his knife raised so that Lynx could see it. With a single strike, the knife disappeared from Lynx's view, the Russian stopped yelling, stiffened, and his mouth opened but no sound came out.

Lynx grabbed the pistol from his hand. The Russian's eyes were still agape as he collapsed to the floor of the compartment.

Ivan quickly entered and closed the door. Lynx immediately checked the collapsed Russian's pulse on the neck artery and found none.

Ivan extracted his knife from the Russian's back and wiped the blood onto the Russian's uniform. He then walked over to the window and opened it. Without asking, Lynx helped him lift the dead Russian into position to be thrown out the window—now *unquestionably* Lynx's favourite garbage repository—of the speeding train.

Lynx looked out and down at the view. They had been crossing a wide river on a bridge high above the water with nothing between the train window and the river below—a perfect disposal location for an unwanted body. It would float down the river without a trace of whence it had come.

Ivan closed the window and the two men sat down in the compartment, facing each other.

"The debt is paid, my friend," said Ivan. "I owed you. The one in the church last night had me cold. This one had you. Now we are even."

The two agents broke into laughter, happy to have found such a clean solution to such a messy problem. They bantered back and forth, Ivan again professing his deeply held hatred of the Russians, the MKGB, and the Russian army. He despised their exploitation of fear, their ruthless suppression of divergent viewpoints, and their iron-fisted approach to control.

Already Lynx had noted a pattern with him. Loose and fun-loving like himself, his mood could quickly change at the mere mention of anything Russian. Lynx pondered quietly to himself, *Ivan has some history that has embedded his hatred of Russians, and some day maybe I'll find out what it is—but not right now.*

The rest of the trip to the border was uneventful. Their papers were checked only once, now a routine. Still puzzled why the Russian had objected to his passport, Lynx handed it to Ivan for examination.

"Well," said Ivan as he looked through the document, "I don't know what it was that got him so excited either, but he paid a price. I was only too happy to charge the price he asked for. It's like I was a vendor, selling death."

Once across the border, Ivan passed the vial to Lynx, asked Lynx to "Say hello to Sir Richard for me,"[23] they shook hands, he wished Lynx good luck, and the two men parted company.

---

23 Sir Richard White, MI-6 Head, 1956-1968.

Lynx went straight to an empty compartment on the Paris-bound train, happy in the thought that this mission—his last—would soon be over. He would deliver the microfilm to Sarge, break the news of his intended retirement from the Service at the debrief. And—the best part—how he and Susan would meet shortly in London and she would later join him in Canada.

The train slowed, stopped, and several people got aboard, including a young woman who opened the door to his compartment. She said something in French that Lynx did not understand, but he presumed that she was asking if the seat in the compartment was taken.

He did not reply, but motioned her to sit down, to which she gave a charming "Merci" reply.

Lynx studied her sitting across from him in the compartment as the train resumed its westward journey. She was in her early twenties, a striking dark-haired beauty, about 100-110 pounds, wearing a long dress that went well down past her knees.

Before long, she spoke again in French, and Lynx still couldn't comprehend. He was a Canadian, of course, and even though one of the languages spoken in his country was French, he spoke only English.

The young lady then launched into a Slavic language; Lynx was not sure which one. Slightly embarrassed, he kept his eyes down to the floor to avoid eye contact, only to have her launch into yet a third language, this time probably Polish. Lynx began to wonder, *Why is she so eager to converse with me?* His suspicion antenna went up, but his built-in alert system remained quiescent, so he was not unduly alarmed.

Then, when she finally blurted out, "Do you speak English?" he was totally taken aback, and absentmindedly replied, "Yes"—even though his desire to converse with her was low.

"Oh, this is good," she continued with a slight accent. "I thought I would have to travel all the way to Paris with no one to talk to. My name is Jezzebel. And yours is?"

"Robert."

"We are acquainted now, yes?" she continued, smiling sweetly.

She was a knockout all right, but Lynx had known many beautiful women—most of them cold-hearted and consequently was wary of getting involved. Besides, he thought, *Susan has happened, and she is cut from a cloth that this chick could only imagine.*

"How far do you travel?" she asked.

Too many questions, thought Lynx. *Why does she want to strike up a conversation so badly with a complete stranger—a man at that—on a train? This is not normal behaviour.*

As she sat waiting for a response, Lynx finally decided to say, "To the next town."

"Oh," she replied, "that is too bad. I had hoped that we could be together longer than that." As she delivered a come-hither smile, she added, "What is the name of the next town?"

That was it. *She has an agenda, and I don't know what it is, so I'm getting out of here,* thought Lynx. Without responding, he promptly picked up his kit bag, opened the door, and closed it behind him without saying a word.

He had to find another compartment. He was already in the last car on the train, so there were plenty to choose from. Two cars up the train, he found a compartment with a priest sitting as its lone occupant.

Lynx motioned at the empty seat in international sign language, asking if it was taken. The priest shook his head as he continued working his way through his rosary beads, looking straight ahead, lips moving, praying in silence.

Lynx put his kit bag down near one end of the seat, intending to use it as a pillow but also facing the door. He sat down a few feet from it, laid his head on the kit bag, and was soon fast asleep.

He slept for six hours. When he opened his eyes, dawn was just emerging, and the priest was now asleep. Feeling hungry, Lynx quietly moved towards the door, picked up his kit bag, left the compartment, and closed the door behind him.

He went to the dining car and ordered bacon, eggs, toast, and coffee in English. The food came and it was delicious—just what he needed.

As he sat digesting the meal and sipping coffee, thoughts of Jezzebel returned. *Why so many questions? Just who was she? Am I getting paranoid?*

When he had finished breakfast, he made his way back to the compartment and the priest was still asleep. Moving cat-like, he re-entered the compartment, sat down, and had soon dozed off. When he awoke, the priest was watching him.

Speaking with a slight accent, the priest asked him in English, "Are you all right?"

"What?" replied Lynx, surprised that here was yet another English-speaking traveller—a French priest, no less.

"A while ago, you were asleep and dreaming, and you spoke in English. That is why I asked if you are all right."

"Yes. I'm all right," replied a startled Lynx. "I didn't know that you could speak English."

"Oh, yes. I speak five languages."

Now feeling uncomfortable again, Lynx started weighing the situation. He started wondering, *Am I experiencing the usual mixture of randomly picked compartmental companions, or are they agents of another organization who are onto me? Maybe I should move to another compartment.*

As he sat there studying the priest, he called upon his observational skills, thinking *He could be a priest. His shoes are old and scuffed. When he was sleeping, I noticed a hole in the sole of one. His hair is long, going grey. He wears a priest's hat with a brim, old and well used. His open jacket reveals a priest's collar. It is also old, soiled, and unkempt.*

If he's not a priest, Lynx concluded, *whoever dressed him up knew what they were doing. Hell, he's a priest. He* has *to be a priest. Everything says that he's a priest. I'm just getting overly paranoid.*

Finally sucking up his paranoia, Lynx almost blurted out, "Father, are you hungry?"

"Yes. But that's all right. I'm used to that."

"Let's go down to the dining car. I'll buy you breakfast."

"Thank you, young man. But you don't have to do that."

"I want to," he insisted. The priest's thin, almost malnourished frame now preyed on Lynx's conscience.

"All right. I'll accept your kind offer."

In the dining car, Lynx ordered the priest the same breakfast he had just eaten, along with a coffee for himself to sip while the priest ate. When the food arrived and was placed before him, the priest closed his eyes and gave thanks for his food.

Now Lynx was certain that he was a real priest. His mood eased, and any residual tension he was feeling evaporated.

"You're not eating?" he inquired of Lynx.

"I ate earlier while you were sleeping," he replied.

"I heard nothing. Where are you from?"

"North America," replied Lynx, thinking, *That was a sufficiently vague answer.*

"I've never been there. Which city?"

"A small town on the west coast," he lied.

"Then you're a long way from home."

"Yes."

When he had wiped his plate clean, he sat back in his chair and pronounced that the meal was "delicious. Young man, I thank you for your kindness."

"Where are you going, Father?" inquired Lynx.

"Austria. I'm a monk in a monastery in West Austria."

Lynx would be spending the next two days aboard the train. At least he could count on unthreatening company for the next few hours.

After they had made their way back to their compartment, Lynx asked, "What is your name, Father?"

"Cadieux. I'm Father Cadieux."

"You're French?"

"Yes. I was born in a small town near Paris."

When the train lurched, Lynx's kit bag fell off the seat and when he bent over to retrieve it, his jacket opened, exposing his holstered Beretta. Father Cadieux spotted the gun, and a look of surprise came over his face.

"You carry a gun?" he asked.

"Yes, Father Cadieux. I do."

"Are you a criminal or a robber?"

"No."

"Well then, why do you carry a weapon?"

"Father Cadieux, I am sorry that you have seen my gun, but I'm not a robber. I carry it for protection," which—in an odd sort of way—was true.

"Perhaps you are a policeman?" he continued.

"No, I'm not. Look, Father, the best thing to do is to forget that you saw my gun. It's better that you know nothing more," which, too, was true. Lynx felt a little pride at having answered the priest's questions so honestly—vaguely, but honestly. Lying to a priest would somehow seem more sinful than lying to an everyday Joe, even though Lynx was not a Catholic.

"I see," replied the priest, giving Lynx an icy stare. "You are into something that you obviously want to keep secret, and I will ask no more about it. All right then, young man, what is your name?"

"Robert. Robert Hammond."

"Very well, Robert. What shall we talk about? How is your soul with God? How do you feel about God?" he smiled as he finished the question, now into territory in which he was most comfortable.

"I don't think much about God, Father Cadieux. In my life, there isn't much time to think about God."

"Into which religion were you born?"

"Protestant. My mother took me to church regularly when I was a boy."

"Was she religious?"

"Very."

"Are you married?"

"I was. I'm now separated."

"Any children?"

"Yes," replied Lynx, the questioning now getting a little too close for comfort. "Father Cadieux, no more questions, please."

"Just one more. Do you believe in God?"

"Yes," replied Lynx, thinking about the Russian agents he had killed, the Thou-shalt-not-kill commandment, and how he would one day seek forgiveness for that.

"Your mother taught you that?"

"Yes, but let's change the subject. Believe me father, it would be better for both of us."

That did it. Father Cadieux finally let the subject drop, asked no further questions, and the two travellers explored all manner of subjects for the next few hours. Lynx found out that the priest was a humble, well-educated man. He had graduated from a university in Paris and held three degrees.

When lunchtime came, they ate together. Father Cadieux was travelling without food or money, causing Lynx to wonder, *How long has it been since this man of God—in his sixties—has eaten?*

When the time came for the priest to get off the train, the two men stood in the compartment facing one another. The priest placed his left hand on Lynx's forehead while he made the sign of the cross with his right. Speaking in Latin, the priest blessed Lynx, who found the gesture uplifting.

It was 10:00 p.m. local time, and Lynx walked with the priest to the platform between two cars. The priest took his hand and held it.

"Mr. Hammond, may the Lord be with you. I think there is much danger ahead for you. Be careful, my son."

"Father Cadieux, I have enjoyed our conversation. Thank you for your blessing."

"Robert, thank you for your kindness to an old man," said the priest as he stepped off the platform of the stopped train and disappeared into the night.

Lynx watched him go, turned, and went back to his compartment. There was still a long way to travel.

Lynx got comfortable in his compartment, and was enjoying the solitude and cozy warmth of the cubicle. He didn't want to remove his jacket because that would require hiding the Beretta in his kit bag. Lowering the window slightly would decrease the temperature inside the compartment. He got up to do that, but had forgotten to lock the compartment door and had his back to it.

Too late. The next thing he heard was "Robert! Don't make any fast moves. I have a gun on you."

He recognized the voice immediately. It was Jezzebel. Lynx began turning to face her as slowly and deliberately as possible so as to not trigger any panic moves. He could see that she had a small automatic trained on him. Gone was whatever striking beauty had been there earlier, now replaced by a revulsive scowl.

"Robert or Lynx, whatever your name is, all I want is the microfilm. Don't try anything funny. I will shoot, and if I may say so, I am a very good shot with a pistol."

Lynx, his mind racing, trying to understand how she would know his code name, looking for openings, playing it cool, simply replied, "Jezzebel, I have no idea what you are talking about."

"Don't move, you English pig," she continued, switching into her normal Russian accent. "We are going to leave the train. You are my prisoner. We are going back to the Ukraine. Where is the microfilm? Where is it, pig?"

"Jezzebel, I have no microfilm," stated Lynx as calmly and matter-of-factly as he could, now facing her fully. Lynx focused on the gun held in her left hand as he contemplated the question, *How will I get that weapon away from her?*

Screaming at the top of her voice in the closed compartment, she roared, "No more talk, Lynx. I want that microfilm. Now!"

Suddenly the train lurched unexpectedly as it was in the process of decelerating—the opening Lynx had been looking for. In a flash of calculated action, he made his move.

A full half second before she could react, Lynx had grabbed the gun in his right hand while she was still off-balance from the lurch of the train. Now with his adrenaline at full throttle and in a most ungentlemanly manoeuvre, he slammed the open palm of his left hand into her jaw, delivering more power than a clenched fist. It hit her like a baseball bat, and she went down.

Her eyes rolled and she was dazed, but she seemed to bounce back. Amazingly, she managed to kick Lynx in the leg, knocking him off-balance. Her little automatic that Lynx had grabbed only a second before flew out of his hand and slid on the floor into one corner of the compartment.

Realizing immediately that Jezzebel was highly trained in self-defence, Lynx knew that his life depended on keeping her on the floor.

Calling his own self-defence training into action, as quickly as he could and in rapid succession, he got into position to put his right arm around the left side of her neck, grabbed her right arm, lifted it over her head, placed his left arm on the right side of her neck, and locked his two arms together. He had her in a "no escape" hold.

The karate Master Yamoto had taught him well. Applying the pressure causes the victim to lose consciousness in about nine seconds. Death will ensue if the pressure is prolonged.

Feeling the pain, Jezzebel screamed, "You English pig! Let me go! I'll kill you! Let me go!"

Well, this was precisely why Lynx would *not* let her go.

She tried punching Lynx with her one free hand while kicking with both feet, but Lynx clearly had the upper hand.

She was a Russian agent. She knew his code name. She had seen his face. That left only one option. Sarge's "direction" flashed through his mind—Jezzebel had to die.

Suddenly the door to the compartment opened. The conductor stuck his head in and said something in French.

As he held Jezzebel in his clutches, Lynx shouted at him, "In English, please!"

"Okay, then. What are you doing to that young woman, monsieur?"

"Get this English pig off of me!" screamed Jezzebel.

"She tried to rob me," said Lynx, still holding her on the floor.

The conductor came into the compartment and picked up her pistol off the floor. "You say she tried to rob you?"

"That's what I said. Yes, she did," said Lynx, maintaining his hold on her.

"This is her purse?" asked the conductor as he picked it up and emptied its contents onto the seat. "What is this?" he asked quizzically as he picked up three passports on the seat.

He examined each of the passports, said something in French, looked down at Jezzebel, and stated in his finest but practiced English-with-a-French-spice, "Madam, you are under arrest. Monsieur, let her go. She is now in my custody."

Lynx released the young woman and the conductor took her by the arm. Strangely, she didn't resist, and went quietly.

"Please, monsieur, follow me. I have to take you both to the Chief Conductor."

The threesome—Lynx, Jezzebel, and the conductor—walked down the train corridor through car after car until they finally reached the Chief Conductor's office. A ten-minute conversation in French ensued. All the while Jezzebel was pointing at Lynx, shouting repeatedly, "He's a spy! He's a spy!"

Finally the Chief Conductor approached Lynx. "Your passport, sir, if you please," he asked of Lynx.

Lynx passed it to him. He leafed through it and asked, "You are with the British Diplomatic Corps?"

"Yes, sir."

"And your name is Robert Hammond?"

"Yes, it is," replied Lynx, holding his breath in case something untoward should surface. Jezzebel, now being held by the train security was not resisting arrest, *a good thing*, thought Lynx—because she could give them serious grief. Unconstrained, she was capable of strategically placed karate kicks that would instantly qualify any male recipient for the soprano section of a choir.

"Mr. Hammond, you say this woman tried to rob you. She says that you are a spy. We don't believe her. She has three different passports from three different countries in her possession which is a felony, and for which we will be turning her over to the police. You, sir, may continue your trip. I am sorry for any inconvenience you may have experienced."

Lynx took a deep breath of relief as he returned to his compartment and sat down. The microfilm was still safely held in a hidden pocket. Thinking, *I, too, am in possession of a few different passports, and fortunately they didn't check that out. If they had, I would be under arrest alongside Jezzebel. She'll be in their custody, say, two or three days, by which time I will be back in London. But she knew my code name, and now has seen my face. Sarge is not going to be happy with this development. He has a leak—and he'd better get it fixed!*

Killing a male enemy agent was one thing, but killing a female agent—even if she was a Russian MKGB agent—was another matter. It was purely psychological, but nevertheless, another matter. Just one more dimension to the spy agency business that Lynx was liking less and less.

Shortly after, the train made an extended stop. Lynx guessed it was to wait for a police pick-up of Jezzebel. That took her out of the equation—for the moment—but who knows where or when she'd turn up again?

According to the plan, Lynx would to get off the train about twenty miles outside of Paris, in a small town for pick-up, and that would be the end of the mission. That juncture was still a day and a half away. All he did for the intervening time was eat and sleep, alone in his compartment aside from going to the dining car.

In the quietude of his compartment, he studied the map of his pick-up point intently. He memorized the names of the towns in the area and focused on not missing his stop.

At his designated stop, twenty miles outside Paris, Lynx stood between two cars and the train slowed down. It looked like clear sailing from here on to London. *Perhaps Susan will already be there in London, waiting for me,* he thought.

It was 5:30 a.m., and the sun was rising in the east as the train came to a full stop. Lynx stepped down onto the station platform. He looked for the gap between two buildings as noted in his instructions and headed for it. The parking lot where a car waited should be behind the left-hand building.

He quickly spotted the designated black car, one of only five cars in the lot, confirmed that there was no one in sight, and moved to the left front fender. The key was sitting on top of the left front tire, just as his instructions from Sarge had said.

Lynx slid his kit bag into the front seat on the passenger's side, adjusted the seat, started the engine, and backed the car out of its parking spot. It was a right-hand drive, an embassy car, made in

Britain of course. Lynx was unsure initially which side of the road to drive on, and a few oncoming cars giving blasts on the horn soon convinced him that the right-hand side of the road was the correct one. It felt strange to be driving down the road with the shoulder whizzing by in a blur below his elbow.

He navigated the few streets between him and the road to Paris based on his memorization of the map, and he made it onto the road to Paris without incident.

The time had advanced to 6:00 a.m., and he was well on his way. *Twenty miles to go*, he thought.

He suddenly realized that there was a blue car in his rear-view mirror. His stomach gave a twitch—that "something's wrong" feeling again, when he least needed it. He could see in the rear-view mirror that there were four men in a car—a smaller, left-hand drive European car—a short distance behind. He sped up. They sped up. He slowed down. They slowed down.

Dammit! Jezzebel must have gotten the word out that she hadn't been able to intercept me, thought Lynx. *No choice but to keep moving.*

Then the blue car tried to pass him. Thinking, *If they get out in front, they will be able to stop me,* Lynx floored the gas pedal and the driver of the blue car did the same. The blue car, now in the left-hand passing lane, was keeping pace with Lynx in the right-hand lane. The two cars were speeding down the roadway, almost side by side with no oncoming traffic in sight.

As the blue car sped up again, this time right alongside Lynx, he spotted a gun in one man's hand.

Lynx touched the brakes. The blue car moved ahead a fraction of a car-length, giving the gunman no time to aim his weapon. Lynx turned his steering wheel hard to the left towards the blue car, now just slightly ahead of him and braced for the impact. As his front left fender caught the rear of the smaller French car, his much heavier British car caused the rear of their car to skid slightly to the left.

Now in continuous contact with their car, Lynx continued to apply pressure by turning his steering wheel even harder left, causing their car to skid further sideways and his own front wheels to also skid slightly. Lynx's car was now pushing hard against theirs as they sped down the road in continuous contact. Once again, Lynx was *Bullitt's* Steve McQueen, reliving his stock car days.

The driver of the blue car lost control, whereupon Lynx relaxed his steering wheel and pulled ahead of the blue car as it started fishtailing from one side of the road to the other. The fishtailing worsened with each successive swerve, and finally, after a few swings back and forth, it veered off into the ditch.

Lynx watched in his rear-view mirror as long as he could and couldn't see anyone climb out of the car. He had sustained enough damage to the front left fender of his own car that the police would easily spot it and, of course, have questions.

A few minutes later, he passed through a small town at slow speed and spotted a garage. *Probably one that could fix bent front fenders,* he thought. Lynx stopped, went back to it, and found the owner just opening the place up for the day's business.

He said something in French that, as usual, Lynx could not understand. Lynx pointed at his badly bent front fender, pulled out a roll of large designation French francs that would have choked a horse, and started peeling them off, one by one. The obvious message was, "Fix this, and these are yours."

The garage owner's eyes opened wide, and he nodded his head eagerly in acknowledgement that he knew what Lynx wanted: Yes, he would fix the fender.

Just then, a woman of voluptuous proportions wandered by, evidently closing down business after a slow night. Hoping to participate in the action, she could smell easy money and offered her services. She said something incomprehensible to Lynx in French, and her message was clear—made even more explicit as she pulled up her mini-skirt, already so short as to be scarcely classifiable as a skirt at all, exposing virtually her full upper leg almost to the point of revealing her crotch.

The mechanic smiled at Lynx and raised his eyebrows as she continued to proposition Lynx. He rejected her repeatedly, saying "No! No! Not now!"

The woman persisted, trying to get Lynx to follow her—to somewhere.

Lynx attempted to let her down easily. He spoke to her as politely as he could in the circumstances, saying, "Look, lady, I'm just too busy right now to go anywhere with you."

In the exact reverse of what he intended, she extracted fresh energy from his statement, perhaps thinking they may be converging on a basis to do business. She gamely attempted to keep things moving forward, responding, "Oh! You . . . speak. . . H'englayze! I . . . speak. . . H'englayze!"

To complicate matters, a police car was now cruising by, eyeing Lynx's damaged front fender. His already high anxiety level went even higher. Desperate to move forward with the repair of his fender, Lynx handed the woman a handful of large denomination French francs from his considerable supply, saying simply, "Here!"

She smiled broadly through her overdone lipstick, responded, "Merci," turned, and sashayed off down the street.

The mechanic waved Lynx into his garage and started to repair the damaged fender. By 10:30 a.m., it was fixed—not a perfect job, but more importantly, the damage was concealed. Lynx handed the mechanic a good wad of francs that he took gratefully. Several "Mercis" were spoken alternately by each man in a two-way, one-word conversation, the same word being repeated at least twice by each party. Without further ceremony, Lynx got in the car and drove off towards Paris.

In the Paris suburb designated in his instructions, there was a small hotel with Room 217 already booked under the name of Robert Hammond. Lynx picked up the key at the front desk. He intended to be there just long enough to change clothes.

He went up to the room and there, as organized by Sarge, was a Canadian military uniform in the closet. Lynx promptly put it on. As instructed, he left all unneeded passports and other papers in the room for someone to pick up later—as well as the car, which he left parked in the hotel lot. Lynx also left his Beretta and knife in his kit bag in the room, as there was no need to be armed from this point on.

He dropped the room key at the front desk and stepped out onto the street. He walked past the parking lot, only to sight two men, one sporting a bandage over his right ear—probably Russian agents from the blue pursuit car episode—standing beside the black car Lynx had left parked there.

They, of course, had no idea what he looked like. Jezzebel had probably found a way to alert them that she had been unable to intercept Lynx. She, of course, would have recognized him immediately —but she was now in police custody.

Walking down the sidewalk whistling the tune *Goodnight Irene*, Lynx hailed a cab and instructed the driver with a single word: "Orly."

"The airport it is," replied the driver, looking at Lynx in his rear-view mirror. "Canadian?"

"Yes," replied Lynx. After all, he was wearing a Canadian military uniform.

"I used to live in Pittsburgh," volunteered the driver, and the conversation proceeded from there. He had been in the American army and came to France after being discharged five years earlier. He had stayed there ever since, "loving every minute of it."

Lynx checked his wristwatch as he got out of the cab at the airport: 12:15 p.m. In forty-five minutes, a Canadian four-engine aircraft would land and Lynx would step aboard for the flight to London, his mission completed.

At precisely 1:00 p.m., right on schedule, a big Argus aircraft taxied up to the terminal, shut down its engines, opened its cargo door, and Lynx climbed aboard. He settled into a seat, the engines were restarted, and in a matter of minutes, he was aloft, bound for London as the sole passenger. The crew went about executing their duties, and no one spoke to him for the entire flight.

When the aircraft landed in London, a black car was waiting. A Secret Service agent got out and asked Lynx if he was Robert Hammond.

When Lynx replied in the affirmative, he asked Lynx to follow him to the black car. Lynx got in, the agent got into the passenger side of the front seat, and after an hour's drive, they stopped in front of yet another big grey brick house.

"Maurice is waiting inside," said the agent, as Lynx got out of thc car.

Lynx went through the front door, closed it behind him, and there was Sarge standing beside an open door, just down the hallway.

"Good to see you, Laddie," he said, pausing for just a second before asking, "Got the film?"

"Yes," replied Lynx as they entered the room and he placed the vial into Sarge's waiting hand.

"Much trouble?"

"You won't believe what I've been through, Sarge," replied Lynx,..

"Well, then, let's get on with the debriefing, shall we?" he said, placing the tape recorder on the table and hitting the "Record" button.

Lynx started relating events since he had left Sarge in Paris, omitting the parts about his relationship with Susan—for now. When he reached the part where the Russian soldier had her on her knees, her hands tied behind her back, Sarge shut down the tape recorder.

"With the recorder off, tell me what happened, Laddie," he said. Lynx later thought, *Why was Sarge interested in that particular detail? Is he perverted?*

Lynx described how the Russian was about to commit an unwelcome sexual act, and how he had then inserted his knife in the precise location to deliver the most efficient result.

Satisfied, Sarge turned the tape recorder back on.

Sarge stopped the recorder again when the church scene was reached; then he stopped the recorder a third time when Lynx was describing Jezzebel's appearance in Lynx's compartment with her gun.

Here, Lynx wanted to make sure that Sarge got the message. "Sarge, she was a Russian agent who knew my code name—and of course, she saw my face. At great length. You have a leak!"

"She's dead, I hope," interjected Sarge.

"No, Sarge, she's alive and presently in the custody of the French police—unless her organization has managed to spring her out, a possibility I wouldn't rule out. She didn't resist arrest in the slightest when she was turned over to the French police. The way things are unfolding with the leak situation we have on our hands, nothing would surprise me. And we do have one, Sarge—maybe more than one."

This had clearly started to worry Sarge. Lynx assured him that he couldn't have done anything differently to get rid of her. Unless, of course, he had known that she was a Russian agent from the beginning—just as she evidently knew that he (Lynx) was on the other side.

After Sarge's usual second-guessing, they went through the entire debrief again, this time without any tape turn-offs.

"What's done is done," mused Sarge as he passed Lynx his airline ticket home.

When Lynx informed Sarge that he was going to stay at the Cumberland Hotel for a few days, Sarge asked with a smile, "Oh, really. Who are you seeing?"

"Susan," came Lynx's one-word reply, having decided that he might as well tell him now.

Suddenly taking on a sombre air, Sarge invited Lynx to "sit down a minute, Laddie. I've something to tell you."

Sarge's tone caused Lynx to brace himself mentally. Sarge came around the table and sat down beside him.

"Susan's dead, Laddie," Sarge said simply.

Lynx was stunned. He couldn't speak for the better part of a minute. He fought back the tears, and was finally able to get out the word "How?"

"She made contact successfully in Moscow and went to the designated house to retrieve the microfilm, but the house was under surveillance. She got into a gunfight with three Russian agents, and she killed two of them before the third one shot her. I'm so sorry, Laddie. Better tell me about the two of you."

Lynx levelled totally with Sarge—how they had fallen for each other, their intention of ending their espionage careers after this last mission, how they would live together in Canada—the whole story, sobbing his way from aspect to aspect, the floodgates wide open.

Sarge placed his hand on Lynx's shoulder and offered him a drink. Wiping the tears from his face, he accepted. Sarge poured him one that Lynx almost quaffed in a single gulp. It helped with the pain, so he had another. This time he nursed it a little, but still it went down much faster than usual.

"Susan was a wonderful woman," said Sarge somewhat wistfully. "I have known her for a long time, and she will be greatly missed. But then, romance has no place in this business—it's something we discourage at every turn."

Lynx had only the two drinks. He headed for Heathrow and his flight back home in a state of total dejection—feeling as if his life, his plans, and his future were now shattered, destroyed beyond all retrieval. *How could there be hope?* he wondered, as he now faced the prospect of reverting to the lonely world of the espionage agent on an open-ended basis—and no one to share it with.

With Susan gone, the thought of ending his relationship with Sarge never crossed Lynx's mind.

Chapter Six: **Operation Spearhead**

It was 1965, and Lawrence was lost. He was living in Toronto, working at de Havilland, and had separated from Elsie the year before (1964). His children were still living in a foster home in Wyevale, Ontario. He had difficulty sleeping and when he was able to, nightmares occurred regularly. Invariably, he would wake up screaming, and in a sweat. He would quickly realize that it had all been a nightmare, but each one felt real and painful. PTSD had settled into a regular, embedded pattern.

Wary of taking pills or other medication, he thought his only refuge was the bottle, rum in particular—not daily, but almost. He tried to lead a normal life, still doing aircraft engine work and immersed in the wonders of de Havilland's merchandise—which seemed to be the main anchor to retaining his sanity.

A few empty months went by after his return from Beslan. One afternoon, he stopped at a small restaurant for a coffee and a doughnut. The only person in the restaurant was behind the counter. He ordered a coffee, she poured it with a smile, and they engaged in friendly conversation. Her name was Paula, a single mom with a daughter, separated from her husband. Lynx could feel a chemistry building between them, and he asked to see her again. She agreed, and they soon became an item. They went dancing, to the theatre, and drive-in movies together. Paula had soon become a factor in keeping Lawrence sober. He felt that she was becoming a substitute for Susan, and found himself falling for her.

Try as he might, he could not behave like a regular, everyday person, knowing that Sarge might contact him at any moment and request another mission. He now knew in no uncertain terms that his double life was not normal. He realized that he had developed a resignation-to-reality philosophy insofar as his MI-6 involvement went. It was like he like he was on a train, going down the tracks, verging on the out-of-control, and he might as well enjoy the ride. There was no denying that the danger inherent in MI-6 work was exciting. One marriage had already failed, the secrecy of unexplained absences being a prime cause—but that was just the price of doing business. If Sarge contacted him for another mission, would he be able to resist the temptation? He simply didn't know.

A few months after they started seeing each other, Paula announced that she was pregnant, and they got an apartment together.

Then, a few months later, Sarge showed up again. Lawrence started to look at his MI-6 boss a little askance, and realized that time was taking its toll. Now well into in his late forties, Sarge's hair was thinning on top. When they had met in 1952, it had been dark. It was now a salt-and-pepper grey. He stood about five foot six and weighed about 160 pounds. He had been a Regimental Sergeant Major, and still had the swagger of one. He could still shout orders and, when necessary, go into an outrage with the best of them, delivering the volume of a bull moose. And despite his many moods and imperfections, deep down, Lawrence admired him.

It had been several months since the Beslan mission and the unforgettable Susan episode; Sarge opened the conversation with that subject. He started by expressing his regrets that things had not worked out for them. Lynx played it cool. But when Sarge pressed him for details on how close they had gotten, Lynx cut off the conversation cold turkey; the memories were just too painful. Besides, he was now with Paula, and she had become an adequate substitute—and "adequate" was the word. At that time, Lynx felt that no one would ever be able to match Susan as a soul mate, if for no other reason than she understood the realities of MI-6 work.

Lynx did not mention Paula to Sarge. He wanted Lynx to go on yet another training exercise—to an army base for weapons refresher training, including an exercise to build up resistance should he be captured by the Russians—perhaps anticipating a need. It was 1966.

Lynx agreed to the exercise. Sarge made the necessary arrangements with de Havilland and promptly took him to Camp Borden for the week. As soon as he entered camp, Lynx was met by four men in Russian military dress. They grabbed him, put him in behind-the-back handcuffs, and dragged him into a bare room. It had no windows, no furniture, and no blankets—nothing but a naked light bulb hanging from the ceiling. That light bulb would be left on for the next three and a half days.

The exercise started immediately. They wanted to know who he was, what was he doing here, who did he work for, and why was he here? When he repeatedly replied Robert Hammond and gave a fake ID number but told then nothing more, they slapped him around for the rest of the day, the entire interrogation peppered with profanities. Then, when he mistakenly gave them a different ID number, they intensified the abuse. Exhausted, his memory started to lapse and to this day he still does not remember much of what happened from then on. Sleep deprivation continued for three more days as they tried to break him down. At one stage, Lynx almost lost it and nearly hit the leader with what could have been a fatal blow. The exercise had almost gotten out of hand.

When Sarge showed up, the exercise ended. Lynx took a shower and got dressed in civvies. After dinner with the exercise team, Lynx went drinking with them and the leader told him that what he had experienced would be mild compared to what the Russians would do in actuality.

On his return from the exercise, Paula, of course, wanted to know where he had been. He concocted a cockamamie story, the first of a series that eventually drove Paula back to her husband.

In June 1966, Paula gave birth to Kate, Lawrence's second daughter. Paula never prevented Lawrence from seeing his new child, but that simply added yet another complication to his already complicated life.

Lawrence stayed in touch with Paula, but the magic in their relationship had evaporated over his unexplained absences. Other women—mostly one-night stands—re-entered the picture and his booze consumption went up.

As the next six months unfolded, Lynx started having health problems. His nerves started acting up. He drank too much and Sarge made contact several times, probably sensing that he was in danger of losing one of his crack espionage couriers.

Sarge appeared in the spring of 1967, and—again having made the necessary leave of absence arrangements with de Havilland—he took Lynx off into the woods north of Trenton for a two-week retreat, complete with map, compass, and provisions. Sarge's purpose was to dry him out and refresh his survival skills. He would drop Lynx off at some untoward location, give him a target return time—typically two or three days—and await his arrival back at their camp. Despite his age and without exception, Lynx excelled at these exercises. By the time he went back to work at de Havilland, he could sense his old self returning.

About three months later, Sarge appeared out of nowhere, and that very Centennial (1967) summer night, Lynx and Sarge were aboard a flight bound for England. Sarge had made all the necessary arrangements with de Havilland. When Sarge had put the question, Lynx could hardly wait to get on board, his borderline, out-of-control train ready—once again—to go down the tracks. As he sat winging his way across the Atlantic, prepared to re-enter the frenzied world of espionage and put his skills back to work, Lynx still had no idea what this next assignment would be.

Awaiting the pre-mission briefing, Lynx sat in a London pub sipping rum while Sarge, as usual, sipped water. Sarge was tense but somewhat talkative, and he told Lynx that he suspected a mole was on the loose in his organization.

Wisely, Lynx just sat silently and listened. *Didn't I uncover evidence of that on his last three missions—Prague, Poland, and Russia?* he thought pensively. *Russian agents had been everywhere on all three missions. And that information had been duly relayed back to Sarge. Was he only now, nine years since my Czech mission, waking up?*

Lynx considered Sarge to be a bulldog, relentless in the pursuit of any objective he aimed at. *But he was slow off the mark on this one*, he thought. Sarge implied that he had been losing men at an alarming rate, and cautioned Lynx almost as if he fully expected enemy agents to intercept the mission.

"Trust that feeling that you get, Laddie. It's kept you out of trouble several times now. You'll need it more than ever for what's coming up," he warned Lynx.

Foregoing the hood this time, a few minutes later, Lynx and Sarge met with six army officers. One of the officers called the meeting to order and turned the chair over to "Sir Richard."[24]

He simply invited Sarge to lead the briefing. Sarge stood up and started in: "Gentlemen. This operation is called Operation Spearhead, to retrieve microfilm from Poland—Warsaw, specifically. The papers in front of you include all the necessary detail and the pick-up points. My agent, Lynx here, will be taken by submarine to the designated point on your maps, take a train to Warsaw, pick up the vial of microfilm, and exit the country."

One of the officers interrupted. "Sir, Major Austin here. How is he to come out of the country?"

"I know who you are, Major Austin. That has already been predetermined between Lynx and myself," replied Sarge.

Appealing to the chair, the Major persisted, "Sir Richard. This is a briefing for an army operation. We need to know the method of extraction of this courier from the country."

"Major Austin," replied Sarge, picking up his papers from the desk and placing them back down. "It is my privilege to inform you that,

---

24 Sir Richard (Dick) White, head of MI-6 from 1956 to 1968.

what my courier does or doesn't do—how he travels, exactly where he goes, and such details—are at my discretion, and my discretion alone."

Major Austin was visibly upset, almost sputtering. "This is highly irregular, sir. Highly irregular," he said, and then sat down. The tension level in the room was rising. The officers started exchanging uneasy looks.

Sarge was getting angry, his face reddened like Lynx had seen it many times. This time it was a little deeper shade of red than average.

Continuing, Sarge simply finished the briefing with, "All right then. Lynx leaves at 2100 hours on the submarine. The operation is a go. "

Taking Lynx by the arm, they exited the room and proceeded directly to the boat docks, Sarge talking into his ear as they went. "Keep your wits about you, Laddie. You will meet the submarine in the North Sea. A speed boat is waiting to take you to it." He passed Lynx a letter to be opened later. "This gives you further instructions Be particularly careful at the first pick-up point. It's right in the centre of Warsaw. I've taken every precaution I can, but the going could get tough."

Then he went into a deep silence for the rest of the trip to the dock, almost sulking.

Lynx sat thinking, still taken aback by the last few minutes of the pre-mission briefing. *Something is bothering Sarge,* he thought. *Major Austin—who had ignited Sarge at the last pre-mission briefing—had made him angry. Sarge is a perfectionist, and Major Austin was questioning him a little too much about his plan.*

Lynx picked up his kit bag containing his 9-mm. Beretta, knife, small .25-calibre, five-shot automatic, passports, and everything else he would need for the four-day trip into Poland. Sarge had seen to that.

Kit bag in hand, Lynx stood on the dock. They shook hands, Sarge got back into the car, Lynx got aboard the speedboat, its engines roared to life, and the moorings were cast off. A sailor took Lynx below to stow his kit bag and his fifth mission was under way.

The speedboat was fast, but they had a long way to go. Once they were under way, the skipper informed Lynx that they would be rendezvousing with the submarine in the Baltic, not the North Sea.

Strange, thought Lynx. *Why not the North Sea, like Sarge had said?*

When the waves got bigger, the bouncing of the boat precluded any sleep during the crossing. It slammed into one wave after another, until finally the helmsman cut back the throttle slightly. The bouncing eased, but still not sufficiently to permit sleep.

Below deck, Lynx took a seat at a table for what seemed like hours, when suddenly, the bouncing ceased completely. Lynx went up on deck to see what was happening. The sea was now calm, the sky brighter, and the engines were put back at full throttle. It was 4:00 a.m., and the sun was rising in the east. With the throttle full open, the speedboat was almost flying low.

"How much farther to the Baltic?" Lynx asked the captain, who had taken the wheel.

"Your boss wanted me to rendezvous with the sub an hour ago, but it'll be another hour before we reach the submarine," came the answer.

Why did Sarge want me there so quickly? wondered Lynx. *There must be some mistake. Sarge said we would rendezvous with the submarine in the North Sea. Now the captain is—again—telling me the rendezvous will take place in the Baltic Sea. Sarge was purposely misleading someone. What gives?*

Lynx decided to go below and open Sarge's letter.

It began:

> Lynx,
>
> If Point A is blocked, go to Point B. I suspect the KGB will be watching and waiting at Point A. The location of Point B is hidden in the margin of this note. Use a match to reveal it.
>
> Good luck,
> Sarge

What the hell? thought Lynx. *Sarge suspects someone of being a mole, and is using me as bait. This sounds like he knows that Point A will be intercepted.*

Lynx now knew that this mission—his fifth—was going to l snags. The first four hadn't exactly been smooth sailing. Not them had gone off without a hitch, and now here he was with this one on his hands, complications a virtual certainty.

By nightfall, the speedboat had reached the waiting submarine and pulled alongside. Using long poles with fittings attached to their ends, sailors held the speedboat clear of the sub while Lynx jumped onto its deck. Seconds later, the speedboat had disappeared into the black of night.

The trip in the submarine was a short one—a mere six hours. Lynx was told to get ready to disembark as the vessel surfaced. On the submarine deck, two sailors held a small inflatable steady while Lynx got in, and then they jumped in and headed towards the Polish beach.

Five minutes later, Lynx was standing ashore, watching the small inflatable disappear into the darkness. It was 2:00 a.m. Polish time. He turned and started walking inland.

The surroundings looked familiar. *Could it be the same place I landed in 1962 on the Petroff mission?* he wondered. As he looked around at a few landmarks, which were only visible as outlines in the darkness, he concluded that it was. Taking a reading from his compass, he determined that he was heading south and knew—from his prior visit—that it would lead to a road. Four minutes later, he reached the road, turned left onto it, and continued walking towards a small village where he, again, knew he could catch a train to Warsaw.

He walked down the road for about an hour and could see lights coming from a village up ahead. He started looking for a place where he could spend the day out of sight. According to the train schedule that Sarge had included in his pack, the next train would not leave until 9:00 p.m. the next evening.

He reached a bridge over a small stream with trees and brush along its banks. Underneath the bridge and its immediate surroundings would be a good place to lay low for the day. Picking a spot beside a large tree, he set down his kit bag, took out his weaponry, and put it on, not knowing when it might be needed.

By this time it was well past 3:00 a.m., and Lynx hadn't slept for several hours. He sat down against the tree so that the brush around its trunk provided good cover and was soon fast asleep.

He went into a dream almost immediately. He imagined that he was in a gravel pit with large, earth-moving machinery—diggers, backhoes, bulldozers, earth-movers, and big trucks—that were all around him in the dark. The bottom of the gravel pit was six inches deep in mud, and he was lost. He was all alone and couldn't find a way out.

He suddenly awoke with a start, shook his head trying to clear his mind, and realized that he had been dreaming. His PTSD demons were playing games again.

Then he could hear giggling coming from behind him—now clearly not a dream. Without making a sound, he peered out from behind the tree to see two young girls walking down a path, talking and laughing as they skipped merrily along. He watched as they disappeared from sight and glanced at his watch. It was 7:15 a.m. and, now with the benefit of daylight, he looked around and confirmed that he had selected a good hiding place.

Lynx was thirsty, and there was a small stream only about ten feet away. It was a good five feet wide and fast running. He spotted a discarded beer bottle, took it to the water's edge, and washed it out. Satisfied that it was clean enough, he filled it with water, smelled it, confirmed that it had no odour, and drank his fill. He went back to his hiding place by the tree, arranged his kit bag as a pillow, and fell asleep.

When he awoke, it was 11:30 a.m., and now he was hungry. He took some rations out of his kit bag and washed them down—terrible tasting as they were—with plenty of water. He still had about nine hours to kill before the train would depart and hunkered down to do it, counting only three additional people—two women and one man—that passed along the nearby path over the course of the afternoon.

All day long, he could hear trains coming and going, off somewhere in the distance.

At about 6:00 p.m., with only three hours to go until his intended train would depart, he had another helping of rations, which he again washed down with plenty of water.

At 8:40 p.m., he started out towards the train station, which was only two blocks away. Before leaving the path, he noticed a man staggering towards him carrying a vodka bottle in one hand. As soon as they were close enough, the man put his hand out for money and said something in Polish.

Assuming that he wanted a handout, Lynx went to pass him and he grabbed Lynx's shoulder with one hand. His eyes opened in a look of fright as Lynx grabbed his wrist, twisted it up behind his back, gave him a shove, and let go. He staggered forward, turned towards Lynx, and started shouting something in Polish.

Lynx backed away, cautiously. When he got far enough away, Lynx turned and walked briskly towards the train station, glancing periodically over his shoulder. The man continued shouting at Lynx in Polish.

Right on time, the 9:00 p.m. train pulled into the station. At the ticket wicket, Lynx said one word to the attendant—"Warsaw"—and raised one finger. Lynx passed him some money, he passed a ticket to Lynx, and the transaction was completed without a single additional word being spoken.

Lynx boarded the train and started looking for a seat. As he entered the first car, there were only five passengers in it. Lynx took a seat as far away from them as he could, neither knowing any Polish nor wishing to engage in any conversation. Soon he was fast asleep in the seat, his kit bag once again functioning as his pillow.

Some time later, he awoke with a start because there were people shouting and laughing at the other end of the car. Four soldiers had arrived, and they were drinking from a bottle that one of them was holding, taking turns at good long "pulls." Sitting near them was a young girl, quite pretty, that they were harassing. One of the soldiers was attempting to undo her blouse.

Feelings of anger welled up in Lynx as he watched, unable to intervene, even though he was certain that, with his karate training, he could easily disable the entire quartet in short order.

An old gentleman finally got up and said something to the soldiers. One of the soldiers walked up to him and pushed the man so hard that he fell sprawling to the floor.

Unable to contain himself any longer, Lynx started to get up from his seat when a huge shape—a muscular mountain of a man, his upper body clad only in a T-shirt, every muscle rippling—passed him, moving with dispatch towards the soldiers.

When one of the soldiers saw him coming, he shouted to his companions and they momentarily looked his way. A hasty assessment of their chances in a hand-to-hand fight began as the powerhouse of a man walked toward them. One of the soldiers, sensing that they would probably absorb some serious causalities if a fight broke out, opened the door of the car and the four soldiers made a hasty exit.

The big man helped the elderly gentleman to his feet, said something to him in Polish, turned back towards Lynx, and started walking back down the aisle. As he passed Lynx, he smiled broadly. Lynx smiled back.

The rest of the ride to Warsaw included many stops—virtually every town—but was uneventful. Lynx dozed off and when he awoke, it was 7:15 a.m.

At the outskirts of Warsaw and an hour before they would reach the main station, Lynx's gut started churning. Trouble was brewing "somewhere ahead" and he raised his caution antennae to full alert. Remembering that Sarge had warned the MKGB would "likely be waiting" for him at the pick-up point, he surmised that they might also be waiting for him at the train station.

They had a way of taking an in-depth approach to anything they undertook, and always seemed to have plenty of manpower.

To avoid—or at least reduce—the probability of that happening, Lynx decided to de-train at the next stop in the Warsaw outskirts.

As he stood on the platform, he sighted a taxi, walked over to it, and told the driver the downtown Warsaw address. He had memorized and practiced it repeatedly out loud. The taxi driver invited him into the cab and they drove off towards the requested destination.

The driver watched Lynx in the rear-view mirror and asked, "You're English?"

"How did you know?" Lynx wanted to know.

"I see all kinds of people in this business. I can tell a mechanic from a banker, a secretary from a housewife. And you, my friend, are English," he replied with a smile—a friendly smile.

"Sure, but how did you know? Was it the way I spoke the address?"

"Well, you spoke the address with a slight accent, and that was okay. It was just your mannerisms. I can't explain it any better than that, but I just knew."

The ice had been broken, and Lynx was satisfied that the driver was legitimate, not involved in the Cold War, and most importantly, not likely an informant. Consequently, they conversed freely as they drove downtown.

As they approached Lynx's requested destination, the driver pulled over, turned towards Lynx in the back seat and said, "Something is wrong."

"What?" asked Lynx.

"I don't know, but there are MKGB agents everywhere. All around."

Looking up and down the street and feigning innocence that would evidently get him a second opinion free-of-charge, Lynx replied, "I don't see any. Where?"

"Look at those two men over there. MKGB."

The two men he had pointed out were walking away from the car, only their backs visible.

"The two men standing in that doorway over there. MKGB." He pointed with his hand below the windows of the car so that only Lynx could see.

There were two men wearing brown raincoats standing in a doorway. Lynx agreed with the driver's assessment, and he got the message. Lynx remembered Sarge's If-not-A-then-B instruction and gave the driver the alternate address. He nodded, and they drove off. As they left, it became obvious to Lynx that the area was crawling with MKGB agents. His driver continued to point them out.

Twenty minutes later, they arrived at Sarge's designated "B" address, back out in the suburbs. The driver pulled up in front of it, pronounced it MKGB-free, turned to Lynx, and asked for the fare.

Lynx pulled out a wad of Polish notes that was a goodly four or five times the expected amount. He passed it to the driver and said, "This is for you, my friend. Are you with the Polish resistance?"

"No. But I know some of them."

"Kindly forget this address, if you follow what I mean," replied Lynx.

"What address?" replied the driver, smiling.

Lynx got out of the taxi, closed the car door, and the taxi drove off.

Lynx approached the house, which looked identical to all the others he could see down the street, each with a small front lawn. He proceeded inside the unlocked door of the outer porch, and was about to knock on the inner door when it opened and a man stood looking at him.

The two men studied each other for a few seconds, when the man standing in the doorway asked, "Lynx?"

"Yes."

"Come in, please."

"Lynx, the MKGB are looking for you. They know your code name, what you look like, and they know about the microfilm." He paused. "My name is Michael. Your boss has contacted us, and he wants you to stay here."

"For how long?"

"Until the danger has passed."

"Days? Weeks? How long?"

"Lynx, I don't know for sure. But probably a month."

There was a sofa in the living room and Lynx sat down on it, his mind racing. *No one except me and Sarge know the country exit plan*, he kept saying over and over in his mind, *so what's the problem? Hey, I couldn't stand the stress of a month staying hidden from the authorities. The nightmares are already bad enough; they would only worsen. My work would suffer. People back home would be worried sick. Leaving promptly is really the only option.*

Lynx studied him. Michael was in his early forties, bald but with dark hair remaining on the sides of his head, about five foot eight, 155 pounds, quite muscular and fit.

"Lynx, would you like something to eat?" asked Michael.

"Yes. I would."

Michael introduced Lynx to his wife Maria, a beautiful woman about his age. Lynx sat down at their dining table and enjoyed a delicious meal.

By this time, it was 12:30 p.m. and, as Lynx sat sipping his coffee and enjoying a cigarette, he was deep in thought, weighing the options and trying to decide what to do.

Finally he asked Michael, "Did you know how I was to leave the country?"

"No. No one told me. Why?"

"I just wondered. We have a leak in our London operation. I'm convinced of it. Someone is feeding the Russians information. Only my boss and I know how I will leave the country. That is our strongest suit right now."

"You mean the MKGB know that you are here somewhere in the country, but don't know your escape route?"

"That's right. So I could leave without them knowing where, when, how, or what route I'd take—without them knowing *anything*."

"Lynx, they are watching for you. They have an incredible network out looking for you. Trains, roadblocks, everything is under surveillance. And apparently, many of them know what you look like. It's the biggest manhunt I've ever seen."

"When do you contact my boss again?" asked Lynx.

"Later tonight, at 2300 hours," replied Michael.

"Okay, Michael. I'm going to leave at 2200 hours. Tell him to give me an extra two days to get out."

"Lynx, don't do this. Stay here with us. We'll keep you safe until the danger has passed, and they've stopped looking for you. Then you'll be able to leave safely."

"Michael, I can't stay here for a month. That's thirty days! I'd go nuts!"

"We would be honoured to have you stay with us."

"I know, Michael. But that would be an unreasonable imposition, and I don't want to endanger you and your wife."

"Well, it looks like you have made up your mind."

"I have. Do you have a backpack that I could carry some food in?" asked Lynx.

"Of course. But I wish you'd change your mind."

"I'll be okay. Don't worry."

It was a fateful decision that would haunt him for the rest of his life.

While Michael went out to get maps of Poland between Warsaw and the Baltic Sea, including back roads, Lynx and Maria started stashing a supply of food—including some of her homemade cookies—into a backpack, and Lynx readied himself for what he knew would be an ordeal.

When Michael returned with the maps, he and Lynx poured over them at great length, plotting Lynx's escape route. Now Michael knew the escape route too, but Lynx had no choice other than to trust him, thinking, *He has to be reliable. After all, he's in touch with Sarge—unless he's a double agent. Whatever happens, it's a risk I've taken, and probably not a big one.*

The agreed plan was that Michael would drive Lynx to the edge of the city—about thirty kilometres north. Michael insisted they take his car and he would leave Lynx there on his own. They did so and encountered neither roadblocks nor police in that leg of what was to be a complex and lengthy journey.

As they stood talking at the side of the road, Michael wished Lynx good luck, and asked one final time if he had changed his mind. When Lynx answered "No," Michael promised to contact Sarge at 2300 hours on his radio to update him on Lynx's decision—that is, to go it alone back to the Baltic coast. Michael passed a vial of microfilm to Lynx for delivery and they parted.

Day One

A 450-kilometer journey to meet his submarine pick-up lay ahead. Lynx turned from watching Michael's car disappear into the night towards Warsaw and started walking north up the road.

Now faced with the reality of getting out of the country on his own resourcefulness, Lynx mulled over the options. Walking that distance, of course, was not an option, nor were trains, buses, and the like because of the MKGB net. That meant finding a vehicle of some sort to steal—probably a car or truck would be the least obvious. Stealing a motorcycle was another possibility. He hadn't ridden one in several years, but it was like swimming—once you know how, you never forget. It made his wish list.

The first stretch of road was totally uninhabited. There were no houses, only trees and fields on either side of the road. After about five kilometres, a car passed him and he got off the road into the ditch to avoid being seen. Then he spotted a car parked near the road at the end of a long driveway. Its door was unlocked. He put his kit bag and backpack on the ground beside the car and sat down in the driver's seat.

The interior lights came on quickly, so he immediately removed the light bulb. There was no key in the ignition. Feeling under the dashboard, he had soon located the ignition switch wires and tore them free with a quick yank. Searching for the power supply wire from the battery, he scraped the switch wires across the bottom of the dashboard until a shower of sparks indicated that he had found it.

He put the gearshift into neutral and started looking for the starter wire. When he found it, the engine turned over momentarily. He looked around and all was quiet. He picked up his backpack and kit bag and put them on the front passenger seat. He twisted the wires together and touched them with the starter wire. *Presto!* The engine started.

With the engine idling, he put the gearshift into first gear, released the clutch slowly, and pulled the car out onto the road heading north, he headlights off for the moment to avoid drawing attention. *knows? Maybe the owner is still up*, he thought.

After a few hundred yards, he turned on the headlights and checked the dashboard gauges. All indicators—oil pressure, alternator, and fuel tank about half full—looked good. Hoping for more gasoline to avoid stopping for gas, a half tank was better than nothing, and he accepted the situation. *It is what it is*, he thought, *but at least I'm no longer walking.*

The night was warm, and he opened a window for fresh air, alert for roadblocks as he motored down the road. It had been about 1:00 a.m. when he had stolen the car. By 3:00 a.m., he stopped and sipped coffee from his thermos, had a cigarette, and then got back on the road.

By 5:30 a.m., he started looking for a place to lay low for the day and saw a small laneway exiting the road. He checked the map and had gone only about 110 kilometres. He backed the car into the laneway, shut down the engine, and walked down the lane to confirm that it was not a driveway with a house farther along it.

Back at the car, he took his backpack and kit bag out of the car, sat leaning against a tree, ate some grub, closed his eyes, and fell asleep.

At about noon, he awoke, stretched, checked the car, and looked around—not a soul was in sight. He went back to the tree, sat down, and again was soon asleep. He awoke again at about 2:30 p.m., checked his Beretta and the small derringer in his leg holster, sat back, and started waiting for nightfall.

At dusk, he put his kit and backpack back into the front seat and touched the two wires together to start the car—nothing. The battery was dead. He had made the mistake of leaving the wires connected together with the battery wire, resulting in the battery power being drained. *Damn*, he thought.

He wrapped the wires together, opened the car door, and pushed the car down the lane towards the road. A slight grade enabled him to easily get back in once the car was moving. He popped the clutch at the right moment with the gearshift set in first gear, and the engine came to life. He was back in business.

To conserve fuel, he kept the speed down, the tank now reading a quarter full. From the moment that he had stolen the car, he had known that fuel supply would be an issue, and sure enough, at about 11:30 p.m., the engine began to sputter. He pulled over to the side of the road and consulted the map. He would have to leave the main highway and managed to make the sputtering car go another few hundred yards, where there was a small crossroad onto which he turned. Surprisingly, the car kept running until he had reached the next intersection, onto which he turned to continue north.

After a short distance, the car sputtered to a halt, this time for good.

Day Two

He decided to abandon the car. After strapping his kit bag to his backpack for the best hands-free walking, he started out on foot, continuing north. After a long right curve, followed by a left curve, he could see lights coming from a few farmhouses and could hear roosters crowing. It was about 4:30 a.m., and the light of dawn was showing. The immediate priority had once again become finding a place to lay low until nightfall.

He found a place to hide for the day, checked the map, and concluded that he had covered another eighty-five kilometers, totalling about 150 kilometers with the car for the two days. Since abandoning the car and walking all night, he had covered about eighteen miles.

He ate some bread and drank the remaining coffee, realizing that with the coffee now gone, he would soon need to find a source of water.

He slept under a canopy of trees and awoke at 10:30 a.m. as the dappled sunlight hit his eyes through the leafy branches. He quickly came to full alert as he heard footsteps approaching and had soon determined that an animal was walking towards him, five or six footsteps at a time. As a cautionary measure, he pulled out his Beretta, screwed on the silencer, and waited.

As the noise came ever closer, he was even more certain that it was an animal. Sure enough, a big hound soon popped out of the bush.

The dog came right up to him, its tail wagging—a good sign—and he petted the animal for a few minutes.

"Okay, boy, off you go," he instructed the dog. It seemed to know what that meant and had soon scampered out of sight.

Lynx laughed to himself over the matter and tried to sleep, but was unable to. He checked the map and his slow rate of progress began to worry him. Finally, he drifted off to sleep. When he awoke, for a few moments, he couldn't get his bearings, unable to recognize anything around him, but slowly all came back to him—probably a disorientation effect of PTSD.

He glanced at his watch. It was 3:10 p.m. and he was still unable to sleep or even close his eyes. He started to think: *How would I react if I awoke and someone was standing over me? Too slowly, with dire consequences*, seemed to be the answer.

That did it. He decided that he would simply not go back to sleep—it was too dangerous.

The time had now advanced to 3:30 p.m. There was full visibility, and he decided to move on—with caution, of course. Food was low, and he would soon need water.

As he walked down the road past several open fields, a faraway farmhouse appeared in the distance with a horse grazing not far from the road. He approached the horse, and he seemed gentle enough, allowing Lynx to stroke his face. A halter was hanging on the fence nearby.

Hey, he thought. *I could preserve my strength by riding the horse, if he'll let me.*

He took the halter and stroked his head several times before slipping it into place and doing up the buckle. The horse seemed to welcome the move. *Now to mount the animal without a saddle in place*, he thought.

Lynx recalled that someone had told him horses prefer to be mounted from the right. He went around to the right-hand side of the horse, it stood still, and Lynx made his move, more or less hopping up onto his back. Lynx had only ridden a horse twice before, but the horse made no untoward moves and seemed comfortable with Lynx aboard.

He grabbed the two rope reins hanging from the halter, half-whispered "giddy-up" into the horse's ear, and the animal started to trot forward. Lynx steered him onto the road and they were making pace—not terribly fast, but moving well, certainly faster and consuming less energy than walking.

When dusk arrived, they crossed a bridge over a small stream. Lynx dismounted, led the horse down to drink, and filled his thermos.

He remounted, and they rode off into the night. Over the course of the next half hour, they met only one car coming towards them, spotting the headlights well before the driver could see them. Lynx quickly dismounted and led the horse into the roadside brush until the car had passed.

Day Three

At about 4:00 a.m., Lynx stopped, dismounted, and let the horse graze at the side of the road while he ate the remaining food from his backpack. When he remounted the horse, the animal seemed reluctant to continue in the same direction they had been travelling, preferring to go in the opposite direction—home.

Lynx persevered, and soon had the horse going north again. At about 6:00 a.m., he dismounted and the horse started to trot off back down the road in the direction from which they had come. When Lynx tried to catch the rope dangling from his halter, the horse started to gallop.

Lynx got the message: We've gone far enough. The horse was telling him, "I wanna go home."

Lynx stood on the road watching the horse disappear in the distance and then started to look for a place to spend the day. He saw a spot off in the bush beside the road, walked there, and sat down. Although there were no large trees around, he curled up on the ground and went to sleep.

Day three had ended, and he was still about 170 miles from the Polish border. He wondered whether he could make that distance in a day without food, and planned on getting water as he went. But having no food was emerging as a serious problem.

Day Four

He slept until noon and awoke—hungry. He took a sip of water from his thermos and drifted off back to sleep. Glancing at his watch when he awoke, it read 5:10 p.m. and the sky was overcast; rain sometime soon seemed a likely prospect. There were no large trees in the immediate vicinity, only second-growth saplings, say up to two inches in diameter. He was out of food, had only a cup of water in his thermos, and a single cigarette left.

Still a long way from the Baltic Sea, he was getting annoyed repeatedly from the constant need to convert kilometers to miles on his map. So he took a piece of paper and marked it off in miles to use as a gauge in measuring his progress. With 170 miles to go, one conclusion seemed inevitable: He had to find another car to steal.

As he got to his feet, his stomach growled. He stretched, picked up his kit bag and backpack, and started trudging down the road. As he walked, he pondered his strategy. *A detour will be needed to find a car,* he thought, *but that investment in time will pay off if it enables me to reach the Baltic Sea before midnight.*

It occurred to him that leaving a stolen car and horse in his wake would be a trail that the Russians would soon pick up on—either through the police or checks that their army might follow up on. One way or another, when they put two and two together, they would track him down. That meant that getting to the Baltic seashore was becoming increasingly urgent. He wondered repeatedly, *How long would Sarge's pick-up force wait?* To that, he had no answer.

As he proceeded on foot down the road in full daylight, twice he had to take to the roadside brush as cars approached.

By 8:30 p.m., it was getting dark, and the cover of night would be a welcome advantage. Off in the distance, he could see the lights of houses. He gradually realized, as he approached the top of a shallow hill, that there was a village a short distance ahead.

He looked for a hiding place to observe the scene from a distance and made a plan for securing food, water, and—above all—a car.

Why didn't I notice the village on the map? he wondered.

By 9:00 p.m., he had located a hiding place in an alley between two buildings in the village. It was quite inconspicuous from most vantage points, and with the cover of darkness, would serve him well in case someone came down the road.

While he waited in the alley for better darkness, he reduced his kit bag contents into the backpack and discarded some of the clothes that would no longer be needed to reduce the volume. *Better manoeuvrability in case of action*, he thought.

As he sorted through his pack, he noticed his lock picks. They were wrapped in a cloth and he carefully placed them at the top of the backpack for ready use. *After all,* he thought, *I'm in the vicinity of buildings with locks. I might need them.*

He heard a noise in the street and peered around a corner of a building to see two boys playing with a ball. One would toss the ball at a wall, it would bounce off, the other would catch it and repeat the pattern. Lynx had no idea where they had come from, but was unconcerned because they were walking away from him.

He suddenly realized that the odour of freshly baked bread was wafting from a bakery just down the street in the direction that the boys had gone. The boys disappeared from view as they turned a corner, and Lynx moved silently down the alley towards the rear door of the bakery.

In his state of extended hunger, his olfactory sense almost became overpowered by the scent of the bread. Lynx tried the bakery doorknob, and the door was locked.

He quickly retrieved the lock picks from his backpack and inserted his best guess as to which one would work. In a few seconds, the tumblers clicked into the unlocked position. He slowly pushed the door open, looking for any sign of an alarm. There was none. The interior of the room appeared as black as the ace of spades.

Great, he thought, *That means that no one is in the shop.*

Instinctively, he reached for his Beretta, and then the silencer. His eyes darted around as he screwed it into place.

As his eyes got accustomed to the darkness, he gradually realized that he had entered the bakery's storeroom. There were boxes piled high in several places and a variety of machinery positioned throughout the room. At the far end of the room, there was a door that led to another part of the bakery. A shallow beam of light coming under the door gave just enough light that he could now discern the features of the room.

However, there was a downside to the light coming in under the door. That meant that someone—*people, how many?*—were in the next room, which was the front room of the bakery. Lynx moved stealthily towards the door, hunger now becoming increasingly all-powerful—perhaps dangerously.

He reached out and placed his hand on the doorknob, slowly turned it, and pulled the door towards him. He opened it the smallest of cracks so that he could see into the room. The sweet smell of freshly baked bread increased dramatically, almost overwhelmingly.

Lynx peered through the crack in the doorway and could see a rack of freshly baked loaves to the right of the door. Close to the front of the store, a man stood at a counter doing something with his hands on the counter. His back was facing Lynx.

Lynx opened the door enough to enter the room. He was now taking chances he would not normally take—but hunger can do that to a person.

The rack of bread was about three feet from the door opening. Keeping an eye on the man, Lynx reached for a loaf of bread. The man's Sixth Sense—Lynx wasn't the only one with it!—kicked in, and he turned around just as Lynx's outstretched hand was closing onto a loaf of bread.

The man shouted something in Polish just as he spotted Lynx's Beretta and immediately changed his demeanour from policeman to frightened victim, his eyes now at full shutter.

Lynx, of course, had no intention of harming him in any way, contrary to what he would have done had the man been MKGB. He was a shopkeeper and Lynx was stealing his bread.

As Lynx reached for that loaf of bread, in a phenomenal time-dilated but compressed flashback, his mind cast back to his childhood, when he had stolen a toy 1934 Ford car from Karch's General Store in Midland. His mother had told him that it was too expensive. It was about ten inches long, with red and black fenders, wire wheel rims, and spare tires set into the front fenders. He had hidden it in their back yard. When his mother found out what he had done, she took him by the ear, reminding him of the Thou-shalt-not-steal commandment as she scolded him all the way down to the store. She stood outside, arms folded on her chest, waiting as ten-year-old Lawrence went into the store to tell Mr. Karch that he had stolen the toy. He said he was sorry for doing so and was now returning it, tears running down both cheeks. Mr. Karch looked out the front window of the store, saw Lawrence's mother standing there in her apron, and took the toy car from the boy without a word of acknowledgement. Afterwards, Lawrence left the store post haste to go home with his mother, only to get a razor strap spanking.

In a split second, this vivid memory of childhood guilt flashed through Lynx's mind. He completed his grab of the loaf of bread, stepped back, closed the door behind him, dashed across the storeroom and out of the building—his prize in one hand, his Beretta in the other.

Knowing that he now had to get away from the village as quickly as he could, Lynx was still hesitant because he didn't know which direction to go. East would take him back to the main road where he would almost certainly be arrested—either by the police, the MKGB, or the Russian army. He had soon decided that west was best, intending to turn north as soon as he was convinced that it was safe.

He ran about a hundred feet in the easterly direction after turning a few corners and found a parked car, pointing in the same direction as he was running—now west, according to his built-in compass. He tried the door, opened it, and quickly glanced around to see if he had any pursuers.

Seeing none, he slipped his backpack off onto the passenger seat along with the loaf of bread. He hurriedly ripped the wires off the rear of the key switch and started the process of finding the correct wires to hotwire the car. Within a few minutes, he had started the car and took off, turning the headlights on as he went.

He wanted to turn north as soon as he could, and without any police or pursuers, felt he had made a clean getaway. Reaching over to the passenger seat, he grabbed the loaf of bread, tore off the end of it as he drove, and wolfed it down.

He realized that the police would now be on the lookout for an armed bread thief. If they connected that with his recent car and horse thievery, or brought others into the chase—the MKGB, the Russian army—who were already searching for a fugitive British agent, there were at least three organizations ready to take up his trail. One way or another, trouble ahead looked like a certainty.

At the next intersection, he turned north again but noticed that the gas tank was less than a quarter full. He maintained a moderate speed in an attempt to stretch the gas mileage to its maximum. Overall, he was encouraged that—so far—there was no one in obvious pursuit.

After a few more ravenous bites of bread, he realized that half the loaf was already gone. More seriously, he was completely out of water.

He crossed a bridge over a small stream, stopped the car, and left it idling by the side of the road as he filled his thermos from the shallow trickle.

He quickly got back into the car and resumed his northward progress. He sipped on the thermos of water as he went. It didn't taste the best—but it was water.

When a streak of lightning suddenly lit up the sky, Lynx knew that rain would almost certainly follow. Sure enough, it started to rain heavily a few minutes later. The rain was so heavy that the windshield wipers simply could not cope. Visibility was limited, and he decided to pull over until it had subsided. The downpour continued for an hour. It stopped almost as suddenly as it had started.

Day Five

About two hours after Lynx had stolen the car, the gas tank was empty and he had only gone sixty-five miles. That left about one hundred miles to go. His best option seemed to be to find another car to steal.

By 1:30 a.m., in the black of night—no moon—Lynx found himself walking down the road, still northbound. As the lightning flashes continued, only a sprinkle of rain fell. Then, by about 2:30 a.m., the heavy rain resumed. Lynx got off the road and into the bush. He pulled a rain poncho from his backpack that he made into a crude shelter by suspending it from four small saplings.

As he sat attempting to remain as dry as possible in the downpour under the poncho, he drew his hand across his forehead. He suddenly realized that it was very hot, and that he was not feeling well.

As the downpour continued, he sat with his head between his knees and his arms encircling his knees to conserve heat. He sighted a large tree that was suitable for leaning against and moved the poncho over to it for better shelter. Now that he was feeling weak, that minor activity took all the strength he had.

How could this happen? he wondered. *Was it the bread? More likely the water.*

He sniffed the water in his thermos and it smelled swampy, so he emptied the thermos onto the ground. He formed the edge of the poncho into a crude spout and let the rainwater drain into his thermos. He rinsed out the thermos and refilled it.

It was 3:45 a.m. Lynx was tired and feeling weak. He closed his eyes and fell asleep. When he awoke, his watch read 6:15 a.m., and it was still raining. His only option was to stay put, and he drifted off to sleep again.

By noon, Lynx awoke. The rain had stopped and the sun was shining. He tried to stand, and after a shaky attempt, managed to get up onto his feet. He could hear laughter somewhere nearby. He quickly drew his Beretta and the laughter suddenly seemed to be coming from another direction, but he couldn't see anyone. Then it came from yet another direction. Lynx turned so fast towards it that his balance and fell down. All strength seemed to have ebbed is body.

The voices started to reappear. "What's the matter, Lynx?" said one. "You have to get up and get moving."

"Who said that?" he asked out loud, his eyes unable to focus, the surroundings appearing blurred.

"Come on, buddy. Get with it," the voice said again. "You'd better get moving before they catch you."

"Where are you?" asked a trembling Lynx.

"I'm right here, buddy," the voice replied.

"Who are you?" asked Lynx, still unable to see. That voice, one he hadn't heard in almost ten years, was Nomad's. *How could it be? Nomad had been shot a long time ago,* he thought.

"Nomad?" he said out loud.

"Right, buddy. I'm going to help you escape."

Lynx shook his head and suddenly realized that he had been hallucinating. There were his PTSD demons again—and the ghost of Nomad—haunting him. He felt drowsy, so he sat down and leaned against the tree.

He fell back asleep, and when he awoke, it was dark again. His watch read 12:30 p.m. He had been asleep for almost twelve hours. He wondered if he was too weak to travel. As a test, he stood up, and felt not bad—not great, but not bad.

He took down the poncho, put it into his backpack, ate what was left of the bread, and sipped rainwater from his thermos for a few minutes while he collected his thoughts. Feeling refreshed, any fever he may have had had at least partially broken and he started walking along the road, heading northward.

Five miles up the road, his strength gave out and he stopped to find a place to lay low for a few hours. He stepped off the road into some brush and medium-sized trees, curled up on the ground, and was soon asleep.

Day Six

When he awoke, it was 10:00 a.m. He got up, stretched, and had no food to eat but still had some clean rainwater in his thermos.

The fever had subsided a little, but he clearly had not yet shaken it. And without food, he would be unable to regain his strength. He was certain that at least three organizations—the police, the MKGB, the Russian army—were now looking for him. He hoped that the police would keep his local transgressions—stealing a loaf of bread and a car—at the local level. There seemed no obvious reason why they should involve the other two.

He laid low and decided that he could benefit from a little rest. He sipped on the water, closed his eyes, and before he knew it, awoke with shivering chills. His wristwatch read 6:00 p.m. Minutes later, his fever had skyrocketed and he was soaking wet with sweat from the fever. Perhaps it was finally about to break.

He waited patiently and fell asleep. When he awoke, it was dark again. He checked the time; it was 10:00 p.m. The sky was overcast, making the blackness of night total. He somehow mustered the strength to get up and started down the road again, putting one foot ahead of the other, painful step after painful step.

As midnight approached, he could see a light in the distance coming from a house off to the left of the road, with an old, half-ton pick-up sitting in the driveway. Even though an outside light was on, the house sat in total darkness.

Lynx had his doubts that the truck would start. He looked into the rear cargo compartment in the dim light and found a shovel, a hoe, wooden boxes, and a five-gallon pail. Alongside the pail was a one-inch hose, about three feet long, ideal for siphoning gasoline.

Lynx tried the truck door and it opened. To his surprise, the key was sitting in the ignition. He smiled to himself as he tossed his backpack onto the seat, got in, put the gearshift into neutral, and rolled the truck under its own steam down a slight grade on the gravel driveway and back onto the main road, facing north.

He turned on the ignition key on, pressed the start button beside the key switch, and the engine started. He shifted into low gear and was off down the road once again. Even though the engine was missing on one cylinder, the other five seemed to be healthy and the truck was making good speed.

He checked the all-important fuel gauge and found—once again—that it was just over a quarter full. The pattern was now clear. The Polish leave their gas tanks well below full whenever they park a vehicle.

Lynx was now two days late for his pick-up and his anxiety level on that issue was rising. Every day's delay increased the risk that the submarine would be detected as it surfaced daily to charge its batteries—in Polish waters, a place that the British government would not want their submarine to be discovered. The international embarrassment could be substantial.

Day Seven

By 2:00 a.m., the truck engine temperature gauge was reading "hot" and, not wanting the radiator to boil over, Lynx stopped for an hour to allow it to cool down. At 3:00 a.m., he resumed driving down the road, looking for a source of water to top up the radiator. By 4:00 a.m., he stopped at a bridge over a river about twenty feet wide and flowing fast. He filled the radiator and his thermos, and he stopped again a little farther along the road—this time because he lacked the strength to continue.

He located a grove of trees down a lane and drove the truck into the grove to hide it. He walked about twenty feet from the truck and collapsed on the ground, exhausted.

It was 11:30 a.m. when he awoke, but was feeling better. He stood up and felt weak, but was able to remain standing.

The truck was low on fuel and he had to find a car from which to steal enough gasoline to complete the journey—and get some food. He took a sip of the water in his thermos and found the taste nauseating.

From that simple test, he concluded that he most definitely had something impure in his system. As he leaned against a tree in the grove, he craved a cigarette. He slid down the trunk of the tree into a sitting position, closed his eyes, and realized that he could not travel without undue risk until after dark.

When he awoke, it was dusk. A check of the map revealed that he had only covered twenty miles since stealing the truck, leaving eighty miles to get to the Baltic coast.

He got into the truck, started it, and headed out onto the road again, determined to find a car from which to top up his gas tank. The first thing he noticed was that the traffic had increased substantially on the road, most of it oncoming. The missing cylinder made it difficult to keep the truck at any speed. That was exacerbated by an unusual amount of smoke coming from the engine compartment—to the extent that he could smell it in the driver's cab.

According to the map, there should be a small village just up ahead. He reached it at about midnight and drove slowly through the streets—which were empty—looking for a parked car from which to steal some gasoline. He had gone almost through the village before he sighted a good prospect beside a field with no house nearby. He stopped the truck behind the car, looked around, and there was no one in sight in any direction.

He quickly put some gasoline into the five-gallon pail using the hose as a siphon and poured it into the truck's gas tank, bending the rim of the pail into a crude spout to make the transfer easier and minimize spillage. He repeated the procedure with a second trip, bringing the added fuel up to about five gallons.

He was soon on his way again, now with less than eighty miles to go and a goodly five gallons of additional gas in the tank. The thought that he would now likely make it to the Baltic coast gave him renewed strength. His adrenaline was surging.

Day Eight

By 4:00 a.m., he had covered forty more miles but the old truck was beginning to falter. It steadily got slower and slower and refused to respond to its gas pedal. Finally, it quit completely.

Lynx pulled over to the side of the road, tried to turn the engine over, and it would not respond. The engine had seized completely. He checked the map and concluded that he was still thirty miles from the coast.

He got out of the truck and started down the road on foot. After about three miles, he stopped from exhaustion but managed to find a resting spot alongside the road. His strength was steadily dissipating. and he had no idea how much longer he could keep this up.

He could not even remember when the last time was that he had washed his face. Thinking, *I must stink to high heaven. High heaven. That's one of mom's favourite expressions*—he collapsed beside the road and fell asleep.

When he awoke, he believed that without food, he would not likely survive this day. He gamely gathered up his backpack and started walking north once again. He was now four days overdue at the designated Baltic pick-up point, and had no idea how long his pick-up team would wait.

He walked all morning, and by noon had covered between three and four miles. He stopped and sat by the side of the road. A car passed but didn't stop. *Good,* he thought. *I haven't been seen.* He drank the remaining water in his thermos, got to his feet, and started to walk again. By 3:00 p.m., he had covered only an additional three miles.

He spotted a farmhouse and a farmer was working in an adjacent field. It looked like the farmer was hoeing vegetables. A roadway leading up to the farmhouse was about three hundred feet long. Lynx could see a large barn at the rear of the house and some cattle in a field beyond. Smoke was coming from the chimney of the house. The farmer's wife was probably cooking something up.

It had now been almost three days since he had eaten. Lynx decided that he had to get some food almost at any cost, got an idea, and headed up the laneway towards the farmhouse. The farmer looked up from his work as Lynx approached. Lynx put on his best smile and nodded. As the farmer started speaking Polish in an unwelcoming tone, Lynx put his fingers up to his ears and shook his head, hoping that the farmer would understand that he also couldn't hear. He then pointed to his mouth and shook his head, signalling—he hoped—that he also couldn't speak. *Get it? I'm deaf and dumb,* he thought, hoping that mental telepathy might help.

The farmer looked at Lynx and waved him away. Then he started speaking in Polish, pointing back towards the road, indicating that Lynx get off his property. Lynx persisted, and signalled through charade-like actions that he would chop wood in exchange for food.

Again, the farmer shook his head. Undeterred and desperate, Lynx persisted, hoping that the farmer would relent. His demeanour suggested that he was about to reject the idea again when his wife appeared in the doorway of the house. She started scolding the farmer in Polish, wagging her finger at him. Then she turned towards Lynx and bid him to follow her.

The couple were both in their late fifties, the farmer about five foot ten and weighing about 165 pounds—a lean specimen, the result of manual labour. His wife, on the other hand was only about five foot five, and quite stout. In her long blue-flowered dress with a white apron, she led Lynx to the woodpile, showed him where the axe was, turned, and walked back into the house.

Lynx had invented a job for himself, applied for it, and got it all in the space of a few minutes—albeit with a somewhat rocky interview. Now faced with doing the job, he wondered how much strength he could muster in exchange for some great-tasting food. Sliding his backpack off onto the ground, he noticed that the farmer was watching him intently for a few minutes before he went back to his weeding.

Lynx had split only two pieces of firewood when he heard the farmer's wife behind him. He continued working because he was supposed to be deaf.

She tapped him on the shoulder. He turned towards her and she had a glass of lemon drink in one hand and a plate of cookies in the other that she was offering to him. Lynx stopped chopping and accepted them. She gave him a big smile, turned, and went back into the house.

Wary of exposing his ravenous hunger, Lynx nibbled at the plate of cookies and sipped at the lemon drink as he worked. He was so famished that he could have devoured the entire presentation in a few mouthfuls. The food was tasty beyond belief, and he could almost feel his strength returning with each successive nibble.

Then the wife reappeared with a plate of cookies and a lemon drink for her husband. He chatted to her, and although Lynx couldn't hear what they were saying, he thought it was probably along the lines of *How dangerous it is to let a stranger—one who looks like an escaped prisoner, perhaps a killer, all dishevelled—come into their yard, and let him case the place for purposes of who knows what.*

Lynx could see her trying to calm him down, thinking she presumably is trying to dissuade her husband's concern with, *"He's just a hungry traveller, deaf and dumb at that. How could he be a killer?"*

Lynx finished the cookies and lemon drink, continued chopping wood for over an hour and sat down for a rest. He couldn't imagine how he had summoned the strength. By then, it was about 5:00 p.m.

The farmer's wife reappeared again and Lynx played it dumb as if he hadn't heard her coming. This time, she had a loaf of bread in one hand and a roll of Polish sausage in the other. Lynx's mouth watered.

The farmer was with her. She must have scolded him because he extended his hand to Lynx and he shook it. The farmer smiled and stepped back beside his wife.

She handed the food to Lynx and pointed at the pump, meaning that he could wash up there. Then the old farmer placed his hand on Lynx's shoulder, pointed at the barn, and put his head down onto his arm, indicating a sleeping position. In international sign language, he was inviting Lynx to sleep the night in the barn.

The couple waved at Lynx as they went back into the house. After washing up, Lynx went out to the barn, opened the door, and there was a huge pile of hay on which to bed down for the night.

He slipped his backpack off and started snacking on the Polish sausage. He sipped from his thermos that he had refilled at the pump. The sausage and bread were both homemade. Lynx sat, chewing every bite fully, trying not to wolf it down, his taste buds in overdrive with the extravaganza of tastes emanating from the food. He relished the moment.

He ate his fill and stowed the remainder of the food in his backpack. He felt drowsy, lay down on the hay, and was soon asleep.

Day Nine

At around 6:00 a.m., Lynx was awakened by the distant sound of approaching vehicles. He cracked open the barn door, only to see a black car coming down the lane, followed by a large army truck. The truck cargo bed was covered with canvas. When the truck stopped, about a dozen soldiers jumped down onto the ground.

Lynx had seen enough. They had come for him. His only surprise was that it had taken them so long to track him down. He had expected this development days ago.

He picked up his backpack and took off on the full run out the back door of the barn, out of sight of the farmhouse and its military visitors. He kept the barn in his line-of-sight with the farmhouse as best he could.

He knew that he was about twenty-five miles from the Baltic coast. With compass in hand, he verified the direction of due north and ran through the brush and fields, skirting farmhouses and staying off roads as much as he could. They would have great difficulty running him down with vehicles of any kind with that strategy.

Every time he came to a road, he would check first before crossing it. If the way was clear, he would take it. If not, he would detour around any risk he uncovered. In the background stood the ominous question: *Will the submarine still be there, waiting?*

After twelve or thirteen miles on compass bearing only, Lynx had to rest. As it was, he continued to be amazed at the strength he had somehow summoned. He stopped and checked the map, but could not tell precisely where he was. There were no visible landmarks—no tall buildings, church steeples, obvious standout hilltops, or the like.

While poring over the map and struggling to get his bearings, he nibbled at the Polish sausage and sipped a bit of water.

After looking in vain for a visible landmark, he noticed a railway track on the map that ran to the Baltic coast. He reasoned that, if he could find those tracks, he would be able to navigate his way to the submarine pick-up point fairly easily. He would just have to hope that his pick-up team had waited.

Suddenly he could hear dogs barking in the distance. Tracking dogs were one eventuality that he hadn't anticipated; with tracking dogs, they would readily overtake him.

With renewed resolve and energy from the Polish sausage, he took off again on the dead run, but the sound of the barking was increasing, indicating that the dogs were gaining on him. That meant one thing: they had let the dogs go, running freely ahead. Lynx knew immediately that his pursuers had thereby committed a strategic error.

Lynx found a hiding spot, crouched down, and waited, his heart pounding. From the barking, he deduced that there were two, perhaps three dogs, and they were getting closer.

He readied his Beretta by fitting it with the silencer. Then he spotted them in the distance. There were two of them, and they looked like Dobermans, sniffing the ground as they followed his scent. Then one looked up, spotted Lynx, and stood erect, its ears up and charged.

Knowing that he would get only one shot off before the dog was upon him, Lynx waited until it was about fifteen feet away, took careful aim at its chest, squeezed the trigger, and *zip!* The dog went down without a sound.

The second dog had heard the *zip!* of the silencer, looked up, and charged. Lynx fired, and it too went down, but this time with a howl, still alive. Lynx ran over to it and finished it off with a second bullet.

Lynx looked up towards where the dogs had come from and there stood a soldier with two leather leashes in one hand and an AK-47 under the other arm. As the soldier raised the machine gun towards Lynx, everything went into slow motion.

Before the soldier could level the machine gun at him, Lynx fired the Beretta twice in rapid succession, both bullets ripping into the man's chest. The soldier was dead before he hit the ground.

Lynx turned and ran towards the train tracks—thinking that was still a good idea. When he reached the train tracks and started following them, he came across a bridge that was marked on the map. He realized immediately that he was now five miles too far to the east of his Baltic pick-up destination. *Five miles!* he thought. *Hey, I'll have to do better.* Remembering that attitude is everything in difficult circumstances, he fought off all thoughts of discouragement, silently vowing, *I'll make it up*.

It was about 3:00 p.m. but his determination had somehow recharged. He backtracked west for the next three hours and by 6:00 p.m., had reached a spot close to where he had shot the dogs. Curiously, there was no sign of any military follow-up. He then turned north, reckoning that his targeted extraction point was now about seven miles ahead; he was still pumped and the adrenalin was flowing like never before. With his attitude now positioned for success, his confidence was high that he would make it to the Baltic coast.

He sat down to rest a mile farther along his compass course. Still feeling sick, he finished off the remaining food and drank the rest of his water, knowing that he still had six miles to go.

Holding his compass course, he stopped to rest every mile, now tired beyond description. But around 10:00 p.m.—with extreme perseverance—he had reached the Baltic seashore, very close to his targeted pick-up spot. Now all he had to do was to lie low until midnight, and hope that the submarine had waited. He hid in a clump of bushes and nodded off.

He was awakened by the sound of soldiers on each side of the bushes, prodding and poking the underbrush with the muzzles of their AK-47s. They were laughing and talking as they made their way from one set of brush to the next.

Lynx looked at his watch. It read 10:55 p.m. He replaced the five bullets he had fired earlier in the day in the magazine of his Beretta as quietly as he could and drew his five-shot Derringer from its leg holster.

There were about thirty soldiers looking for him, and he had resigned himself that he was going to die that night—but he had also resolved to take as many of them with him as he could. It was going to be a lop-sided fight-out—like the one immortally captured in the final freeze-frame of the 1969 blockbuster movie *Butch Cassidy and the Sundance Kid*.

He decided to make his peace with God Almighty before all hell broke loose, and quietly whispered his final prayer: "Father in heaven, you are Lord of all. I am truly sorry that I never stayed close to you, like my mother wanted. She tried her best to bring me to you. But I went in another direction. I'm sorry, Lord."

Lynx felt relief that he had finally made peace with his Maker and braced himself for the coming battle. It was going to be bloody—and probably short.

Suddenly, one man's voice was heard above all the others, and the soldiers—who had been jovially poking away at the underbrush—all fell silent, listening to their commander. He was shouting in Russian. Lynx held his breath, wondering if he even had the strength to move if necessary—thinking, *Their commander is likely giving orders for them to shoot anything that moves on sight.*

Lynx knew that once the battle started, he was vastly outnumbered and would ultimately lose, but he might as well make every shot count.

When the Russian commander stopped shouting orders, the soldiers started to move en masse towards his hiding place. *Here we go,* he thought. But to his great surprise, the group of soldiers continued on past him as they moved along the shore, leaving only one sentry behind.

When the group of about thirty soldiers was a good three hundred yards on down the beach, Lynx checked his watch. It read 11:31 p.m.

Lynx still had two plastic C-4 explosive packets in his pack, so he dug them out and set the timers for a twenty-four-minute delay. They would explode at 11:55 p.m.

Now to deal with the lone sentry they had left behind. With the silencer on, he could terminate the problem with a single shot from his Berretta. Lynx could see him standing about eight feet from his hiding spot, which was three feet inside the bushes. As he took aim, he had second thoughts: *What if he makes a noise on being hit? That could alert his companions and lead to serious trouble. A guaranteed silent death would be far better—and safer for me.*

Lynx holstered his Beretta. He inched silently towards the unsuspecting soldier and watched from a few feet behind. The soldier lit a cigarette. Lynx summoned strength he didn't think he had, fuelled by sheer determination that came from somewhere deep inside. As the soldier stood there contentedly smoking his cigarette, Lynx reached out at blinding speed with his right hand and placed it over his jaw. As he pulled it back towards him, his left hand went simultaneously to the back of his head and pushed, delivering a fatal snap of the neck.

The dead soldier fell to the ground without a sound. The glowing ember of his cigarette lay on the ground—still alive, but without an owner.

Shaking with emotion from this action but alert even in his weakened condition, Lynx scanned the area to see if anyone was nearby. He dragged the dead soldier's body into the bushes, grabbed the C-4 explosives from his pack, set the timer for seven minutes, and placed them near the far end of the bushes.

He rifled into his backpack and grabbed a small, inflatable, one-man life raft in a plastic bag—including an air canister for inflating. A cord was attached to a valve that, when activated, would inflate the raft.

At 11:52 p.m., Lynx stepped into the waters of the Baltic Sea. The water was cold, and he waded out. Right on cue, the C-4 explosives ignited with a deafening blast and Lynx pulled the cord to inflate the raft. The sound of AK-47s firing could be heard in the distance.

Muzzle flashes could be seen going in many directions—but none seaward, where Lynx was.

Standing chest-deep in the water, Lynx scrambled to get into the raft but was unable to make it for lack of strength. He tried a second time with the same result. He decided that drowning near the shores of the Baltic would simply not do after all he had gone through to reach this point in this mission—his fifth and final. Lynx made a third determined effort to get into the raft—and this time, he made it.

While guns were still rattling on the shore, Lynx used his hands as paddles and headed straight out into the calm waters of the Baltic Sea. He was five days past his designated extraction date.

It had been a gargantuan, nine-day struggle to get here since leaving Warsaw. Now the single, remaining question became, *Had they waited?*

As he continued out into the calm Baltic waters, about three hundred yards offshore, his inflatable brushed up against the submarine halfway between its bow and conning tower in the pitch black night.

They *had* waited! His heart jumped with emotion. The mission was over and a success.

Unable to climb out of the raft for lack of strength, Lynx pulled his Beretta from its holster and tapped against the submarine hull with the butt—three dots, three dashes (dots with a pause between them), and three dots—a Morse Code "SOS."

"Who goes there?" came the response in a Scottish accent.

"Lynx," he answered.

"Well, come on up then, Laddie," replied the watch.

"I haven't got the strength," replied Lynx. Even though he was elated, elation did not translate into strength.

"Come on, I'll give you a hand," replied the watch, reaching down to connect with Lynx's outstretched hand as he held his backpack in the other.

Their hands touched, he grabbed Lynx's wrist and pulled him up and out of the raft in a single, practiced motion. He then set Lynx down in a sitting position while he pulled out a knife, punctured the raft, and sunk it.

He had a large handlebar moustache, and even in the darkness, Lynx could tell that it was red—like the hair on his head.

"Let's get you below and warmed up," said the sailor as he helped Lynx to his feet, over to an open hatch, into the submarine, and down a ladder.

The light got brighter as Lynx descended the ladder. At its bottom stood an officer, awaiting his arrival. It was the captain.

"You're a lucky man, Lynx," he said as Lynx stepped off the bottom rung. "This was the last night I was going to wait for you. We knew from radio broadcasts that someone was being hunted down, and they said that they were looking for an escaped convict. But then yesterday, they changed that to a manhunt for an escaped killer. That's when we knew that you must be close." Extending his hand, he continued, "I'm Captain Anderson of Her Majesty's Submarine Swordfish."

"Pleased to meet you, Captain, and many thanks for waiting," replied an exhausted Lynx.

"There's a man over there that wants to see you," said the captain, pointing to a man in dark glasses about ten feet away.

Lynx walked over towards the man, thinking, *Who wears sunglasses in a submarine in the middle of the night?* He was a Secret Service agent, presumably sent by Sarge. He extended his hand without saying a word, palm up. Lynx knew that he wanted the microfilm. He fished it out of a pocket in the shoulder of his shirt and handed it to him.

As the agent closed his hand on the vial, he asked, "What do you want first—food or sleep?"

"Food," answered Lynx, his stomach growling.

Lynx staggered under his own steam to the sailor's mess. Perhaps the cook was expecting him; he already had bacon and eggs ready. Lynx, his hands shaking as he ate, managed to eat only half the breakfast before he slipped off his chair onto the floor—out cold

The next thing Lynx remembers, there was a man kneeling beside his bunk. It was the boatswain, the big Scot with the handlebar moustache.

He had carried Lynx over to his bunk. The doctor standing beside him had something in his hand. Lynx felt a prick on one arm and the lights faded out.

When he awoke, the Secret Service agent was shaking him, now without his sunglasses on. "How are you feeling, Laddie?" he asked.

"Pretty woozy," replied Lynx.

"We've been at sea for over twelve hours. There is a launch alongside, waiting to take us to London," he said. "Think you can make it?"

"Sure," replied Lynx who tried to stand up. He didn't make it all the way up, and the Secret Service agent caught him. He was unable to stand without assistance.

"Don't worry about it, Laddie," said the Secret Service agent. "We know that you've had a rough time of it." He helped Lynx towards the hatch.

The agent shook his head at the captain, who shouted some orders. A sailor slipped a rope around Lynx's waist and slid it up his chest, under his arms. Using the rope as a sling, they lifted Lynx up and out the hatch and lowered him onto the starboard deck of the submarine.

The sea was rough that day, and the submarine was experiencing a slight side-to-side roll. Two or three sailors were using long, specially designed poles to keep the launch from bashing against the submarine's hull. The big Scotsman with the handlebar moustache stood beside Lynx on the deck, steadying him.

They strung a line from the sub to the launch through a small davit-like crane that could hang out over the side of the sub and would enable lowering Lynx down onto the launch in a boatswain's chair. They put him in the chair and, controlling it with a second line, carefully transferred him to the launch.

A medic aboard the launch took Lynx below to a bunk, and Lynx immediately passed out. The Secret Service agent jumped aboard the launch, and the launch was cast off. The next thing Lynx knew, they were at a dock somewhere along the Thames in London.

As they helped Lynx into a waiting black car, Sarge held the door open for him. Sarge got aboard, gave some instructions to the driver, and off they went. Turning to Lynx, Sarge's first remark was, "God, Laddie-Buck, you look awful."

"Thanks a lot," replied Lynx, with a clear inflection of *Yeah, sure, what did you expect*?

"I'm so happy that you made it back okay, but I gather there were a few problems," said Sarge. "By the way, not only do you look awful, you also smell bloody awful!"

"Sarge, I've been on the run for over a week, without even washing my face."

"Well, we're taking you to a military hospital and the nurses will give you a bath."

"You know, Sarge, I might enjoy that."

"Now you listen to me, you little rascal. You keep your hands off those nurses."

"Don't worry about it, Sarge. I'll be a perfect gentleman."

That was all Lynx could take at that moment in terms of a conversation, and he blacked out again. He had lost twenty pounds during the nine days the mission's exit leg. When he awoke, he was in a hospital room with the shades drawn, the door to his room open an inch or two. He closed his eyes and went back to sleep.

When he awoke, it was daylight and a lovely nurse with long, dark hair was standing over him, wearing a white nursing uniform and a starched nurse's cap.

When she noticed that Lynx had opened his eyes, she said, "Good morning, Robert. Are you feeling better?"

It took a few seconds for Lynx to undergo a mental fast-rewind as he tried to remember who Robert was. He started to remember how Sarge had introduced him in 1958 to an American Secret Service agent as Robert Hammond. Then, in 1965, he had travelled under that name on a British diplomatic corps passport into Russia. He concluded that Sarge must have given her his identity as Robert Hammond.

The nurse continued talking. He asked how long he would be staying there, and she told him that he would be staying in the hospital "until he was well." A doctor then came in with a stethoscope dangling from his neck like doctors do, and Lynx asked him the same question.

"Let's just see before I answer that," he said as he checked Lynx's chest and heartbeat. "Sounds good," he said as he stood back from his patient and sat down in a bedside chair. "Maurice brought you in here two days ago."

"Two days ago!" said Lynx in surprise. He couldn't believe that he had been unconscious that long.

"Yes, Robert, you must have gotten some bad water somewhere. The antibiotics you are now on will have you well in no time. Nurse Trudy and I will be the only ones to tend to you. To tell you the truth, Maurice brings a lot of young men in here—sick, shot up, sometimes with broken bones—and I'm not allowed to ask any questions. I'd really like to know what's going on."

He looked at Lynx, his eyes full of questions.

"Sorry, doc. I can't tell you anything," replied Lynx.

The doctor slapped both hand on his knees and stood up, saying, "I knew you'd say that." As he headed for the door, he turned to Lynx and said, "Is it so secret that you can't even tell the doctor who's treating you?"

"Sorry, doc," repeated Lynx.

Two days later, Sarge came into Lynx's hospital room with street clothes for him that, as usual, fit perfectly. Considering Lynx's twenty-pound weight loss, that in itself was an achievement. Sarge, of course, had long since had all his measurements, and presumably had made some adjustments. Lynx was still weak, but by then had progressed onto solid food and was gaining strength with each passing day. He had, however, developed a severe tremble in both hands.

When he left the hospital, both the doctor and the nurse were there. Nurse Trudy gave him a hug, and the doctor shook his hand and wished him well as he followed Sarge out the door to a waiting car.

As they drove down the road, Sarge set a tape recorder between them on the seat and he began taping Lynx's blow-by-blow account of the mission.

Part way through the debrief, Lynx looked at Sarge and asked, "Why did you tell me that I would be transferred from the high-speed launch to the sub in the North Sea when you knew that the transfer would take place in the Baltic Sea?"

Sarge shut off the recorder and said simply, "Too many ears listening. Sorry, Laddie." Making direct eye contact, he continued, "I found out just after you left who our leak was. You were already off the sub and in Poland. It was Major Austin. That's why he wanted to know what our exit plan was so badly—so the double-crosser could let the Russians know."

Lynx was stunned. "But he's British Army."

"Yes, he is. But he was being run as a Russian mole from their embassy. He was an MKGB agent."

"So, what happens to them now? Are they in jail?"

"No, Laddie, they aren't."

"Are they going on trial?"

"No."

"So, what happens to them? Nothing?"

Turning to Lynx, Sarge said, "Well, the Russian mole. He . . . He had a terrible accident. His car ran into a concrete bridge doing about eighty miles an hour. He was killed on impact."

"And the major? Where's he?"

"Well, it seems he had a medical condition. He sleepwalked."

"Yeah. So?"

After some hesitation, Sarge continued, his demeanour suddenly changing into a mellow mood. "Apparently he went sleepwalking one night in his apartment when his wife was visiting her mother, and he was alone. His apartment was on the twentieth floor, and the poor man apparently sleepwalked off the balcony. He, too, was killed on impact."

Then, smiling, he added, "Saved us an expensive trial. But it did accomplish one thing. Our leak has been fixed."

"I hope you're right about that, Sarge."

"We lost a lot of couriers because of him. Some were caught alive, tortured, and Lord knows how they were treated before they died. The Russians are ruthless when they want information. If they think you can tell them something, they don't exactly play by the Geneva Convention rules. That's why I let each member of each team know only what they have to know to execute their part of a mission. That way, they are far less likely to know anything of value to the enemy, even though the enemy may think that they do know something of importance. I can't do anything about that. But I'm already sleeping better knowing that he is not informing on us anymore."

Then, Sarge switched the tape recorder back on and continued the debriefing.

Later, during the trip into downtown London, the driver made a detour to the back entrance of a house. There were Secret Service agents everywhere. They entered the house through the back door and Sarge led him to a room. Standing there in front of Lynx was HRH the Duke of Edinburgh and Prime Minister Harold Wilson, among others. Sarge introduced Lynx as his agent who had "recently" brought "the goods out of Poland," and Lynx shook hands with both men. The Duke acknowledged Lynx's valuable work and remembered Lynx from an extended game of darts "with the boys" in the Edmonton airmen's mess in 1962.

To this day, Lynx has no idea what was in that microfilm vial, but it was information that the British certainly valued highly. It was just after that that the USSR began to disintegrate.

On the flight back to Canada, Lynx had a lot to think about. He had just narrowly escaped with his life. In fact, just before his rendezvous with the submarine only days earlier, he had concluded that his life was over, outnumbered thirty-to-one and surrounded by heavily armed military while he was on the Baltic coast. He was highly skilled, but no amount of skill can handle those odds. Sure, he would have taken a few of them with him. But it was purely fortuitous that the Russian soldiers moved on down the beach when they did.

He was still sick from the contaminated water, his nerves were on edge, and the possibility of another mission loomed. Susan had told him that three was the usual limit, and she had been in a position to know.

Would he accept another assignment from Sarge? As tired, relieved, concerned, and drained as he felt on that flight home, not likely.

Lawrence was released from MI-6 work in 1978. When Sarge was doing so, he indicated that he would like Lawrence to consider becoming his personal bodyguard. His skills and abilities were, of course, important but Sarge acknowledged that Lawrence's unique Sixth Sense was rare. Sarge believed that it set Lawrence apart from other agents who had worked for him.

When Lawrence declined, Sarge left the door open. "If you ever change your mind, give me a call. You have my number."

Lawrence never pursued the option.

Epilogue:
Sarge, PTSD, and Lawrence's Post-MI-6 Life

Sarge, of course, is a prime mystery character throughout this narrative. Lawrence Fox met him in 1952, almost immediately after he enlisted in the RCAF. It would be a good many years before Lawrence would know who he truly was.

Sarge's name was Maurice Oldfield. He was born November 16, 1915, on the family farm near Derbyshire, England, the eldest of eleven children. He studied history at Manchester University, and had World War II not intervened, in all probability he would have become a renowned medieval scholar.

Oldfield joined the British Army during World War II. Most of his wartime service was in Egypt at the Security Intelligence Middle East (SIME) in Cairo, a counter-intelligence organization, whose purpose was to counter the activities of hostile agents in the region. That was to be an apprenticeship for his later work in the British Secret Service.

In the early Cold War era, following the dropping of the Iron Curtain in 1946, Oldfield was responsible for Soviet counter-intelligence in MI-6. He was functioning in this position during the period that Lawrence Fox worked for him as an espionage courier.

Oldfield knew his way around the Free World espionage circles of his day. For example, he knew Kim Philby well. Oldfield even alerted Philby—the notorious British double agent—that there were leaks to the Soviets from the Los Alamos atomic project and from the British embassy in Washington. Ironically, Philby already knew about those leaks—he was their prime source.

Oldfield also knew William Stephenson of the biography *A Man Called Intrepid* and Oshawa's Camp "X" fame. Oldfield visited him at least once at his Bermuda home—a juicy tidbit he once let slip in conversation with Lawrence.

Oldfield was appointed head of MI-6 in 1973 under Conservative Prime Minister Edward Heath. He served in that position for five years and was knighted by HRH Queen Elizabeth II in 1975. He retired in 1978.

Sir Maurice Oldfield died on March 11, 1981.

PTSD

Lawrence Fox suffered from PTSD in the form of nightmares, which began the same day that his first mission partner Nomad was shot (November 6, 1956). They recurred frequently. He was still experiencing them over twenty years later.

In 1964, Lawrence hit on the "crazy" idea that writing poetry might help steer his mind away from those nightmares. Several years later, he had written twenty-four poems on a variety of subjects. One day in January 2011, he saw an ad in the Midland library for a contest, typed out an entry on the computer, and soon four of his poems were published in two books, *Island Magic* and *Mists of Morning*. Although the benefits cannot be quantified, writing poetry seemed to help dissipate the nightmares. One of his favourite poems, *The Wanderer*, is appended.

Alcohol, of course, offered easy refuge from PTSD, and Lawrence deployed that option extensively at times. He would sometimes drive off alone in his car with a bottle of rum to a favourite remote field, put the keys under a floor mat, and turn up country music loud on the radio. He would then polish off the bottle of rum over the next hour, taking care to not dilute it with too much 7-Up. Those drinking binges provided some momentary escapism, but also delivered many painful hangovers.

In 1968, Lawrence met Georgette, the year after his near disastrous—and last—eleven-day mission Operation Spearhead into Poland. Six years later, in 1974, he finally divorced Elsie and married Georgette. Their marriage lasted seven years. When Lawrence told Georgette about his MI-6 work, she was so upset that she left for three months. After thinking things over, she came back and theirs became a roller-coaster relationship that featured a long series of furious fights followed by frantic lovemaking—with the some periods of calm interspersed, of course. Between times, Georgette assisted Lawrence greatly in coping with his PTSD demons.

Georgette weaned Lawrence off a prescribed PTSD narcotic that was almost certainly addictive. She also coached him steadily away from drink. By 1978, he had largely shaken his PTSD demons, had quit drinking, and was working for Canadian Protection Services. One day, his fellow workers invited him for a social drink and he hadn't touched a drop in over three months. He was pleasantly surprised to find that his favourite drink—white rum and 7-Up—tasted terrible. He then knew that he had essentially beaten the problem. The nightmares still recurred, but were far less severe.

Lawrence's Post-MI-6 Life

Lawrence's post-MI-6 life has had some interesting and colourful moments. He had a job working as a Private Investigator for Percy Parks of Great Lakes Security. His assignments included drug busting in downtown Toronto.

One of his most interesting cases involved assisting a major Sarnia petrochemical company solve a $40,000,000 gasoline theft case. The company's Chief of Security was flummoxed on how to handle the case, and Great Lakes Security brought Lawrence to his assistance. His work contributed greatly to identifying the culprit—but no charges were laid. Instead, the company bought all the mortgages on the perpetrator's trucks and equipment and foreclosed on them. That put him out of business. Not a single word about the entire episode appeared in the media.

In 1978, at the Bancroft Gun Club, a Dr. Emery had a Dan Wesson 357 Magnum five-shot, a pistol that had changeable barrels and cost about $1,500 at the time—a very expensive weapon. When he asked Lawrence if he would like to try it out, Lawrence said he would. Still a crack shot even though his nerves were a still a little shaky, he emptied the weapon in a rapid-fire burst at a target, thirty feet away. His barrage of bullets totally obliterated the bullseye.

"Larry," said Dr. Emery, "you're not shooting my gun anymore."

Lawrence could still keep a tin can in the air by emptying a pistol from twenty feet, each successive shot sending it back up into the air.

In 1983, Lawrence expressed interest in a job with the Bank of Nova Scotia's security operation. When he met with Charlie Angus, their Chief Security Officer, Lawrence outlined his experience and security-related skills. Charlie had him fill out an application form. When Lawrence asked how much of what he had just told him to include on the form, Charlie told him to "include whatever you want."

When Lawrence handed the completed form to Charlie, he simply said, "Well, Larry, there are thirty-five guys ahead of you, but when can you start?" He stayed fifteen years.

Lawrence was moved immediately into the Executive Protection branch. He was armed with the usual shoulder-holster weapon and added a Raven-Arms .25-calibre, five-shot derringer that he carried in a sleeve holster. That way, if he ever had to put his hands up in surrender, he could get a shot away, as he had done at least once on MI-6 duty.

One day, the Yugoslavian ambassador came to see the BNS Chairman with two bodyguards.. The hair on Lawrence's neck stood on end as soon as he saw them—MKGB agents! His first reaction was that he should shoot them both. Instead, to avoid them identifying him, he quickly retreated to the elevator and went down to the ground floor of the building. It, too, was crawling with MKGB agents. So he stepped right back into the elevator and made himself real scarce.

In 1985, Lawrence joined the Humber Valley Flier's (Model Airplane) Club in Toronto. When they found out his level of prowess in that recreational pursuit, they immediately made him Chief Flying Instructor, a position he held for ten years.

Lawrence's airplane model-making achievements border on the legendary. Before he was finished, he had built and sold about forty model Fireflies for two hundred dollars apiece, engine not included. They could execute stunts—stand up on a wing, do a falling leaf, fly upside down, and even flat spin. Over the years, he built at least a dozen different models—one, a twin-engine Donyer-217, a ten-pound model that featured retracting landing gear and a fully functional parachutist operating out of a bomb bay door. He built a four-engine Lancaster from scratch that weighed twelve pounds; it also featured retractable landing gear.

In 1981, Lawrence met a Polish woman called Eufrodita. He promptly divorced Georgette and took up residence with Eufrodita. In 1996, they were married and in 1998, they moved to Barrie, Ontario. On discovering his model airplane prowess, the Barrie Model Airplane Flying Club promptly appointed him Chief Flying Instructor.

On at least one occasion, Lawrence's MI-6 experience came in useful when he was married to Eufrodita. When her family wanted out of Poland, Lawrence advised them to "Take a boat trip to Germany, jump ship, and ask for asylum." They followed his advice and swiftly immigrated to Canada.

A succession of stressful years followed. In 1999, doctors found a (98%) blocked artery in his neck, which they cleared by an operation. In 2000, tragedy struck when his son Larry died in Vancouver. In 2001, he was hospitalized with a stroke that took over a year to subside and left him with restricted movement of his right side. It was about that time that he met Gary and Margaret Taylor at the Barrie Model Airplane Flying Club. They became close lifelong friends and supporters.

In 2002, Lawrence and Eufrodita separated, and in 2003, he came back to his hometown of Midland, Ontario, a location he considered a safe haven. For recreation and to keep his mind sharp, he joined bridge clubs in Victoria Harbour and in Midland—the Full Deck Club. Soon, he had become treasurer of the Full Deck Club, a position he held for seven years.

In 2005, Lawrence and Eufrodita divorced. Sadly, that same year, tragedy struck a second time when his son Carl died. The stress of losing a second son was so intense that, after eight days in the Newmarket Hospital, Lawrence had quadruple bypass surgery. Over the intervening years, he has survived several heart attacks. At the time of this writing (October 2015), he had accumulated twelve stents throughout his cardiovascular system.

In 2011, Lawrence met Leona Pilon who was to become the love of his life, even exceeding the intensity of his short-lived relationship with Susan during his MI-6 mission into Russia in 1965. Lawrence and Leona were married on November 7th, 2015.

Life goes on.

One day in 1978, at a restaurant in Bancroft, Ontario, with Georgette, Lawrence saw two soldiers sitting at a table and went over to look at their hat badges to see where they were from. They exchanged some small talk, and when one of them asked Lawrence whether he had been in the military, he said that he had, having left the RCAF in 1962. When Georgette piped in with "That was when you left Military Intelligence," one of the soldiers said to his pal, "Military Intelligence? Tell them about that guy that's getting you to do all that training."

"Yeah," said the second soldier. "My best area is marksmanship, and I've done a lot of rifle and pistol work, then karate and kick-boxing training for this guy. Now he wants me to go to Ottawa to learn Slavic languages when everyone else is going to Gagetown. I'd far rather go to Gagetown with the guys."

"What's he look like?" asked Lawrence.

After the soldier had described Sarge to a tee, Lawrence offered this advice: “Keep your mouth shut, and don’t tell your buddy anything more.”

Sarge was still recruiting.

The Wanderer

by Lawrence A. Fox

The wanderer is without time, without reason.
His endless pace carries him from season to season.
Roaming restlessly, from place to place.
What does he think, this man, who uses not lace?
The world is his home, his abode.
And, as he strolls down that winding road.
What more could he ask, or want?
The stars at night, do not taunt.
He travels light, under moonlit night.
Then, nature booms out, testing its might
Raging torrents, with fury unfolds,
Off in the distance, thunder rolls.
On he plods, without hesitation.
What, or where will be his destination?

Appendix A: Lawrence A. Fox Chronology

1935 September 5: Lawrence is born.

1943 Lawrence gets a job at Steer's White Rose gas station.

1949 Lawrence's father buys him a single-shot Cooey .22 rifle.

Lawrence buys a bike for $55.00, pays in eleven $5.00 instalments.

1950 Lawrence lands his first job, plowing fields in Stoney Lonesome at $2.00 a day.

1951 Lawrence gets a job on the *Midland City* for three months (May–July) at $100 a month.

Lawrence works at the new Roxy Theatre in Midland.

1952 October 20: Lawrence enlists in the RCAF. He signs on for three years and reports to Saint-Jean, Quebec, for an eight-week Bootcamp. He meets Sarge as one of five selectees from fifty.

1953 January: Lawrence is deployed to Camp Borden and takes an Engine Mechanics course. He is called from a classroom and Sarge reappears.

February: Lawrence leaves Camp after a shouting match with Sarge.

Lawrence serves fourteen days for going AWOL.

April: Lawrence reports to Lachine, Quebec base in the 4-Transport Operational Training Unit (4-TOTU); night after night, he is with Sarge on the range.

July: Lawrence hitchhikes Dorval to Midland for R&R. The next day, he reports back to base. He goes for orienteering training with Sarge in Resolute Bay within a day of his return; he celebrates his eighteenth birthday there.

1954 January: Lawrence's squadron is deployed to CFB Trenton.

Lawrence buys a 1936 Ford coupe and converts it into a stock car. Spring, he meets Elsie who never misses a race.

September: Lawrence takes parachute training at CFB Goose Bay, Labrador.

September 4: Lawrence marries Elsie; they live in Belleville, Ontario.

1955 Spring: Lawrence takes stealth training with Gurkha-Jack near Marmora.

Lawrence takes a Flight Engineer's course.

April 8: Lawrence's son Carl is born.

Lawrence re-joins the RCAF, and he signs on for five more years.

1956 Spring: Lawrence's in-line stealth entry exercise at CFB Goose Bay, Labrador is successful. It is his last training exercise before signing on with HMSS.

June 24: Lawrence's son Larry is born.

Lawrence undergoes a variety of training, including a five-person survival exercise near Bancroft, Ontario.

November 4: One thousand Russian tanks move into Budapest at dawn.

November 5: Lawrence meets Jenny.
Pre-mission briefing for **Operation Retrieve** into Hungary; he departs London at 2205 hrs.

November 6: Lawrence jumps at 3:15 a.m.
At ~ 1100 hrs. Nomad is shot.
Gets picked up at ~ 3:00 p.m. for his return flight to the UK.

1957 April 28: Lawrence's son Arthur is born.

Lawrence makes three flights to England on North Stars for training and cargo delivery; he stays at Jenny's apartment when in London.

1958 June 4: Lawrence's daughter June is born.

Lawrence takes intrusion training with cat burglar Charles.

Lawrence starts teaching six teenagers how to build model airplanes in his CFB Trenton basement.

July: Lawrence embarks on **Mission 2 to Prague** and brings out Strawinski.

Lawrence takes a weekly karate lesson from Master Yamoto for two months.

Lawrence goes to Switzerland with Sarge and waits about eighteen hours for a "no show."

1959 Sarge shows Lynx a photograph of his lead Russian spy in a motel room in Trenton, a high-ranking Russian officer (Susan's husband). Sarge gives Lawrence a lighter 9-mm. Beretta. Lawrence and Sarge fly to Phoenix for blueprint symbology training.

Lawrence spends three months (Nov–Jan) in Goose Bay, Labrador. Elsie stays in Trenton.

1960 Lawrence discovers Elsie's infidelity, and is granted a compassionate transfer to CFB Namao, Edmonton.

1961 December: Lawrence is charged with attempted murder. The court case drags on for ~ nine months.

1962 February 26: Lawrence's son Wayne is born.

March: **Mission 3 into Poland**. Lawrence brings the Petroff family out.

September 25: The Attempted Murder court case is resolved.

November: Lawrence gets an honourable discharge from the RCAF.

December: Lawrence and his family move to Ontario.

1963 January: Lawrence starts in the Riveting Dept. at de Havilland in Downsview, Ontario.

1964 August: Lawrence separates from Elsie; an extended custody battle begins.

Lawrence starts writing poetry as a PTSD coping therapy.

1965 Sarge arranges a two-week LOA through Hawker Siddeley with de Havilland for **Mission 4 into Beslan**, Chechnya;

Lawrence falls in love with Susan en route. A few months later, Lawrence meets Paula and they become an item.

1966 June: Lawrence's daughter Kate is born.

Sarge sends Lawrence to Camp Borden for a simulated "Russian prisoner" training exercise.

Lawrence's children are adopted as a unit into a home in Oakville, Ontario; they stay for seven years.

Lawrence's health problems appear, his nerves start acting up, and his drinking binges increase. Sarge makes contact several times.

1967 Sarge takes Lawrence into the woods north of Marmora for training to dry him out and sharpen his skills.

Lawrence runs into Edward Petroff at de Havilland. Sarge gets Lawrence a new job at Douglas Aircraft, Malton.

Mission 5, Operation Spearhead into Poland, planned for four days; it takes eleven days.

1968 Lawrence meets Georgette.

1974 Lawrence divorces Elsie and marries Georgette; she leaves for three months when told of his MI-6 work.

1978 Although inactive in MI-6 for about 11 years, Lawrence is still experiencing PTSD nightmares.

Lawrence meets two soldiers in a Bancroft restaurant; one soldier describes Sarge to a tee.

1980 Lawrence receives a registered letter from Fred Gibson, signed by Pierre Elliot Trudeau, authorizing the start of a Secret Service organization, later CSIS; Oldfield and Lawrence Fox are the only two names in the letter. Gibson invites Fox to participate, and on learning that there would be dangerous and unarmed work, Fox declines.

Kate, age fourteen, is told that Lawrence is her father.

1981 Lawrence meets Eufrodita and moves in with her; he divorces Georgette.

Lawrence's father dies at age seventy-six from a burst aorta.

1983 Lawrence is hired by the Bank of Nova Scotia as an Executive Protector; he stays for fifteen years.

1985 Lawrence becomes Chief Flying Instructor of the Humber Valley Flyers Club; he holds the position until 1995.

1988 Lawrence's mother dies at age eight-two of bowel cancer.

1996 Lawrence marries Eufrodita.

1998 Lawrence moves to Barrie, Ontario with Eufrodita.

1999 Doctors discover an artery in Lawrence's neck, 98% blocked, which is cleared with an operation

2000 Lawrence's son Larry dies in Vancouver; Lawrence starts searching for an inner peace from a higher authority.

2001 Lawrence has a stroke; movement of his right hand and leg become restricted.

Lawrence meets Gary and Margaret Taylor at the Barrie Model Airplane Flying Club

2002 Lawrence separates from Eufrodita.

2003 Lawrence returns to Midland, a safe haven.

Lawrence joins bridge clubs in Victoria Harbour and Midland (The Full Deck); he becomes treasurer of the Midland club and holds the position for seven years.

2005 Lawrence divorces Eufrodita.

Lawrence's son Carl dies; he was living at the Salvation Army on Jarvis St. in Toronto.

The stress of Carl's death causes Lawrence heart complications. Eight days after admission to the Newmarket Hospital, Lawrence has a quadruple bypass operation.

2011 Lawrence meets Leona Pilon.

2015 November 7: Lawrence marries Leona.

Selected Resources

Deacon, Richard. *'C': A Biography of Sir Maurice Oldfield, Head of MI-6*. London: Macdonald, 1985

Dorril, Stephen. *MI-6: Inside the Covert World of Her Majesty's Secret Intelligence Service*. London: Fourth Estate Limited, 2000. Also published in the USA by The Free Press, a Division of Simon & Schuster Inc., 1230 Avenue of the Americas, New York, NY 10020.

About the Author

Robert Popple was born and raised in Penetanguishene, Ontario and attended Midland-Penetanguishene District High School (Class of '59). He obtained a B.Sc. (Engineering Physics) from Queen's University in 1963. He pursued a thirty-two year career with the former Ontario Hydro in their nuclear-electric programme.

He owns his own consulting company, RTP Associates Inc., that partners with specialists to undertake organizational effectiveness assessments of nuclear-electric stations.

He and his wife Heather currently reside on Vancouver Island, British Columbia. They have three grown children—Catherine, Beth and Steven—and four grandchildren—Cameron, Leo, Adelaide and Bridget.

Other Books by Robert Popple:

Left: *Northern Belle: The Life Story of Haliburton's Ethel Curry, Including her Connections with the Group of Seven*, RTP Publications (2003)

Right: *John Arpin: Keyboard Virtuoso*, Dundurn Press (2009)

Printed in Canada